Doing Phenomenology

PHAENOMENOLOGICA

COLLECTION FONDÉE PAR H. L. VAN BREDA ET PUBLIÉE SOUS LE
PATRONAGE DES CENTRES D'ARCHIVES-HUSSERL

63

HERBERT SPIEGELBERG

Doing Phenomenology

HERBERT SPIEGELBERG

Doing Phenomenology

ESSAYS ON AND IN PHENOMENOLOGY

MARTINUS NIJHOFF / THE HAGUE / 1975

To The Memory of
ERWIN SPIEGELBERG
1901–1938

ISBN 90 247 1725 6

PRINTED IN THE NETHERLANDS

ACKNOWLEDGMENTS

I am indebted to the following copyrightholders for permission to reprint here, in the original or in slightly amended form, the articles listed next: *American Catholic Philosophical Association,* "How Subjective Is Phenomenology?"; *American Philosophical Quarterly,* "Toward a Phenomenology of Experience"; Duquesne University Press, "Phenomenology Through Vicarious Experience"; *Encyclopaedia Britannica,* "Phenomenology"; Harvard University Press, "The 'Reality-Phenomenon' and Reality"; Johns Hopkins Press, "The Relevance of Phenomenological Philosophy for Psychology"; Martinus Nijhoff, "Change of Perspectives: Constitution of a Husserl Image" and "On Some Human Uses of Phenomenology"; *Philosophy and Phenomenological Research,* "Critical Phenomenological Realism" and "Phenomenology of Direct Evidence"; Quadrangle Press, "A Phenomenological Analysis of Approval"; *Review of Existential Psychology and Psychiatry,* "The Idea of a Phenomenological Anthropology and Alexander Pfänder's Psychology of Man"; and John Wiley & Sons, "On the Right to Say 'We': A Linguistic and Phenomenological Analysis."

PREFACE

Substantial encouragement for this volume came from the editors and readers of the Studies for Phenomenological and Existential Philosophy (SPEP) at Northwestern University Press. But its publication has been made possible only by the unqualified and unabridged acceptance of the Editorial Board of *Phaenomenologica*, which at the time was still headed by its founder, the late Professor H. L. Van Breda, who welcomed the manuscript most generously. This makes his untimely passing even more grievous to me.

The stylistic copy editing and proof reading were handled efficiently by Ruth Nichols Jackson, secretary of the Philosophy Department. In the proof reading I also had the able help of my colleague Stanley Paulson.

I dedicate this book to the memory of my late brother, Dr. chem. Erwin Spiegelberg, at the time of his death assistant professor at the University of Rio de Janeiro, who preceded me by two years in emigrating from Nazi Germany. When in 1938 he put an end to his life in an apparent depression, he also did so in order not to become a burden to his brothers, who were on the point of following him. Whatever I, more privileged in health and in opportunities in the country of my adoption, have been able to do and achieve since then has been done with a sense of a debt to him and of trying to live and work for him too.

Washington University
Saint Louis, Missouri
May 1974

CONTENTS

PART ONE

TO THE THINGS
(ESSAYS *ON* PHENOMENOLOLOGY)
    1

PART TWO

AT THE THINGS
(ESSAYS *IN* PHENOMENOLOGY)

INTRODUCTION: THE OLD AND THE NEW

I. THE GOAL

The title of this book calls for an immediate explanation. The phrase "doing phenomenology" is clearly a loan from the arsenal of analytical philosophy. Its implication is that phenomenology can be practiced in a way comparable to the way analytical philosophy is "done." I would like to demonstrate this here. I would even like to show that phenomenology is itself a kind of analytical philosophy. Only it is more than analysis, especially analysis of language.

This is not a completely new book. What I am offering here consists mostly of essays published over nearly forty years in scattered places, some only in German. What is new about them is chiefly the new pattern I have imposed on them. It tries to make new sense of the old material. However, this also requires the addition of several unpublished pieces, which I held back for maturing. The most important of these are the two dealing with "Ways into Phenomenology" and the one on "Criteria in Phenomenology." Thus, while this volume is a collection it is a collection with a difference based on the new context in which the parts are to add up to more than their sum.

I shall first try to explain the genesis of the main ingredients of the new *Gestalt*. Their historical sequence was determined chiefly by concrete needs, not only in thinking through unresolved problems in my own mind, but in attempting to present phenomenology to outsiders. Thus the essay on "The Phenomenon of Reality and Reality" was still a response to a German challenge. The pieces on self-evidence and on criteria in general tried to answer those I encountered in the States. But the major challenge for me has always been the need of demonstrating phenomenology concretely by *doing* it rather than by talking *about* it. This is in fact my major goal in this volume. But on the way to it certain roadblocks have had to be removed.

The need of tackling these roadblocks is one reason which makes me feel uneasy, if not slightly dishonest, about the choice of my main title. For what I am offering in the first part of this volume is seemingly not yet phenomenology done but preparatory road-clearing. However, I hope that in so doing I have been able to show how this operation itself can be carried out with the decisive help of phenomenological tools. Also, I do not think that such preparatory work is merely pre-phenomenological. If there is anything to the overworked slogan *Zu den Sachen* (To the "things") as the most common denominator of phenomenological philosophizing, its primary sense is that of a movement toward the things, implying that there is a way to travel that is by no means always short and smooth. Only at the end of the road have we arrived "at the things" and can begin the actual research.

But why not a new book instead of such a patch-up solution? Collecting one's own production and realigning it for display is certainly a questionable undertaking, in which laziness and vanity may have their fair, or rather unfair, share. At least I can plead these mitigating circumstances:

1. With time running out and more important unfinished business claiming priority all I can still plan in this area is to improve on what I have tried before.

2. I believe there is an urgent need right now for demonstrating phenomenology through smaller pieces of the type I have supplied in these essays.

3. I would like to be frank about a more personal motive for presenting this collection: By doing phenomenology on the phenomena themselves I would like to undo as far as still possible my dubious reputation of being merely a historian, if not a mere chronicler of phenomenology. True, I had better resign myself to the fate that my historical introduction to the Phenomenological Movement, a tour de force at its best, cannot be stricken from my record for some time; for I myself consider my perspective on the history of phenomenology one-sided and temporary. At least I would like it to be understood that my role as a historian was not a matter of free choice but one more or less forced upon me by accidents of my academic history in which the filling of

an urgent need of historical information was the only way for me to regain the freedom for later independent work of my own.[1] The time when I have reached such freedom is late indeed. But at least I can still hope that I may match some of my questionable record as a metaphenomenologist by direct contributions to the development of phenomenology itself. The present volume is a first attempt at such a rehabilitation. Given more of a period of grace I shall try to do better on more substantial projects.

II. THE NEW PATTERN

I would like to comment first briefly on the general layout of this volume. Its two major parts "To the Things" and "At the Things" coincide with the division into essays *on* phenomenology, focusing on issues crucial for the understanding and defense of phenomenology, and essays *in* phenomenology, presenting some of its fruits in areas other than phenomenology itself.

Part I is subdivided into two sections. Section A is an attempt to interpret the meaning of phenomenology. The way to this goal is through surveying its scope, discussing ways of entering into it, developing its methodology, showing how far it can be extended in entering even experiences of others not directly accessible to the phenomenologist, and finally considering the question of how far phenomenology as such can be put to wider human or existential uses. Section B is made up of attempts to defend such an enriched picture of phenomenology against some of the epistemological challenges that, as far as I can see, have not yet been met explicitly enough. They include attacks on its essential subjectivity, its reliance on self-evidence and its lack of adequate criteria. I am trying to meet them by developing better defenses through phenomenological means. I also want to supply the groundwork for an alternative to Husserl's phenomenological idealism by a phenomenology of our consciousness of reality without returning to a "naive realism" or a critical realism in the traditional sense.

After thus clearing the way "To the Things" in Part I, Part II, "At the Things," brings samples of phenomenology done in various de-

[1] See my 'Apologia pro bibliographia mea,' to be published in the near future in Philip Bossert (ed.), *Phenomenological Perspectives*, The Hague: Martinus Nijhoff, 1975, X, 279 pp.

tached areas, frankly all originating from specific occasions on which I tried to demonstrate phenomenology in action. Topics in general epistemology and metaphysics, psychology, sociology and anthropology predominate, but theory of values is also represented through an analysis of the key concept of approval which tries to show that what is unanalyzable for analytic philosophers need not be so for phenomenologists.

III. THE INGREDIENTS

I shall now comment briefly on each item in this collection, partly for the sake of those who are particularly interested in historical background and information about significant alterations. I should also point out that, especially in my earlier English pieces, I have made stylistic changes without always identifying them. When I began writing in English my active vocabulary was somewhat limited. Also the help which I could enlist, and without which my transition from German to English would have been impossible, was not always sufficiently trained in philosophy to protect me, my suffering readers and the English language from blunders and infelicities. In retrospect I now often feel embarrassed about these early attempts. But I believe that my struggles have not been entirely in vain. While I know that I shall never achieve the freedom of expression I once enjoyed in my native German, I owe to my linguistic reeducation a new discipline of thinking and expression which makes me ashamed even of my earlier German style.

The first item in the section about the meaning of phenomenology is an article which appeared in the *Encyclopaedia Britannica* between 1966 and 1973. In the 1974 edition only the lead and the two sections on "Characteristics" have survived almost unchanged; the historical part was turned over to Professor Walter Biemel, who has the exclusive responsibility for all changes and additions. In this book the article is to serve as a concise account of the state of phenomenology today. However it should be borne in mind that originally this piece had to be adjusted to the strait jacket of 4000 words, incidentally the same limit which was partly responsible for the misfortunes of Husserl's own article in the 14th edition of the Britannica, when the translator telescoped it into half its original size. However, in a few places I have brought it up to date in proportion with the original scale.

The following two essays were originally parts of a single lecture on ways into phenomenology given at a workshop-institute on phenomenology at DePaul University in Chicago in 1969. I have now separated its critical and its constructive parts, because the latter part, the presentation of the new workshop approach, required a much fuller account after two further and thus far final runs. I consider this pilot experiment, incomplete though it still is, as my only real contribution to the teaching of phenomenology. At this point of the sequence it might have been desirable to insert a piece about the actual way or method of phenomenology itself. The obvious candidate would have been the final chapter of my historical introduction to the Phenomenological Movement, of which at least a brief abstract can be found at the end of the Britannica article and in the two following essays. What spoke against this inclusion was its length and its easy separate availability from the original publisher, Martinus Nijhoff. All I can do here is to suggest to the more inquisitive and critical reader to consult it at this stage, not as a rule book for step-by-step application but as an attempt to put the main varieties of phenomenological procedure at his disposal and show him how they can be put to use in a specific paradigm case.

Assuming sufficient familiarity with the essentials of the phenomenological method the two last essays in this section take up possibilities of going beyond it. "Phenomenology Through Vicarious Experience" considers an expansion of the procedure itself. It grew out of my initial uneasiness about the attempts to apply phenomenology in a field like psychiatry beyond the range of direct and normal experience. However, in struggling with the problems and considering the achievements of phenomenological psychopathology I came to realize that beyond the boundaries of primary phenomenology dealing with one's own direct and normal phenomena there can be a legitimate expansion through vicarious methods. This extrapolation, if clearly recognized as such, opens up possibilities for other legitimate uses of phenomenology in the human sciences and possibly beyond.

The essay on what I call here "The Existential Uses of Phenomenology" (the original title talked about "Some Human Uses") may seem least in keeping with the spirit of the other items in this collection. However, at the end of the section on the meaning of phenomenology it seems to me in order to consider also its human significance. The basic ideas have been with me for a long time, longer than most of the technical essays. But I would like to make it clear that the exploration of the existential meanings of doing phenomenology is not yet phenomenological existentialism, i.e., the application of phenomenology to problems of human existence. What I am concerned with is the existential meaning of the very doing of phenomenology itself. Phenomenology has no more right to bypass this dimension than any other human enterprise.

The second group of preparatory essays on the rights of phenomenology is an attempt to clear away some of the roadblocks put up in its way mostly by outsiders. But this does not make them any less serious. In fact they should have been tackled long ago from the inside. Also, in trying to defend the rights of phenomenology against some of these challenges, I hope to show that doing phenomenology itself can develop some of the best defenses for meeting them.

The first short essay in this group had its origin in a rather improvised symposium for which I myself had formulated the question of the extent and right of subjectivity in phenomenology. My primary stimulus was the introduction to phenomenology by Professor Quentin Lauer under the rather intriguing title *The Triumph of Subjectivity*. In trying to meet the challenge I wanted to show how an analytic and phenomenological refinement of the question can throw a very different light on the issue. Moreover, I wanted to use the occasion for giving a first idea of the significance of the varieties of phenomenology. I did not want to contest the "subjective" element in phenomenology. But I wanted at least to show that this element does not doom it to utter subjectivism.

"The Phenomenology of Direct Evidence" is a paper which was read at the first symposium on Phenomenology before the Eastern Division of the American Philosophical Association in Philadelphia in 1940. The original title spoke of "self-evidence." The term "direct evidence" for "self-evidence" was substituted by the editor of *Philosophy and Phenomenological Research*. On second thought I wanted to return to the more traditional, if not notorious, term. But on third thought I now believe that there are additional reasons for avoiding the term, based on the fact that it is misleading if applied to propositions; for propositions can never be evident by themselves alone without the states of affairs about which they speak. I also have tried to update the essay by taking account of some of Husserl's later publications and some of the new secondary literature. However, I have omitted an appendix which tried to deal with one of the contemporary critics of self-evidence, Professor Brand Blanshard in his *The Nature of Thought*; it might still be consulted in the original source by those who are interested in seeing how the phenomenology of direct evidence compares with the coherence theory of truth.

The final essay in this section, "The Phenomenon of Reality and Reality," has undergone the biggest changes since its first publication more than thirty years ago. At that time it was broken up in two instalments because of a retroactive limitation of space. The most important change is the reintegration of its two parts. Besides, many sections, especially the one on reality criteria, have been rethought and rewritten. This was actually my first larger paper in English, based on my German drafts for an inaugural university lecture at Munich, in which I wanted to spell out the position of a realistic phenomenology and to think through its problems as they appeared to me from my first American academic foothold at Swarthmore College, where Wolfgang Köhler had developed his transphenomenological realism. While I still think that the paper incorporates my best insights in epistemology on phenomenological foundations, it was the least naturalized of my English papers. I hope by now the English has become at least intelligible, even if the ideas and some of my terminology are not yet fully Americanized.

A general warning is in order for the papers in Part II, which are attempts to show phenomenology in action. They are not trying to demonstrate a method step by step, something which may seem to be suggested in my chapter on "The Essentials of the Phenomenological Method," where one exemple is taken through the paces of such an approach. For one thing, at the time I wrote that chapter a good many of these papers had long been completed without my having conceived of the entire range of possibilities opened up by phenomenology. Rather did my chapter grow out of a critical synthesis of these attempts. I could, and perhaps should, have rewritten them much more thoroughly. And I add in some cases how far I think more could be done now.

On the other hand the informal approach of these papers can be rationalized as a virtue. I want to make it clear that the method recommended in my chapter is not meant to standardize phenomenology. There are many legitimate ways of doing it. Which one and what steps of the method recommended in general will be most fruitful can be decided only in the light of the particular phenomena to be investigated. Their requirements have primacy, not any preconceived set of rules.

There is no coherent theme in these applications. They were prepared for unrelated occasions. In the present setting they are to show the relevance of the phenomenological approach in separate fields of philosophy. The first, "Toward a Phenomenology of Experience," was prepared for a symposium on "Experience" of the Metaphysical Society of America, where I wanted to show the special potential of phenomenology applied to a theme shared by most contemporary schools of philosophy, and at the same time discuss its chances of doing metaphysics from such a basis.

"A Phenomenology of Approval" takes up a problem in the theory of value. Here I wanted to demonstrate that phenomenology can give an analysis of a phenomenon which to analytic philosophers has appeared unanalyzable. It can thus throw a new and different light on its place and significance in philosophy.

" 'We': A Linguistic and Phenomenological Analysis," the Alfred Schutz Lecture of 1972, is a more sustained study of a new subject in social philosophy meant to illustrate at the same time a possible cooperation between phenomenology proper and the "linguistic phenomenology" of the Austinian variety.

The following two essays are not direct applications of phenomenology in the same sense as were the first three. Their primary objective is to indicate the proper place for a phenomenology in such fields as psychology and anthropology. However, by way of illustration the one on the relevance of phenomenological philosophy includes an attempt to relate the psychological field concept and Husserl's life world and to develop them phenomenologically beyond their present radimentary stage. The piece on phenomenological anthropology, in addition to showing the dimensions of a phenomenological exploration of man, tries to provide concrete illustrations by pointing out phenomenological ingredients in Pfänder's psychology of man.

The last short piece in this section, thus far published only in German, was written originally in response to an invitation to contribute my recollections of Husserl to a memorial volume. Although I was fully aware that my acquaintance with Husserl was anything but representative, I accepted the invitation in the idea that I could use it for several purposes, including the one of reestablishing my faded European credentials for the enterprise on which I had embarked at that point, the historical introduction to the Phenomenological Movement in its entirety. But ultimately even more significant seemed to me the challenge of using my perspectives for a phenomenological experiment in historical biography, more specifically in showing how through such perspectives a personality like Husserl's can "constitute" itself. I want to add it here as an illustration of what constitutive phenomenology could do in history. Yet I am fully aware that in the case of my material this is a tour de force. I also have not attempted to relate this sketch to the theory of constitution, and especially to the distinction between active and passive constitution. Most of what I have reported is certainly passive constitution. But in several places I have had to do some active constituting and reconstituting.

Three other pieces of applied phenomenology which I could have added here have been held back for other occasions. For to me their main significance is connected with their subject matter to which I hope to return in a more sustained fashion. The two pieces related to the phenomenology of the self are:

1. "A Phenomenological Approach to the Ego" (*The Monist* 49 (1965), pp. 1-15).

2. "Putting Ourselves into the Place of Others;" ("Toward a Phenomenology of Imaginative Self-transposal"). *Proceedings of the XIth International Congress of Philosophy* (Brussels, 1953, VII, pp. 235-239).

3. "Indubitables in Ethics" (*Ethics* 58, 1947, pp. 35-50), belongs to a group of studies in Ethics and Legal Philosophy. My major remaining project is the systematic investigation of these phenomena as a foundation for a new approach to ethics in which the earlier essays shall be not only incorporated but absorbed.

IV. WHERE I STAND

At this point the reader has a right to expect of me a more explicit statement about my own position and allegiances in phenomenology than I have given him thus far. Even in the final chapter of my historical introduction to the Phenomenological Movement I had tried to maintain neutrality. In the present volume I hope my own stand will emerge at least implicitly and, more important, be under-pinned by evidence.

But before laying down my cards I would like to reaffirm my view that no one, not even Hegel or Husserl, has proprietary rights to a term like 'phenomenology.' It is older than both, and it is in this sense anyone's for the taking – and defining. It is true that Husserl's annexation has given it the greatest enrichment but also compli-cation in its history. But this is no reason to forget its earlier and wider meanings. To restore them was one of the objectives of my historical research. Heidegger was right in his early claim that phe-nomenology means more as a possibility than as an actuality. Never-theless, in this century Husserl's phenomenology was and is the focus of orientation. Certainly for me personally it was the primary point of departure, though modified very soon by Alexander Pfän-der's alternative interpretation. It is therefore in relation to Husserl and Pfänder that I shall try to define my position toward and my reinterpretation of phenomenology.

With all its aspirations to scientific rigor, Husserl's phenomenology never rigidified into an orthodox system. It grew and continued growing to the end, while becoming more radical in its demands. I can identify with its original conception, especially as expressed in the platform of Husserl's yearbook, which stressed the need of a return to intuiting (*Anschauung*) and to essential insights built upon it, and also with most of his objectives in "Philosophy as a Rigorous Science." But, much as I have tried to assimilate his later transcen-dentalism and his radicalized phenomenological reduction, I find myself unable to adopt them fully. I cannot accept the implicit presupposition that all being and even all meaning (the two never being clearly distinguished) have their "origin" in subjective con-sciousness, whatever the unclarified term "origin" may mean in this context. This rejection of "phenomenological idealism" does not keep me from espousing a constitutive phenomenology which ex-plores without bias the way in which the phenomena are established in our consciousness, either by "passive" self-constitution or by more "active" construction. I even believe that thinking through the implications of "passive" self-constitution will reveal much more common ground between the Husserlian position and that of a critical phenomenological realism than it would appear at first sight. Never-theless I consider Husserl's increasing identification of phenomenology with subjectivism an unfortunate and unnecessary narrowing of its original objective, violating the ideal of freedom from unexamined presuppositions.

This qualified disassociation from Husserl's final position will suggest that I identify completely with Pfänder's alternative. This impression is even more plausible in view of my efforts to salvage and revive the Pfänder heritage. All the more is it in order that, beyond occasional hints on previous occasions, I make my position clear. Pfänder was my teacher in philosophy after the winter semester 1924/25, which I had spent with Husserl in Freiburg. Without him my start in philosophy, including my emancipation from him, would have been impossible. But this does not mean that in my own views and studies I felt particularly close to Pfänder's work. The fact that after his death I reluctantly took charge of his papers was due primarily to the circumstance that no one of Pfänder's closer students was in the position to do this. But increasingly I came to realize that here was a phenomenological treasure which must not be lost. Thus not only personal indebtedness and loyalty, but a concern to fill a gap in the record of the Phenomenological Movement, made me usurp the role of advocate for Pfänder's thought.

It is also true that I found Pfänder's emerging conception of phenomenology much closer to my taste than Husserl's. Yet, a critical comparison of my own statements about and practice of phenomenology would show that I am anything but a faithful follower of my teacher. For instance I do not think that Pfänder's start with a type of "linguistic phenomenology" comparable to John L. Austin's, timely as it is, is universally applicable, particularly in areas uncharted by ordinary language. I also have reservations about the way in which Pfänder appealed to essential insights and especially to insights into "basic essences" (*Grundwesen*) as opposed to empirical essences. And, as in the case of Husserl, I feel uneasy, to say the least, about the appeal to self-givenness (*leibhafte Selbstgegebenheit*) as implying a *petitio principii* when used as a final argument in epistemology: Is there any ultimate guarantee that what gives itself as self-present is actually present rather than a clever decoy?

But my main reservations concern Pfänder's final philosophical perspective. I am deeply impressed by his grand vision of a complete philosophy on phenomenological foundations. I am not aware of anything comparable in phenomenological philosophy thus far. On the other hand I am unable to verify sufficiently some of Pfänder's central claims in support of his conception of life as a self-unfolding idea and its key role in ethics. Much as I believe in the significance of Pfänder's phenomenological renewal of an Aristotelian metaphysics, I cannot accept it as more than one actual, besides several potential, extrapolations from the phenomenological evidence. If then I cannot call myself either an orthodox Husserlian or a consistent Pfänderian, where do I belong? I am certainly not in the position to offer a complete alternative. But I hope that the following essays will supply helpful answers to some of the open key questions. In the present context I can merely indicate the direction of my own course.

In one respect my claims for phenomenology are weaker than Husserl's or Pfänder's, in another they are more ambitious. I share with both the conviction that phenomenology can provide a minimum of phenomenal certainty. But it is too small for philosophical "subsistence." However, the quest for any additional "apodictic" certainty (Husserl) or "ultimately final" knowledge (Pfänder) seems to me a will-o'-the-wisp. Any such absolutism is bound to be self-defeating. But the "quest for certainty" is not essential to phenomenology. Phenomenology is not the master key to all locks. Enough if it can unlock some doors and especially the front door. But if in this regard I am more timid than my masters, I am also more daring in advocating the use of phenomenology beyond the range of absolute certainty. Not all the phenomena are fully manifest or even capable of full manifestation. I believe there is this much truth to the idea of a hermeneutic phenomenology that there are phenomena that cannot speak for themselves unaided but need the kind of interpretation that goes beyond the range of what is immediately and fully given. But such interpretations are in need of subsequent fulfilling verification. Else they will remain guesswork, for which phenomenology can never stand. What seems to me to be required is the kind of seek-and-find technique which, at the outskirts of our phenomenological knowledge, pushes out boundaries, picks up clues, pursues them as far as possible even into the half shade, and extrapolates beyond in advance of further searching missions. All such figurative expressions are clearly in need of concrete exemplifications. I hope that the later parts of my essay on the "Phenomenon of Reality and

Reality" and on "Phenomenology of Vicarious Experience" can give a first taste of such a heuristic phenomenology, which might absorb even the legitimate parts of hermeneutic phenomenology. My final hope is that such a self-critical but expanded phenomenology will also leave room for and promote the reintegration of phenomenology with transphenomenological science as a legitimate extrapolation of phenomenology.

PART ONE

TO THE THINGS (ESSAYS *ON* PHENOMENOLOGY)

A. ON THE MEANING OF PHENOMENOLOGY

1. "PHENOMENOLOGY" *

"Phenomenology" is, in the 20th century, mainly the name for a philosophical movement whose primary objective is the direct investigation and description of phenomena as consciously experienced, without theories about their causal explanation and as free as possible from unexamined preconceptions and presuppositions. The term itself is much older, going back at least to the 18th century, when Johann Heinrich Lambert, in his *Neues Organon* (1764), applied it to that part of his theory of knowledge which distinguishes truth from illusion and error. In the 19th century it became associated chiefly with Hegel's *Phänomenologie des Geistes* (1807), which undertook to trace the development of the human spirit from mere sense-experience to "absolute knowledge." The so-called Phenomenological Movement did not get under way until the first decade of the 20th century. But even this new phenomenology includes so many varieties that a fair picture requires a brief sketch of its development.

ORIGIN AND DEVELOPMENT

Husserl's Early Phenomenology

Phenomenology was not founded: it grew. Its fountainhead was Edmund Husserl. Yet even for Husserl the idea of phenomenology as a new method destined to supply a new foundation for both philosophy and science developed only gradually and kept changing to the very end of his career. Trained as a mathematician, Husserl was attracted to philosophy by Franz Brentano, whose descriptive psychology seemed to offer a solid basis for a scientific philosophy. The failure of Husserl's first work, *Philosophie der Arithmetik* (1891),

* *Encyclopaedia Britannica,* 1966-1973, updated.

to secure an adequate foundation for mathematics, in combination with the strictures of Gottlob Frege, resulted in Husserl's systematic examination and repudiation of "psychologism," the attempt to use empirical psychology as the ultimate basis for logic. Nevertheless, the "pure logic," which Husserl now outlined at the end of the "Prolegomena" for his *Logische Untersuchungen* (1900), still required, in his thinking, a parallel study of the acts in which the ideal structures of such a logic were given. So the second volume of this epoch-making work consisted largely of "phenomenological analyses," exploring these acts in their essential structures, in contrast to the merely empirical investigation of their factual modifications studied by psychology.

The most important of these painstaking studies dealt with Brentano's concept of intentionality, the main feature by which he had tried to distinguish psychological from physical "phenomena" (taking this term in the wide sense given it by the Newtonian and positivist tradition). But while for Brentano the "intentional relation" meant merely the reference of our perceiving, judging, or loving acts to their perceived, judged, or loved objects, Husserl found in these acts a much richer structure. Thus in our perceiving of this printed page he would distinguish not only the seeing and the seen but also the perspective aspects through which this page appears and its modes of clarity, and he would study the ways in which consciousness relates and synthesizes the various appearances as they refer to the identical object, the page. Husserl also distinguished between "empty" intentional references and those fulfilled with intuitive content (*Anschauung*), which alone could justify such intentions epistemologically. Besides, these intuitive acts were no longer confined to sense-experience. Even the correlates of such logical connectives as "and," "or," and "if" could be given in a nonsensuous or "categorial" intuition, an extension which opened the way for the recognition of the intuitive givenness of such phenomena as relations, essences, values, and other phenomena, both real and ideal.

Only in the years after the publication of these studies did Husserl develop the idea of phenomenology as a universal foundation of philosophy, capable of converting it into a "rigorous science," a science consisting in the descriptive exploration of the essential structures of the directly given, free on the one hand from the unexamined assumptions of a "naturalism" restricted to the empirical natural sciences, and on the other hand from the relativism implied in the historicism of the *Geisteswissenschaften*. This new scientific philosophy was, however, not meant to supply the cheap comforts of a complete *Weltanschauung* or a speculative metaphysics.

Husserl's Pure or Transcendental Phenomenology

The development of a rigorous or "pure" phenomenology as the science of the essential structures of consciousness by means of correlated studies of the intentional act (*noesis*) and its objective referent (*noema*) involved for Husserl a systematic effort to purify the phenomena of all merely factual ingredients, as studied by the empirical sciences, and of all constructive interpretations. To this end he developed his technique of the "reductions," among which the phenomenological or "transcendental" reduction was the decisive one. Beginning with the suspension of belief in the reality of what seems to be immediately given, like the present printed page, and neither denying nor even doubting its existence, the reductive procedure (*epoché*) aimed at isolating first the field of pure phenomena given with absolute certainty. This field would include each reader's own ego, his acts of reading, and the page as read with all the complexities of its modes of givenness. This immanent region of absolute subjectivity thus coincided for Husserl largely with Descartes' sphere of the indubitable ego, its acts of cogitating, and the objects of cogitation insofar as cogitated about. Adopting Kantian terminology, Husserl also called this immanent region the transcendental consciousness, as distinguished from its transcendent counterpart, the objects of the real world, such as the page meant as part of the physical environment surrounding consciousness. As to this transcendent world, the reduction was to uncover the otherwise hidden ways by which it was constituted in our consciousness, either passively, as it happens in the perceptual experience of this printed page, or actively, as it takes place in predicative judgments or in the constitution or the sense of the sentences as read on this page. Such "constitutive phenomenology" provided Husserl with the main evidence for his peculiar "transcendental idealism" (to be distinguished from Berkeley's idealism with its basis in the empirical mind), according to which the transcendent objects owe not only their being known but also their very being to the constituting acts of transcendental consciousness. Although even other transcendental egos were supposed to be constituted in each one's own consciousness, Husserl believed that he could avoid solipsism by the introduction of peculiar acts of "appresentation," which attested the equal rights of other transcendental egos. The outcome was a "metaphysical" world picture for which Husserl adopted the Leibnizian term "monadology."

In his later philosophizing, consisting largely in the production of a vast number of research manuscripts, Husserl tried to refine especially his studies of the consciousness of time, to which he attributed fundamental importance for the understanding of the structures of all consciousness. But he also sought to open new avenues into his transcendental phenomenology. The one which proved most fruitful was the study of the immediate life world (*Lebenswelt*) of the individual with the ego at its centre, as distinguished from the uncentered objective world of modern Galilean science, which, however, was supposed to have sprung from it. This life world was to provide clues for the study of transcendental consciousness.

The Phenomenology of Essences

A different type of phenomenology, the phenomenology of essences, grew out of a tangential development of the phenomenology of the *Logische Untersuchungen*. Its supporters were Husserl's students in Göttingen and a group of young philosophers in Munich, originally students of Theodor Lipps (1851-1914), who had turned away from Lipps's original psychologism and discovered in Husserl powerful support. The Phenomenological Movement, which now began to take shape, found its most tangible expression in the publication of the *Jahrbuch für Philosophie und phänomenologische Forschung* (1913-30), a phenomenological yearbook under Husserl as main editor, whose preface defined phenomenology in terms of a return to intuition (*Anschauung*) and to the essential insights (*Wesenseinsichten*) derived from it as the ultimate foundation of all philosophy. The 11 volumes of the *Jahrbuch* contained, in addition to Husserl's own works, the most important production of the movement in the broader sense. Of the co-editors, Alexander Pfänder (1870-1941) contributed chiefly to the development of phenomenological psychology and pure logic, but developed also the outlines of a complete phenomenological philosophy which has now been reconstructed from his posthumous papers. Moritz Geiger (1880-1937) applied the new approach particularly to aesthetics, Adolf Reinach

(1883-1917) to the philosophy of law. But the most original and dynamic of Husserl's early associates was Max Scheler, who had joined the Munich group coming from the Neo-Kantianism of Rudolf Eucken in Jena, and who did his major phenomenological work in ethics, where he applied it particularly to the problems of value. The Polish philosopher Roman Ingarden (1893-1970) did major work in structural ontology and analyzed the structures of various works of art in its light and the acts in which they are experienced. Hedwig Conrad-Martius (1889-1966) worked intensively in the ontology of nature. Wilhelm Schapp, Jean Hering, Edith Stein, and others made comparable contributions to other fields of philosophy. None of these early phenomenologists followed Husserl's road to transcendental idealism, while some tried to develop phenomenology along realistic lines.

Heidegger's Hermeneutic Phenomenology

Phenomenology took a new turn in 1916, when Husserl moved to Freiburg im Breisgau, where he was assisted by Edith Stein, Ludwig Landgrebe and Eugen Fink, who, however, emancipated themselves after leaving Husserl. But the main event was the adoption of phenomenology by Martin Heidegger, who had come from scholastic philosophy and the Neo-Kantianism of Heinrich Rickert. Approaching what was for him the supreme question, that of the meaning of beingness (*Sein des Seienden*) through an analysis of the being which we ourselves are (*Dasein*), Heidegger saw in phenomenology the most promising way to uncover the categories of human existence (*existentialia*) for a "fundamental ontology." However, since neither Husserl's phenomenology of transcendental reduction nor the phenomenology of essences proved equal to this task, he developed a new "hermeneutic phenomenology" designed to interpret the ontological meanings of such human conditions as being-in-the-world, anxiety, and care, with results as startling as they were original.

References to phenomenology nearly disappeared from Heidegger's publications after he had abandoned the completion of his magnum opus, *Sein und Zeit* (1927), for a variety of reasons, which involved not only his estrangement from Husserl, who was disappointed in Heidegger as his academic successor for not continuing his own transcendentalism, but also because the approach to being via human existence failed to yield the final answer to his basic question. Still, even in his later works Heidegger claimed the "essential help of phenomenological seeing," much as his methods of philosophizing were otherwise changed.

Phenomenological Existentialism in France

Phenomenology underwent further changes when it was adopted by French philosophy in the form of phenomenological existentialism, a merger which had not yet taken place in Germany, where Karl Jaspers had opposed his philosophy of existence, with its existential appeal to the individual, to phenomenology, with its claims to scientific rigor. Its first French practitioner, Gabriel Marcel (1889-1973), inspired primarily by Scheler, spoke of phenomenology in the context of his metaphysical meditations on human existence, using it as an aid in exploring concrete situations and such experiences as hope, which had been neglected by scientific psychology and objectivist philosophies. Jean-Paul Sartre (b. 1905) found in Husserl's phenomenology the effective method for his descriptive explorations of the imagination and the emotions. However, he moved closer to Heidegger's version in his "essay on phenomenological ontology," *L'Être et le néant* (1943). But even then Sartre defined existence in terms of Husserl's consciousness, rather than Heidegger's *Dasein*, though he rejected Husserl's transcendental idealism as an account of being, the essentially opaque counterpart of consciousness. Since then Sartre's interest in phenomenology has faded.

Phenomenology became even more central in the philosophy of Maurice Merleau-Ponty (1908-61), whose *Phénoménologie de la perception* (1945) was the most original achievement of French phenomenology of its time. Starting from Husserl's late phenomenology of the life world, Merleau-Ponty anchored the phenomena of perception in the phenomenology of the "lived" body in which the perceiving subject was incarnated as the mediating link to the phenomenal world. Such a phenomenology of human "presence" in the world was also to offer in place of the rigid disjunction between idealism and realism an alternative in which consciousness and the world could be reciprocally related. Phenomenology thus became a way of showing the essential involvement of human existence in the world, starting with everyday perception. Important uses of phenomenology can also be found in Paul Ricoeur's *Philosophie de la volonté* (1950, 1960) and Mikel Dufrenne's *Phénoménologie de l'expérience esthétique* (1953).

Ricoeur (b. 1913), who began with a descriptive analysis of the will in all its varieties, stressing the reciprocity of the voluntary and the involuntary factors, has moved recently toward a hermeneutic phenomenology in which the interpretation of symbols in Freudian psychoanalysis, in religion and especially in language are major themes.

Dissemination

Phenomenology spread also to countries other than France. But here its contributions were less original and substantial, and its modifications less pronounced. However, in Belgium, seat of the main Husserl Archives in Louvain since the salvage of Husserl's papers from Nazi Germany by Father H. L. Van Breda, in the Netherlands, in Switzerland, Italy, Spain, where José Ortega y Gasset introduced it, and in the Latin-American countries phenomenology became a major philosophical trend. It was at first less successful in the Anglo-American world, particularly in England, where it was soon eclipsed by the "linguistic analysis" of Gilbert Ryle and by Ludwig Wittgenstein's seemingly anti-phenomenological "philosophical grammar." More recently developments in analytic philosophy, such as J. L. Austin's "linguistic phenomenology," among psychiatrists like R. D. Laing (b. 1927) and a general reaction against analytic thought indicate a change of climate, expressed in new beginnings. The main spokesman of a non-transcendental phenomenology thus far is J. N. Findlay (b. 1903). In the United States, where Marvin Farber (who later became a full-fledged new materialist) obtained a first hearing for phenomenology in the 1930s, it has not yet become fully naturalized. At the New School for Social Research, formerly the University in Exile, Felix Kaufmann, Dorion Cairns, Alfred Schutz, and especially Aron Gurwitsch (1901-1973), who utilized *gestalt* theory, gained a foothold for fresh phenomenologizing. John Wild's (1902-1972) phenomenology of the life world gave it new impetus through his students. Remarkable is also the role of phenomenology in neo-scholastic philosophy all over the world.

Influence

The influence of phenomenology has not been restricted to philosophy. In psychology Brentano and Carl Stumpf had been its pacemakers. In the Goettingen (David Katz, 1884-1958) and the Würzburg (Karl Bühler, 1879-1963) schools and among the gestalt psychologists it had sympathetic allies. Recent phenomenological psychology, headed by the biologist F. J. J. Buytendijk (b. 1887), was inspired by it. Even stronger was the phenomenological impact on psychopathology, where Karl Jaspers (1883-1969) had stressed the importance of phenomenological exploration of the patient's subjective experience, and Ludwig Binswanger (1881-1966), Eugène Minkowski (1885-1972), Erwin Straus (b. 1891) and Henri Ey (b. 1900) had received even more specific inspirations from either Husserl, Scheler, Heidegger or even from Merleau-Ponty and Ricoeur. Indirectly this has also been passed on to Americans like Rollo May (b. 1907) and Carl Rogers (b. 1902). Sociology has been equally responsive to phenomenological stimulation, particularly as developed by Alfred Schutz (1899-1959). In mathematics and physics phenomenological motifs have been passed on through Hermann Weyl, in history through Raymond Aron, in linguistic studies through Roman Jakobson. In the study of religion phenomenology was influential in the work of Rudolf Otto (1869-1937), Friedrich Heiler (1892-1967), Gerardus van der Leeuw (1890-1950) and especially in the later theology of Paul Tillich (1886-1965).

CHARACTERISTICS

Considering the variety of phenomenologies which have thus issued directly or indirectly from Husserl's inspiration, it is not easy to find a common denominator for such a movement beyond its common source. But similar situations occur in other philosophical and non-philosophical movements. Although, seen from Husserl's last perspective, all departures from his own could not but appear as heresies, a more generous view will show that all those who consider themselves as phenomenologists subscribe, for instance, to his watchword "To the Things" (*Zu den Sachen*), meaning by it a fresh approach to the concretely experienced phenomena, as free as possible from conceptual presuppositions, and an attempt to describe them as faithfully as possible. Besides, most adherents to phenomenology will hold that it is possible to obtain insights into the essential structures and the essential relationships among these phenomena on the basis of the careful study of concrete examples supplied by experience or imagination and by systematic variation of these examples in the imagination. Some phenomenologists also stress the need of studying the ways in which the phenomena appear in our consciousness. Beyond this merely static aspect of appearance, some also want to investigate its genetic aspect, exploring, for instance, how a phenomenon, say, a book, constitutes itself in the typical unfolding of our experience. Husserl himself believed that such studies required a previous suspension of belief in the reality of these phenomena (phenomenological reduction), while others consider it not indispensable but helpful. Finally, it should be mentioned that in existential phenomenology the meaning of certain phenomena such as anxiety is explored by a special "hermeneutic" interpretation, whose methodology needs further clarification.

It may also be helpful to bring out the distinctive "essence" of phenomenology by confronting it with some of its philosophical neighbors. In contrast to positivism and traditional empiricism, from which Brentano had started out and with which phenomenology shares the unconditional respect for the positive data of experience ("We are the true positivists," Husserl claimed in his *Ideen*), phenomenology does not restrict these data to the range of sense-experience, but admits on equal terms such nonsensuous data as relations, abstract entities, values, etc., as long as they present themselves intuitively. Consequently phenomenology does not reject universals and recognizes, in addition to the analytic *a priori* and the synthetic *a posteriori*, knowledge of synthetic *a priori* relationships based on insight into essential relationships within the empirically given.

In contrast to phenomenalism, an epistemological position with which it is often confused, phenomenology, which is not primarily an epistemological theory, accepts neither the rigid division between appearance and reality, let alone a thing-in-itself, nor the narrower view that phenomena are all there is (sensations or permanent possibilities of sensations). These are questions on which phenomenology as such keeps an open mind, pointing out, however, that phenomenalism overlooks the complexities of the intentional structure of our consciousness of the phenomena.

In contrast to a rationalism which stresses conceptual reasoning at the expense of experience, phenomenology insists on the intuitive foundation and verification for all formal concepts, and especially for all *a priori claims*; in this sense it is a philosophy "from below," not "from above."

In contrast to an analytic philosophy which substitutes simplified constructions for the immediately given in its complexity and applies "Occam's razor," phenomenology resists all transforming reinterpretations of the given, analyzing it for what it is in itself and on its own terms.

In contrast to linguistic analysis, with which however phenomenology shares its respect for the distinctions of the phenomena reflected in the shades of ordinary language as at least one possible starting point for phenomenological analyses, phenomenology does not think that the study of ordinary language is a sufficient basis for studying the phenomena in all their complexity, which ordinary language cannot and need not try to exhaust.

In contrast to an existential philosophy which believes that existence is unfit for phenomenological analysis and description since it tries to objectify the unobjectifiable, phenomenology holds that it can and must deal with these phenomena, however cautiously, as well as with other elusive phenomena outside human existence.

In the third quarter of the 20th century it remained to be seen whether phenomenology could make solid contributions to philosophical knowledge. To this end it needed to develop rigorous standards, which had not always been observed by some of its most brilliant practitioners, such as Max Scheler, and which were apt to be violated in a philosophy whose ultimate appeal had to be made to intuitive verification. With this proviso, phenomenology may well be qualified, not only to become a bridge for better international communication in philosophy but also to shed new light on philosophical problems old and new, to reclaim for philosophy parts of our everyday life world which have been abandoned by science as too private and too subjective, and finally to give access to layers of our experience unprobed in our everyday living, thus providing deeper foundations for both science and life.

2. WAYS INTO PHENOMENOLOGY:
PHENOMENOLOGY AND METAPHENOMENOLOGY

Proverbially all roads lead to Rome. But not all roads lead there equally fast and equally safely.

This analogy is particularly appropriate to any attempt to choose a way into phenomenology. There is not just one such way but any number of them. Before picking one or building a new road one had better consider this variety. In so doing one ought to bear in mind not only *what* is to be introduced but *to whom* and *by whom*. Perhaps most important, one must be aware of the background and the perspective of those seeking introduction to phenomenology. In this sense all introductions have to be relative, and ideally there ought to be as many introductions as there are persons with different needs. In particular, an Anglo-American student will need a very different introduction than a continental or Latin-American one.

But why call these multiple roads ways *into* phenomenology? Why is it not enough to speak of ways *to* phenomenology, as indeed we spoke of roads *to* Rome? To me this difference indicates much more than the use of different prepositions. It implies, at least potentially, that there can be two kinds or degrees of introduction. One leads as far as the gates of the city leaving the pilgrim wayfarer there alone to enter and find his way by himself; the other way escorts him *inside* the city itself.

This ambiguity attaches even to the English term 'introduction,' one which indicates at the same time the real need and the pitfalls of what is basically a social act – that of introducing. For example, in introducing a person *to* another socially, we certainly make no effort to introduce them to each other's inward personalities and worlds. Beyond providing each with the other's name, we may add minimum information about their stations and backgrounds in order to facilitate their mutual exploring. In other words here we establish contact but no real connection. It seems to me that many of our introductions to a discipline or a subject of study do not amount to much more than such social introductions, allowing a nodding acquaintance but giving no real insight into the subject. In fact, in English the very phrase "introduction to" seems not only conducive to such pseudo-knowledge, but even a contradiction in terms, suggesting at the same time an entering into (*intra*) and merely a leading up "*to*" (*ad*). My point is that there are degrees of introduction, surface introductions and introductions in depth. What I intend to do here is not only to ease the way *to* the gates of phenomenology, but also to give a good look inside what at first must be a bewildering spectacle – a look which will make it possible to distinguish what is genuine from what is fake.

But what exactly does it mean to be introduced *into* phenomenology? Obviously the words "outside" and "inside" are used here metaphorically. What they stand for are differences in the grasp of the subject. "Outside knowledge" indicates the kind of fleeting acquaintance, often second-hand, which might enable one to identify and re-identify an object, to talk about it correctly – but smatteringly. By contrast, "inside knowledge" means a first-hand knowledge sufficient to "do phenomenology," not only to observe it being done, and then merely to accept uncritically its finished product. I mean to suggest that, unless one has a definite idea of how to approach a concrete task phenomenologically, one has not yet been introduced to it meaningfully. But how can this be done?

Any meaningful discussion of ways presupposes a minimum acquaintance with their destination. Hence at this point something has to be said about phenomenology itself, especially for the benefit of those who have been exposed thus far only to the sound of the polysyllabic tongue twister. There would be little point in trying to do this by foisting upon them one of those pocket definitions which rather "wrap up" than "unfold" the subject. What I shall try instead is to give a minimum operational grasp of what it means *to do* phenomenology. In attempting this I do not want to restrict phenomenology to Husserl's increasingly radical – and esoteric – form of it. I intend to interpret the definiendum of a possible final definition in a broader sense, including what is called the Phenomenological Movement, German, French, and even American.

I shall start from the deceptively simple commonly accepted slogan

"To the Things" (*Zu den Sachen*).[1] Its original meaning was that phenomenology aims at a direct investigation of the phenomena. Its peculiar thrust was to get away from the primacy of theories, of concepts and symbols, to immediate contact with the intuited data of experience. In this sense phenomenology represents a reaction against the orientation toward the texts or books, expressed, for instance, in G. E. Moore's notorious confession that, were it not for what philosophers had been saying, he wouldn't have been attracted to philosophy. To phenomenology the primary stimulus of philosophy is what *is* and *appears*, not what anyone thinks or says about it. Yet, phenomenology wants to be more than a mere return to the things, as free as possible from conceptual presuppositions. It wants to see them, and to see them in a new way, namely as phenomena, i.e., as they appear to us, in all their richness, but also in their incompleteness, regardless of whether these phenomena are matched by a corresponding "reality." Take as an example what we really see of a human being when we first meet him. We may begin with his physical characteristics, though most of them are usually concealed by his clothing, and continue with his personal qualities of which we can see at first only very little and indirectly. This is doubly true of his inner life world. Now such seeing is obviously much more than a passive gaping. It involves the intuiting absorption of what confronts us as we approach it with "open eyes." It implies an analytic examination of the structure of the total phenomenon with its elements in context. And normally it will lead to a description of the phenomenon, a description which regardless of all its problems and limitations is apt to sharpen our very seeing.

Now this stage of the phenomenological enterprise, usually called *descriptive phenomenology*, deals only with particular phenomena. At the next stage the phenomenologist tries to determine the typical or essential features of these phenomena, using a method of thought-

---

[1] The closest Husserl came in his publications to using this phrase was in his *Logical Investigations,* where in the Introduction to volume 11, p. 6, (English tr. p. 252) he asked for 'not mere words but the things themselves' and in his manifesto-article on 'Philosophy as a Rigorous Science' (*Logos,* p. 341, tr. p. 146) he asked that research start 'not from philosophies but from the things and problems.' It was only the later Heidegger who asserted that "To the Things" was the basic maxim of phenomenology. See, e.g., his letter to William J. Richardson, *Heidegger: Through Phenomenology to Thought* (The Hague: Nijhoff, 1963, p. XIII) and in his *Zur Sache des Denkens* (Tübingen: Niemeyer, 1969, p. 48).

experiments which Husserl called "free variation in the imagination." Consider, for example, what is essential and inessential to being aware of another being as a human person. This stage often goes by the name of *essential* or *eidetic phenomenology*.

But phenomenology is not only concerned about *what* appears; it is interested at least as much in *how* it appears. This is especially true in the case of consciousness with its direction toward objects other than itself (intentionality). Here it becomes significant to explore the ways in which the phenomena with their many sides are given through various aspects and perspectives, more or less adequately or inadequately. Again, consider the few and only partial perspectives we usually obtain of a person whom we meet in a crowd. One may call this the *phenomenology of appearances*.

Then there is the question of how such phenomena constitute themselves in our consciousness: How, typically, does the picture of another person "take shape" in us, beginning with "first impressions"? This has been called *constitutive phenomenology*.

In addition, some of the more enigmatic and ambiguous phenomena (such as those of human existence) may demand the kind of uncovering interpretation which (since Heidegger) goes by the name of *hermeneutic phenomenology*. But there would be little point in spreading before the reader all the possible dimensions of the phenomenological enterprise. Suffice it if these hints have indicated that doing phenomenology involves a variety of operations which require active and critical "doing."

Now if the above gives at least a first idea, "a phenomenon" of phenomenology, what ways can lead best into the promised land – a land in which phenomenology is not only talked about, but actually undertaken? I shall single out first two more conventional approaches before suggesting, in the next essay, a new way. For the sake of convenience I shall call them (1) the way through the texts, (2) the way through history.

I. THE WAY THROUGH THE TEXTS

By the texts I understand here the authentic writings of the leading self-professed phenomenologists in which they recorded the findings of their search. Here the obvious guide is the central figure of the Movement, Edmund Husserl himself. But in fairness to the historical facts it must not be overlooked that some of the writings of his associates and students, such as Alexander Pfänder, Adolf Reinach, Max Scheler, Dietrich von Hildebrand, Roman Ingarden, Martin Heidegger, and Oskar Becker, as well as the second wave of phenomenologists in France, e.g., Gabriel Marcel, Jean-Paul Sartre, Maurice Merleau-Ponty and Paul Ricoeur, have added substantial contributions to the basic literature.

Unfortunately for most Anglo-American students, these first-hand texts are not accessible directly, but only through the filter of translation. These filters, always a problem, are anything but transparent and far from reliable, especially in the case of the phenomenological literature. With all due admiration for the self-denying and too often thankless job of the translators, there is ample reason to warn against the naive confidence with which the beneficiaries of these translations usually rely on them. At best they are substitutes, or better perspectival appearances, of the one original through the medium of a different language made up of words with different denotations and especially connotations. I have shared enough of the frustrations of translating to know that there are few, if any, exact equivalents for terms which are found in ordinary usage in the original language, but are missing or used only in a different and far from ordinary sense in the target language. There are additional problems in the case of authors who consciously or unconsciously mold, remold, and sometime twist ordinary language or invent new words, as do both Husserl and Heidegger. But granting these special obstacles for the translators, I have to point out that most English translations of the classic texts seriously interfere with an adequate understanding of the originals.[2]

---

[2] As an example of the limitations of one of the best one-man Husserl translations I refer to my 'Remarks on Findlay's Translation of the *Logische Untersuchungen*' in *Journal of the British Society for Phenomenology* III (1972), pp. 195-196. A more serious case is that of the translation of Maurice Merleau-Ponty's *Phénoménologie de la perception* by Colin Smith; see the remarks by Aron Gurwitsch in *Philosophical Review* 73 (1964), pp. 417-22. Something ought to be done about this situation. On the one hand, good translations should receive more prominent recognition. Translators deserve assistance by a central agency. Moreover there should be a center where information about the defects of important translations could be collected and made available on request. The best framework for such services could be a special critical review of translations or a special division in one of the major philosophical reviews. The present Board of Translation founded by Fritz

My conclusion is that ideally only native bilinguals, equally at home in two languages and familiar even with regional variations, such as Husserl's Austriacisms, and having a thorough knowledge of the subject, have a chance to provide us with adequate equivalents of the originals. Short of this, there has to be teamwork between natives of the two languages involved. Besides, phenomenological texts would greatly benefit were they accorded the treatment given Ludwig Wittgenstein's writings, i.e., a presentation of original text and translation side by side, something which has been done only with a few briefer texts of Martin Heidegger thus far. But in no case can a conscientious reader dispense with checking on the original text, especially when the translation is hard to understand.

Assuming then that enough of the original texts can shine through the mirroring substitutes of the translation to make them authentic, we can now enquire how far they lead us to the phenomena themselves. I shall try to answer the question only in the case of a few Husserl texts which by their sub-titles aspired to be introductions to phenomenology. Husserl's case is also pertinent because he himself became increasingly aware of the need for introducing his readers to the more and more radical approach of his later phenomenology, which had left his erstwhile followers far behind.

The first of these three texts, subtitled "General Introduction to Pure Phenomenology," was the *Ideas* (*Ideen*) of 1913. This text, really the first of three projected volumes, begins with a discussion of "Essences and Essential Relations," which systematizes the findings of Husserl's peculiar ontology as developed in his earlier trailblazing *Logical Investigations*. The second part contains a "Fundamental Phenomenological Meditation," which introduces the method of phenomenological reduction with its "bracketing" of reality. But only the third part, after further initial methodological considerations, presents descriptions of concrete structures within the field of consciousness. The last part deals with questions of validity in the light of phenomenological verification.

It must be realized that this introduction was primarily geared to the needs of German readers already prepared by Husserl's earlier work, i.e., the conception of a new "eidetic" or "essential" kind of

Marti at the Southern Illinois University in Edwardsville, Ill. is an important beginning worth recognition and support.

descriptive psychology. Now he wanted them to take an additional step toward a transcendental approach. Even when in 1930 Husserl wrote a special preface to the English translation, he referred to the Lockian tradition merely as background for his new enterprise (incidentally praising Hume as pacemaker of transcendental phenomenology limited only by his bias for sensuous knowledge). But what about this text as an introduction to first-hand phenomenology? Its third part contains indeed concrete accounts of constitution of consciousness, outlining a rich network of dimensions, previously overlooked, and showing particularly the parallelism between act (*noesis*) and object referred to by the act (*noema*). However, one must realize that the *Ideas* remained a torso, with the second (untranslated) volume published only posthumously (1952) and the original third one never even begun. In fact, Husserl himself apparently became increasingly critical of this first introduction as inadequate to his real purpose.

Husserl's second major "Introduction to Phenomenology" had the main title of *Cartesian Meditations*. This attempt had grown out of his four Sorbonne lectures of 1929, themselves a development of his University of London lectures of 1922. But it must not be overlooked that, while the French translation appeared in 1931, Husserl withheld and finally abandoned publication of the German original. His reasons for doing so were partly indicated in his last work, the *Gisis*, i.e., that his Cartesian way was too abrupt and its results empty (§ 43). As far as the original text is concerned (posthumously published in *Husserliana* in 1950) it is chiefly the fifth and longest Meditation, with its first explicit phenomenology of intersubjectivity, which provides concrete and novel material. However, these pieces of direct phenomenologizing have proven more stimulating than convincing. As an introduction to doing phenomenology the *Cartesian Meditations* are probably less effective than the earlier *Ideas*.

There is thus special reason for turning with high expectations to Husserl's last "Introduction to Phenomenological Philosophy" with the main title *The Crisis of the European Sciences and Transcendental Phenomenology*. However, starting at the age of 76, he was unable to complete more than half of this ambitious project before his final sickness and death in 1938. The first two of the projected five parts of this book were published during Husserl's lifetime. But one must be aware of the fact that the most original part III was called back from the editor for reworking, and that it is by no means clear how far he had progressed with this work when he had to stop. Husserl's terminal illness prevented him from beginning the final two parts, which were merely sketched out in a few sentences by Eugen Fink, his collaborator-assistant at the time. Nevertheless, some of the ideas resulting from Husserl's last heroic effort, undertaken while the noose of Nazi persecution was tightening around him, proved to be exceptionally fruitful, even before their final publication by Walter Biemel in 1956. In fact, this new introduction developed two new ways into phenomenology. Their development was preceded by a study in the history of ideas, which interpreted the crisis of the western sciences in terms of the stalemate between objectivistic science (in the Galilean tradition) and subjectivistic psychologism (inspired by Descartes). In Husserl's view, this could be overcome only by a new transcendental approach. The first new way to phenomenology began with the descriptive exploration of the pre-scientific life-world of everyday consciousness and led to its roots in phenomenological subjectivity; the second, less novel, started out from the state of psychology, interpreted as an attempt to become a science independent of the physical sciences, which is in need of a foundation in transcendental consciousness. As far as first-hand phenomenology is concerned, the sketches of the life-world are clearly the most original and suggestive parts of this new work. But it must be realized that for Husserl they had mostly an illustrative function. For to him the life-world was merely a steppingstone toward its subjective origins in pure consciousness.

The upshot of this admittedly slanted survey of Husserl's three introductions to phenomenology is that, while they contain a number of models for direct phenomenological research, their primary emphasis is on developing the *idea* of phenomenology, especially of transcendental phenomenology. Thus at this stage, rather than revealing phenomenology in action, Husserl's phenomenological studies have mostly the function of providing examples from and reports about antecendent findings.

But there is an even more basic limitation for the approach to phenomenology through the texts, whether introductory or advanced. Texts consist of statements and discussions *about* the phenomena. Any study of the texts *as texts* is therefore in a sense meta-phenomenology, not phenomenology proper.[3] Only inasmuch as the texts are used as stimuli for independent verification by a reader who is already emancipated from them can they aid in actual phenomenologizing. Besides, only too often texts tend to become canonical. And such canonization could mean the very death of live phenomenology.

II. THE WAY THROUGH HISTORY

Texts are not always self-explanatory. Even if they were so at the time of writing, they no longer will be for a different readership than the one to which they were originally addressed. This is one reason why even the classic texts are in increasing need of commentaries. While some of these philological commentaries can be restricted to interpretations and clarifications of textual meanings, the major need is that for providing historical background, especially when the texts no longer appear in their *contexts*. *Without* such historical aids the gap between the author and the reader can become unbridgeable, *with* such aids the gap can at least be narrowed, if not closed. This is one of the major reasons why thus far historical introductions and monographs had to be the major form of activity in the teaching of, and writing about, phenomenology in the Anglo-American world. Yet granting this, I must still be frank about the limitations and dangers of such an approach to phenomenology, especially if this becomes the major avenue to it. I feel a particular duty and right to such frankness since I may be one of the prime offenders of what may be called *phenomenological historicism*.

This is not to deny the need for studying and teaching history, including the history of phenomenology. One of its uses may well be that of an introduction to phenomenology proper. But it would certainly not be its *main* use. History is primarily interested in telling and understanding a story, the story of past events, including the story of philosophies and philosophers. Only secondarily is it interested in what they are philosophizing *about*. In such a story even the

[3] The expression 'metaphenomenology' formed after the model of such predecessors as meta-ethics or meta-language is not meant as a mere analogy to them. Specifically it does not merely deal with the concepts of phenomenology (as meta-ethics would) with a language of phenomenology, a task which certainly would make sense. All I have in mind here is any kind of study which does not deal with the phenomena directly but instead with studies of these phenomena, such as their history.

classic texts figure merely as links in longer chains. In this sense one might say that if the phenomenological texts are already at one remove from the phenomena, the study of the history of these texts is phenomenology at second remove. In short, if the philological study of the texts is meta-phenomenology, then a study of their history is meta-meta-phenomenology. In this sense, and studied in this spirit, the historical way to phenomenology can become a flight from the phenomena. Unfortunately, a good deal of the so-called post-war renaissance of phenomenology in Europe is not much more than historicizing Husserl-philology, meritorious in its own right, but dangerous if one forgets that it can be defended only as a means to the end – the return to Husserl's phenomena.

There is another danger: The ideal of objectivity, no matter how problematic, obligates the historian to remain neutral with regard to the issues and to the texts. As far as criticism is concerned, he may be allowed to check his texts for internal consistency. But he is not permitted to challenge them by investigating the phenomena to which they refer and to decide about the truth or falsehood of the texts. This professional neutrality may again divert and alienate the student from a genuine interest in the phenomena.

But the greatest danger is that the study of history will discourage fresh and spontaneous research, especially in the case of the conscientious novice. What Nietzsche said about the boon and bane of history in general also applies to the history of philosophy and phenomenology: "Only strong personalities can stand history; it completely extinguishes the weak." The historical giants can certainly overawe the phenomenological novice if he is told at once how much has already been said and written about the subject and how much he has to read before he is allowed to test his own wings. The study of history may not only sidetrack him from the phenomena, it can paralyze him. From this perspective, I would plead: Better some early dilettantism than mature sterility. What has to be prevented is the castration of present life by its past. Freedom *from* history is as important as awareness and selective use *of* it. In Santayana's terms, we don't want to be condemned to repeating it (though some repetition may be helpful) but we also do not want to be condemned to being history's slaves.

However, after this outburst of anti-historicism I would like to make it plain that I do not think history has to be approached in the spirit of historicism. In fact, by challenging it I want to make room for a more productive use of history, precisely in an approach to phenomenology. A phenomenology at second remove can actually play the role of a double negation, i.e., by removing the remove. A historical relativization of the texts may lead us beyond and below the texts, not only to the "moved" phenomenologists but to the moving phenomena. Thus in defense of my "shady" past I may even point out that I gave my account in the *Phenomenological Movement* the sub-title "A Historical Introduction." This was not in the sense of an introduction to its history but to "moving" phenomenology itself, i.e., to the doing of phenomenology, as I tried to develop it in my last chapter: "The Essentials of the Phenomenological Method." It was also in this spirit that I ended my preface with the sentence: "The ultimate criterion for the success of this introduction will be whether it can entice the reader farther, either to the original sources of this account, or better to the ultimate source for all phenomenological research, the 'things themselves'." In other words, I wanted to lead from meta-meta-phenomenology via meta-phenomenology to actual phenomenologizing.

I have little, if any, evidence that this ultimate goal has been achieved or even promoted. Instead I have heard only too often that my obsolescing perspective of the phenomenological movement was a definitive history, a verdict which now may easily block the way to new research and new perspectives. So I knew, and know now even better, that more and different ways into phenomenology have to be built if phenomenology itself is to return to the phenomena and to become re-creative. It is in this sense that in the following essay I would like to give an account of one such attempt to do phenomenology directly.

3. A NEW WAY INTO PHENOMENOLOGY:
THE WORKSHOP APPROACH

What I would like to present here is a way of doing phenomenology together which, to my knowledge, has not yet been tried systematically. True, philosophy as such has never been done only by solitary reflection but also in groups, for instance by dialogue, if not by the more formalized techniques of the scholastic disputation. In fact, a special term for philosophizing together, *sym-philosophein*, occurs in the *Ethics* of Aristotle, who is otherwise known chiefly as the monological lecturer rather than as the advocate of Platonic dialogue. Husserl himself was fond of using the Greek term when he reached out for others to share his phenomenological quest, only to realize that his longing was in vain and that he had to do his pioneer work by himself. But neither in his seminars, which were usually dominated by his monologues, nor in more intimate conversation did he develop anything like a technique for joint phenomenologizing. There was more give and take in the seminars and colloquia of some of Husserl's early associates such as Alexander Pfänder and Adolf Reinach, and there was a good deal of free exchange in the philosophical societies and discussion circles in Göttingen and Munich before the First World War. But nothing was done to develop such mutual free exchanges into a method of cooperative research. Can this be done? [1] And why should it be done?

My primary concern in trying to develop cooperative phenomenology and its method was to revive phenomenology as a fresh ap-

---

[1] A significant precedent for such systematic group research seems to have been developed by John L. Austin in his Saturday research teams and joint sessions. Here the emphasis was of course on the exploration of ordinary (English) language in the spirit of Austin's 'linguistic phenomenology,' as he nearly came to characterize his enterprise. (Urmson, J. O., 'The Philosophy of John Austin' in *Journal of Philosophy* LXII (1965) pp. 499-508).

proach directly to the phenomena in opposition to mere meta-phenomenology through textual and historical studies which has taken its place especially since World War II in Germany and in the Anglo-American world. I have been disappointed by the relative sterility in recent phenomenological philosophy as far as first-hand research is concerned, especially in comparison with what happened in such countries as France and the Netherlands. What is needed today is a revival of the spirit of doing phenomenology directly on the phenomena, the "things," the spirit which permeated the first generation of phenomenologists. What can be done to reawaken it in a very different setting?

My second concern was to free phenomenology from the seemingly utter privacy and subjectivity, if not solipsism, to which according to certain interpretations of the Husserlian conception it is doomed. What I would like to show is that there is nothing in the nature of the phenomenological approach that confines it to isolated practice, that it can be performed, like any other observation, in groups as well as in isolation, and that these groups could and should communicate.

Now these two concerns are certainly very different. First-hand phenomenology can be done separately and cooperatively, and so can second-hand phenomenology. Moreover, cooperative philosophy need not take the form of phenomenology. However, what I would like to show is that doing phenomenology by cooperating groups may be particularly suited to the doing of first-hand phenomenology. This was the idea behind the pilot experiment of a workshop in phenomenology which took place five times at Washington University between 1965 and 1972 and about which I want to report. I thought that cooperative phenomenology could perhaps overcome the seemingly hopeless stalemate between contradictory "intuitions" of individual phenomenologists. The usual defeatism in this regard seemed to me unwarranted and premature. By concerted effort to explore and narrow down clashes by entering sympathetically and empathically into one another's perspectives and by pointing out overlooked aspects of the phenomena, at least some of the alleged chaos of subjectivities could be overcome in an inter-subjectivity which might better be called co-subjectivity (a term used before and in a somewhat different sense by Gabriel Marcel).

I. THE ORIGINAL IDEA

The idea of a workshop in phenomenology, in which phenomenology would be "done" and not only talked about, came to me only gradually. I wanted to "do phenomenology" within the framework of the American academic setting. In pondering ways which could facilitate the return from meta-phenomenology to the actual doing of phenomenology, I considered (and actually mentioned toward the end of my historical introduction to phenomenology),[2] the possibility of intensive seminars or workshops. Here participants would do sustained work without the interruptions of other academic demands. Independently I had also become acquainted with what seemed to me a rather unique American contribution to education, the summer workshop, a framework which, to be sure, covers a multitude of sins as well as virtues. Would it be possible to use such a frame for the cooperative doing of phenomenology?

What I had in mind first was that such a workshop would consist of a small number of graduate students who would select limited, "bitesize" topics for phenomenological exploration. They would start out by carrying out parallel private investigations of suitable phenomena, preferably not yet covered, and prepare brief written reports of their findings, without any reference to the literature. They would then read these reports to a joint work session for comparing notes, mutual exploration, and finally discussion of seeming and real disagreements. In these, the "director" would serve only as a "facilitator" or "catalyst." The first week would provide basic training through the study of preselected topics. The second week was to be reserved for research on newly chosen topics, to be decided by the group on the basis of suggestions and preference polling.

However, such cooperative group sessions were not to be the only and even the major feature of such a workshop. At least equally as important as the opportunity for exchange and interaction was to be the chance to do preparatory and supplementary work by oneself. Thus at least half the day was to be left free from scheduled group sessions and to be used at the discretion of the members for follow-up studies, and (now, after the direct study of the phenomena) for library check-ups, for the preparation of the next group session, for

---

[2] *The phenomenological Movement* (The Hague: Nijhoff, 1960, p. 646).

spontaneous continued group exploration of the morning topics or other interests, and for consultation with the director and his assistant. ⧵

Finally, there was to be a chance for making personal contact with other phenomenologists and their work. The most convenient arrangement for such contacts was to be through evening lectures, panels and similar events. Preference was to be given to young American scholars at the start of their productive careers, giving them a sympathetic sounding board for their ideas, which the larger professional meetings rarely, if ever, can offer.

II. THE REALIZATION

These ideas were aired first at a symposium of the Society for Phenomenology and Existentialism at Evanston in 1962, which ever since has aided and abetted the experiment. The first occasion to try out the idea came in 1965, when Washington University in St. Louis offered us space in one of its new dormitories for joint living quarters. It was not an easy start. But I shall refrain from telling all about the vicissitudes, the "fumbles" as well as the "hits" of the experiment. A brief survey must suffice.[3]

The first workshop (1965), supported by a grant from the National Science Foundation, attracted only seven participants, all but two of them graduate students; the two exceptions were younger colleagues. However, all responded with an enthusiasm that could easily have misled me into believing that the method had proved itself for any group, particularly since they not only encouraged unanimously a repetition of the workshop in the following year but spontaneously decided to return themselves for concentrated work in one particular area, the phenomenology of language. What is more, they did return with but two exceptions.

The second workshop (1966) faced a very different situation, primarily because it consisted of two groups: the returned "veterans," planning to pursue their special project based on "workbench papers," and a larger group of sixteen "novices," again mostly graduate students. Although this workshop received unexpected generous

---

[3] More detailed reports for each workshop are available in mimeographed form on special request from the Archives of Washington University in St. Louis.

publicity from a British visitor, Professor Wolfe Mays,[4] I personally considered its success as limited. It certainly showed that for optimum results the work groups had to be kept small so that the rounds could be made quickly enough, i.e., not larger than ten participants. Ground rules had to be drafted specifying equal rights, exploratory questions rather than argumentation, tolerance without indifference, and quick feedback in case of frictions. Also, the new group needed more direction for the basic training by way of focusing questions or "practice studies," as we later called them. Besides, the veterans could not pursue their advanced work intensively enough for substantial results because they had to give a helping hand with the new sub-divided group. It was therefore no surprise to me that the final evaluation by this group was less enthusiastic than that of the first.

Thus I was not unhappy when the third workshop (1967) consisted of only one group of ten members, now only new students, the veterans having decided on a separate meeting elsewhere later in the fall (which did not materialize). Now we could try out a more sophisticated and progressive set of practice studies. The ground rules for turn-taking in the work sessions could be made more flexible. In subjective terms, the student evaluation to the final questionnaire went up by one notch from that in 1966.

There was no workshop in 1968 because I had to spend most of the summer in Europe. However, a two-day Workshop-institute offered by the Department of Philosophy at DePaul University in Chicago, consisting mostly of lectures and discussion groups conducted by various faculty members, gave me a chance for describing the Washington University experiment and giving a brief demonstration of what a worksession would be like.

The fourth workshop, slightly expanded in size, took place in 1969. Its chief gain was a systematic development of the practice studies for the first week, leading methodically from the descriptive study of a particular private phenomenon through that of a "public" phenomenon to a study of essential insights through systematic variations in the imagination, next to that of appearances and finally to the genetic constitution of phenomena in consciousness. Also, a more concerted effort was made to organize the research on newly chosen topics during the second week, shifting the responsibility for the

---

[4] See *Philosophical Quarterly* XVII (1967) pp. 262-265.

presentation of theses or of research questions to volunteers among the workshoppers. But the main innovation, triggered by the need of giving the workshop academic credit status for some of the graduate students, consisted in the requirement of a research paper following the two workshop weeks. This led to some encouraging, though not yet publishable papers.

There was a hiatus, this time of two years, between this workshop and the fifth (and probably last at Washington University), again because of my involvement in European projects during the summers. Nevertheless, the fifth workshop showed the largest number of qualified new members from the widest geographical range. While there were minor changes in the practice studies and procedures for the second week, the pattern was practically the same as that of the fourth workshop. The main difference was less in the objectively demonstrable output than in the subjective satisfaction level among the participants. This resulted in first plans for moving the workshop to other academic locations under fresh and younger leadership.

This does not mean that the workshop approach has proved more than its viability. It requires further developments and adjustments, depending to a considerable extent on the availability of better financial backing.

III. THE NEW METHODS

I would now like to give a first taste of what ways of "going to the things" have been developed during these five workshops, and report especially about the technique of the work sessions.

After a general briefing, the first session begins typically with a model demonstration. Having plugged briefly his ears, each member in turn reports on whether and what he has been hearing. After each report the other members in the circle are given a chance of asking questions for further details, but at this stage still without the right of making statements about their own parallel experiences. The same procedure is used for the reports of the other members in the circle. Then an attempt is made to assess the findings, usually with the result that, even disregarding unavoidable outside noises (air-conditioners, etc.), everyone, upon careful listening, has heard *something*. This leads to first observations about the phenomenology of silence, of body noises, their location and the like.

On this basis the mimeographed assignment for the first regular work session (on the second day) is passed out. For this session the participants are asked to prepare written answers to questions about what they can see in a dark room with their eyes closed. This study was finally divided into three parts: an "untutored" part asks the participants merely very general questions about the phenomena observed and their ways of observing them. A second part contains more pointed questions, which are to draw attention to some of the phenomenologically most significant aspects of the phenomena, such as the stability, location and texture of the emerging phenomena and the surrounding field. Finally comments on descriptions of the phenomena by other informants and from the literature are invited as possible aids in developing and attuning what may look at first like highly divergent accounts.

These first examples, beginning with generally neglected and supposedly merely private phenomena, are followed by topics of a more public nature, beginning with three-dimensional visual objects. Again, starting with untutored observations and descriptions, supplementary questions try to direct attention to such neglected features as partial presentation and illumination. In this connection an attempt is made to make the participants aware of what is often called the intentional structure of such experiences, such as the aspects and ways of appearing of such phenomena as transparent objects or passing melodies.

Up to this point no attempt is made to develop what is easily the biggest stumbling block in the phenomenological methodology, the so-called essential intuition or insight into general essential structures (*Wesensschau*). While a responsible phenomenological intuition presupposes the thorough study of particular phenomena as examples, the transition to such general insights is by no means simple. It has to appeal to what Husserl usually called "free variation in the imagination." But certainly this freedom requires a good deal of discipline, if one wants to arrive at valid results. In order to prepare it the workshop had to develop a practice study which, on the basis of varying factors one at a time, attempted to tabulate the result of each such variation, and thus determine what is or is not essential to a certain type of phenomenon.

Similar practice studies were worked out for the exploration of ways of appearance, based for instance on the study of different paintings of the same subject done by the same painter, with Monet's Cathedral Series as the major exhibit. Also, a practice study was prepared which directed attention to the way in which phenomena constituted themselves in the unfolding of our perceptions from incipient stages to a relatively filled-out determination of previously vague anticipations.

It took us more time to develop techniques for stimulating "emancipated" research on newly chosen phenomena during the second week. All during the first week suggestions for such new projects were solicited, collected and finally selected by a preference poll. The topic or topics rating highest were assigned each one session, and one member was to present his findings in more definite form than during the first week. At the same time he would formulate questions for the other members of his group in order to explore their perspectives. They in turn were then to explore his own presentation empathetically. Thus the co-subjective approach was by no means abandoned. But it was now coupled with a more concerted and penetrating analysis of the phenomena, where one member would pioneer, as it were, but without losing assistance and check-ups from his fellow explorers. More important, the presenting member now trained himself not only to stretch his scope of viewing but also to make others see with him.

IV. THE USES AND LIMITATIONS OF GROUP PHENOMENOLOGY

Assuming that the prime need at the moment is to revive the spirit of doing phenomenology by going directly to the "things," why should doing it jointly be a particularly good way?

Here it is important to forestall a misunderstanding. I have no intention of opposing solitary to joint phenomenology. In fact, it is obvious that thus far most, if not all, insights in phenomenology have been achieved by pioneering individual phenomenologists with little aid from fellow phenomenologists. All the more is it important to realize that group phenomenology does not exclude but includes individual work. Even the present brief account should have made it clear that group phenomenology on a serious scale, i.e., after the first model session, begins with an assignment asking each participant to explore the chosen phenomenon by himself before he pools his findings with those of his fellow investigators. Also, the joint phase terminates with the solitary re-examination of the results of the group sessions with a view to reporting changes in one's perspective at the beginning of the subsequent group meeting. Besides, the freedom from scheduled meetings in the afternoon, while not excluding spontaneous exchanges, is meant largely to allow for and promote private study of the common topics. I believe that after such preparation and follow-up group phenomenologizing can achieve much more than spontaneous phenomenological brainstorming can do.

What then can group phenomenology do that cannot be achieved equally well, if not better, in undisturbed solitude? I would like to suggest at least the followings gains of sym-phenomenologizing:

1. It stimulates: One of the most exciting experiences during worksessions is the catalytic effect that remarks and exchanges can have not only on those immediately involved but on the "bystanders," as it were. Very often the give and take during worksessions suddenly opened up new perspectives, if only of a preliminary character.

2. It controls: By this I mean that the need to communicate and to clarify one's reports in answer to exploratory questions may have screening and even sobering effect on less self-critical participants. In this sense intersubjective communication of findings may be a first step in de-subjectivizing and freeing phenomenology from the kind of irresponsible subjectivism with which it is often charged.

3. It intersubjectivizes: Intersubjectivity is at least as serious a concern of phenomenology as a rigorous enterprise as it is of other scientific studies and philosophies. The exchanges among the partners of a cooperative phenomenology team are perhaps the best way available for reaching objectivity for phenomenological results in spite of their subjective bases.

4. It enriches and complements: Clearly one single phenomenologist, even if he has trained his imaginative variation in an attempt to vary his limited personal perspective in order to achieve general insights, is not likely to exhaust all possible perspectives of his subject. Group phenomenology can not only add to his own experience, it can also check and aid his flagging imagination by stimulating and corroborating it.

5. It can attune: Co-operative phenomenology is not merely a matter of exchanging views, of "swapping" reports, as it has been called, or even of registering and, as far as possible, understanding

one another's different perspectives. Such an outcome need not be the "end of the story," it can be the beginning of a new one, the attempt to attune dissonances. But what does it mean to "attune"? The expression is taken from the field of music. Even in this field much remains to be clarified about what is involved in "tuning" and "attuning." But that something can be done about dissonances and about attuning instruments that are out of tune may be indications of what can be tried about discrepant accounts of phenomena. Mutual exploration may reveal that the instruments of description are out of tune, i.e., that the disagreements among the describers are merely verbal, and that a readjustment of the linguistic tools can clear up some discrepancies. But "attunement" is also possible at a deeper level if the dissonances should be in the prelinguistic experiences. Here it is possible to direct and redirect our viewing by "drawing attention" to factors previously overlooked, by pointing out unconscious preconceptions and the like. In the pursuit of such attempts at attunement one of the most meaningful and revealing occurrences may be when one of the partners suddenly exclaims "aha" in a tone of voice indicating that he has not only just become aware of something new but also realizes that he has discovered what the other partner meant all along. Such episodes were among the most rewarding of the workshop experiences. The phenomenology of what is going on in such experiences may throw important light on the process involved in genuine attunement.

In talking up the possible virtues of group phenomenology I have already made it clear that it is meant to serve primarily as a supplement, not as a substitute for solitary phenomenology. But even in this limited role it has its pitfalls. Some of them became apparent when the need for certain ground rules for the work sessions had to be formulated:

1. the rule of turn taking in response to the danger of self-important monopolizing of the exchanges;

2. the rule of exploration against the danger of insufficient communication through ambiguous expression or inadequate inspection; and

3. the rule of tolerance without indifference against the danger of intimidating persuasion.

But there may also be a more general danger of overestimating the value of cooperative agreement. Neither is it the necessary nor the sufficient test of truth. In the absence of cooperative partners agreement becomes meaningless and dispensable. But even where there are other interested partners, their unanimity by itself is never a sufficient test.

Finally, even intersubjectivity appears only in subjective perspectives. So does dissonance and attunement. There is no fool-proof method even in phenomenology. This is equally true of cooperative phenomenology, which is no royal road to *the* truth.

V. INTERIM BALANCE AND UNFINISHED BUSINESS

I hope I have left no doubt about the fact that in spite of all the increasingly positive responses of the participants of the five workshops I am by no means satisfied that the case for the workshop approach is established. There is no demonstrable evidence that after the workshop members emerged with better phenomenologica vision. And there is no indication that they are more immune to meta-phenomenology. There is not yet any output by way of literary production that has found its way into publication.

These realizations suggest caution. They are not reasons for giving up the experiment. Yet they are reasons for modifying it with a view to working for more demonstrable results. For this reason too it is time to replace the most constant variable thus far, the director of the workshop. From that point it may be a blessing in disguise that at this point he has to disqualify himself for physical reasons.

Group phenomenology is unfinished business, but I see no good reason for declaring it unfinishable. What has been "completed" is the proof that such an enterprise can be run and re-run even at decreasing administrative cost and that it can be succesful at least in the eyes of the participants. What remains to be demonstrated to others is that it can produce fruits in the form of publishable results by which it can be known and justify its existence.

4. PHENOMENOLOGY THROUGH VICARIOUS EXPERIENCE*

I. THE PROBLEM AND ITS BACKGROUND

By "phenomenology through vicarious experience" I understand a phenomenology which is based on what one sees not with one's own eyes, but with the eyes of others. How can this be done? More important, how can it be justified?

Before I try to answer these questions I would like to explain my stake in these questions. As part of my unfinished and, if the truth be told, unfinishable undertaking of tracing the impact of phenomenology on extra-philosophical studies, I have become particularly intrigued by the role phenomenology plays in psychology, psychopathology, and psychiatry.[1] I am impressed by the amount and originality of the concrete studies and results attained by such phenomenological psychiatrists as Ludwig Binswanger and Erwin Straus. I am, therefore, in a way flattered by the prestige phenomenology enjoys among them. But, at the same time, I feel a certain uneasiness about it. Can phenomenology really claim credit in their work? Or is it based on a misunderstanding of phenomenology, however productive? Should not phenomenology, therefore, in all honesty and humility decline the honor of all the compliments which it now receives as misplaced and undeserved?

Now as to the reasons for my purist scruples: Phenomenology, not only taken in its strict Husserlian sense but even in its broader senses, aspires to be a direct study of the phenomena as given to the phenomenologist himself without any intermediaries, personal or impersonal. It spurns especially all evidence based on inference and

---

* Straus, Erwin, ed., *Phenomenology: Pure and Applied* (Pittsburgh: Duquesne University Press, 1964, pp. 105-126).

[1] The results have now been published in *Phenomenology in Psychology and Psychiatry* (Evanston: Northwestern University Press, 1972).

on explanatory hypotheses. Now, for the purpose of argument we may assume that we have direct access to the normal experiences of other people with whom we can communicate. But how can any investigation of phenomena which are as inaccessible to the normal range of our experience as those of the neurotic and especially the psychotic person claim to be phenomenological? Isn't one of the main characteristics of mental illness the breakdown of normal communication, the drifting off of our patients into worlds where we can no longer reach them directly, and perhaps not even indirectly? How then can phenomenology propose to enter the world of the abnormal? Isn't the phenomenology which is here invoked really a perversion of the original conception of phenomenology, a pseudo-phenomenology?

II. KARL JASPERS' "PHENOMENOLOGY" OF PSYCHOPATHIC PHENOMENA

In order to substantiate my qualms I shall submit the evidence in the case of Karl Jaspers, whose classic *Allgemeine Psychopathologie* of 1913 contained undeniably – although he, himself, modestly denied it – the strongest impulse for the growth of a phenomenological psychopathology. Jaspers' book began with a long first chapter on "The Subjective Phenomena (*Erscheinungen*) of the Abnormal Life of the Psyche," called in parentheses "Phänomenologie." [2] This chapter, constituting about one-fifth of the book, dealt with the "elements of the abnormal psychic life" as well as with the "general properties and types of psychological processes (*Ablaufsweisen*)," but excluded from its scope the study of the objective symptoms and achievements (*Leistungen*) of the psychic life, which were relegated to a second chapter on the psychology of objective achievements (*Leistungspsychologie*); likewise all connections among the subjective elements, intelligible as well as non-intelligible, were kept out of phenomenology. However, the fact that in a separate article, to which

---

[2] Beginning with the fourth edition (completed in 1942 but not published until 1946) this chapter was incorporated into a new 'First Part,' dealing with the separate facts (*Einzeltatbestände*) of psychic life, an arrangement which toned down the importance of the phenomenological chapter, while still leaving it as the entrance gate to psychopathology. The book was translated rather freely by J. Hoenig and M. Hamilton as *General Psychopathology* (Manchester: Manchester University Press, 1962).

Jaspers referred in the book, he talked about a special phenomenological trend of research in psychopathology [3] shows how much importance he attached to phenomenology at that time.

What then is the objective of Jaspers' phenomenology? What are its methods?

Jaspers leaves no doubt about his answers. The goal of phenomenology is "making present (*vergegenwärtigen*) to our mind the subjective mental experiences, their demarcation and fixation, so that we always mean the same thing by our concepts" (p. 22f). Later he reaffirms even more explicitly that it is "the task of phenomenology to make present to us intuitively (*anschaulich*) the mental states which actually only the patients experience" (p. 47). This second characterization makes it apparent that the phenomenological psychopathologist does not experience the pathological phenomena himself and in actuality. All he aspires to achieve is to make them mentally present to his inspection. In other words, the goal of such a phenomenology is merely imaginative access to phenomena which are perceptually inaccessible. For the German term *Vergegenwärtigung* does not mean making present in actual perception but merely in imagination, "as if" they were perceived.

This becomes even clearer from Jaspers' statements about his *method*. For he states that what is made present in his phenomenology is known only indirectly from the descriptions of the patients which the psychiatrist has to interpret in analogy with his own ways of experiencing (p. 46). The means to be used in this interpretation are characterized in more detail in the article on the phenomenological trend, where the following three ways are distinguished:

1. immersion (*Versenkung*) in the behavior or conduct and the expressive movements of the patient;

2. questioning (*Exploration*) as carried out by the psychiatrist, resulting in information by the patients about themselves;

3. spontaneous accounts (*Selbstschilderungen*) by the patients in writing, about which Jaspers says at once that they are "rarely good, but if they are good, they are very valuable and conditionally usable (*op. cit.*, p. 598).

---

[3] 'Die phänomenologische Forschungsrichtung in der Psychopathologie,' *Zeitschrift für Neurologie*, IX, (1912), pp. 319-408. (Republished in *Gesammelte Schriften zur Psychopathologie*, Springer Verlag: Berlin-Göttingen-Heidelberg, 1963).

Clearly, none of these means will lead the psychopathologist directly to the phenomena as experienced by the patient. Immersion in the patient's behavior, while more than behaviorist account, will give him at best clues for interpretation; questioning will allow him to gather material for his hypotheses; spontaneous descriptions will let him see the patient's own experience as in a mirror darkly.

Why then did Jaspers call this enterprise "phenomenology"? How could he believe, as he did at least at the time, that it had something in common with Husserl's new phenomenology, as introduced in his *Logical Investigations* of 1901? The answer that makes most sense to me is that Jaspers was so preoccupied by the need for investigating the subjective phenomena as the primary foundation of psychopathology that he paid relatively little attention to the questions of the means. Only the "what" mattered, the "how" was a secondary consideration.

In this context it should also be mentioned that in those days it was Husserl who tried to convince Jaspers that he was part of the Phenomenological Movement, while Jaspers himself remained skeptical.[4] Jaspers' relation to, and his increasing detachment from this movement makes an intriguing story, but one which has little relevance to our present concern. The essential fact is that Jaspers' limited use of phenomenology in psychopathology is methodologically unrelated to, if not irreconcilable with, the conception of phenomenology which emphasizes the direct approach to the phenomena as the decisive feature of its method. His phenomenology is defined by its subject matter, the subjective phenomena. To him any method that leads to it is acceptable.

III. DEVELOPMENTS IN PSYCHOPATHOLOGY SINCE JASPERS

It would be misleading to identify phenomenological psychopathology with Jaspers' version of it. Since the appearance of the first edition of the *Psychopathologie*, relations between philosophical phenomenology and psychopathology have become much closer. Ludwig Binswanger was the leading name in this development. But this is not the place for presenting the facts, still so little explored, of the concrete impact of phenomenology on psychology and psycho-

---

[4] *Rechenschaft und Ausblick* (München: Piper, 1951, p. 327).

pathology. I can merely mention the names of the protagonists of this story: Eugène Minkowski, Viktor von Gebsattel, Erwin Straus, F. J. J. Buytendijk, Medard Boss, Viktor Frankl.[5] What is important here is that in the attempt to understand the patient in his world phenomenologically more direct methods than Jaspers' inferential procedures have been introduced and developed. Among these "hermeneutic" procedures are various modifications of empathy and the operation which goes by the apparently untranslatable German term *Verstehen*, an act which aims chiefly at a grasp of the intelligible contents shared by both the understanding and the understood partners. All of these methods try to spare us the indirectness and precariousness of deductive and inductive inferences and merely constructive hypotheses as used particularly in the psychoanalytic theories. This is true also of the deciphering method of Sartre's existential psychoanalysis.

But even these additional techniques do not change anything in the fundamental situation and its problem, which I shall now try to spell out.

IV. THE SCOPE OF THE PROBLEM

In striving for access as direct as possible to be psychopathic phenomena we first have to take account of the basic structure of all consciousness, i.e., primarily of its intentionality, by distinguishing between intending acts and intended objects or referents. On a more encompassing scale this distinction is expressed by the polarity of the experiencing person and his experienced world. The significance of this distinction is that phenomenological psychology and psychopathology really face a double task: that of knowing the person as the center of his world and that of knowing the world of which he is the focal center.

To this general assignment, which is ambitious enough, an even more demanding one is now added, that of crossing the gap between the normal and the abnormal range. By a "normal" person I understand here simply one whose structure is roughly the same as that of his investigator, whereas an "abnormal" person differs in a significant manner from the investigator, to an extent which makes the

---

[5] I have reported more of this story in *Phenomenology in Psychology and Psychiatry*.

transition from one to the other problematic, to say the least. This is obviously only a very preliminary and temporary characterization of normality and abnormality. But it is enough for our purposes. It also makes it clear that the difference between normal and abnormal is primarily one of degree of intelligibility.

What should be stressed from the very start is that such "abnormality" is not restricted to neurotic and psychotic individuals. In this sense comparable "abnormal" features can be found in the case of the genius at the upper end of the scale. Besides, there is the "abnormality" of the saint, the prophet, and of any one who claims privileged religious experience. There may be similar structural differences between members of our generation and the people in other periods of history. Even more important and extreme are some of the differences with which anthropology confronts us, where we approach different cultures and corresponding personalities. Hence, our problem has significance far beyond the field of phenomenological psychopathology.

In the light of these intersecting distinctions of person and world, of normal and abnormal, we can now formulate the following four interrelated problems for the phenomenologist:

1. How to obtain direct access to another normal person;
2. How to obtain direct access to his world;
3. How to obtain direct access to an abnormal person;
4. How to obtain direct access to his world.

V. HUSSERL'S ATTEMPT TO WIDEN THE SCOPE OF DIRECT PHENOMENOLOGY

I shall begin with the first problem, that of how to obtain access to other persons within the normal range. Here phenomenology is reputed to have a relatively simple answer. As a good many philosophers, phenomenological as well as non-phenomenological, have realized, the still wide-spread theory according to which our knowledge of other minds is based on an inference by analogy between a foreign organism and our own is untenable.[6] So is the empathy theo-

---

[6] The main phenomenological critic of this theory, advocated first by John Stuart Mill, was Max Scheler in his book on the nature and forms of sympathy (part III, Section III). Among non-phenomenologists George Santayana (*Reason in Common Sense,* Ch. VI) and more recently Norman Malcolm ('Knowledge

ry, according to which a process of empathy, induced by a tendency
to imitate another person's behavior, leads us to his mind. Max
Scheler had the courage to maintain that there is such a thing as a
direct [7] perception of other selves and back up this claim by specific
examples. However, in so doing Scheler focused merely on the question of how we know about other persons' emotions, attitudes, and
personalities. He did not pay attention to the question of how we
can know what their intentional acts and attitudes refer to, in other
words, to our knowledge of other people's intended worlds. Yet we
can hardly claim that we understand a particular case of indignation
before we know what the indignation is all about. Scheler neglected
this problem.[8]

Now this is a problem which Husserl did face. I believe that he
deserves credit for having initiated in addition to his other achievements an extension of phenomenology which would enable it to approach the problem of the other person and his world more directly
than by inference. My reasons are as follows: In his radical insistence
on absolute or "apodictic" certainty as the foundation of all philosophy and science, Husserl subjected the other person and his
world to the same kind of "reduction" or bracketing as that which he
had applied to all other parts of the "transcendent" or trans-subjective world. Initially this did not mean more than that the belief in
the existence of the referents of our acts be kept in abeyance. But
more and more it came to mean that all the acts in which these
referents were constituted in consciousness were to be suspended,
with the result that eventually these referents appeared as constituted
by consciousness. In other words, phenomenology became a special
kind of idealistic philosophy, a phenomenological or "transcendental" idealism.

We need not enter into the vexed controversy about phenomenological idealism, realism, or neutralism in order to realize that
phenomenology, taken in Husserl's radical sense, has a rough time
with any account of our knowledge of other people, let alone ab-

of Other Minds' in *Journal of Philosophy* LV (1958), pp. 969-78) have criticized
the analogy argument.

[7] The expression 'direct' as applied to cognitive processes, beginning with
perception, is anything but precise, and needs thorough clarification in the light
of the different phenomena to which it is applied. In this essay it means not
more than 'non-inferential.'

[8] See also Schutz, Alfred, *Collected Papers* I, p. 175 (on 'thoughts').

normal people. If it abides conscientiously by its retrenchment to what is known with absolute certainty, it has to stick to the world of the phenomenological subject in its isolation – not exactly a splendid one – and restrict itself to what Husserl calls the "primordial world" of each single transcendental ego.

However, Husserl did not resign himself to the position of philosophical solipsism, much as he thought that philosophical solipsism had to be taken seriously. In fact, from the new Archimedean point of the absolutely certain pure consciousness of one's own Husserl tried valiantly to redeem the belief not only in the "transcendent" world of scientific reality, but also in the transcendence of other persons or egos. Yet this did not prove to be an easy task. Apparently this was one of the reasons why Husserl abandoned his first attempt to tackle it in the second volume of his basic work *"Ideas: A General Introduction to Pure Phenomenology,"* which was to contain an analysis of the constitution of the so-called "intersubjective" world. But fifteen years later he did publish – or at least permitted the publication in French translation of – a much more developed "meditation" on the problem of intersubjectivity, i.e., the fifth of his *Cartesian Meditations*.[9] It is neither possible nor necessary to give a paraphrase of this highly provocative though involved text. Instead, I shall try to single out the chief answers to our problems as they can be culled from the central sections of this Meditation.

Faithful to his original objective, Husserl begins with the analysis and description of the "primordial world" of the phenomenological ego. But in describing the contents of the world, he does not and cannot deny the occurrence of the phenomena of other egos qua phenomena and – something which Husserl emphasized from the outset – of their correlative special worlds. How then can we account for the givenness or, better, for the constitution of such phenomena in our private primordial consciousness?

Here Husserl introduces some of the most interesting and intriguing conceptions of his later philosophy, though unfortunately in an overcondensed and at times rather ambiguous fashion. Thus, Husserl relates the problem of our knowledge of other egos and their worlds to the more general problem of what he calls "appresen-

[9] Additional materials on intersubjectivity have been edited by Iso Kern in *Husserliana*, vols. XIII-XV.

tation," i.e., of the partial givenness of certain aspects of a perceived object jointly with aspects that are fully present. Co-present (*mitgegenwärtig*) in this sense with the front of an object is, for instance, its back. The situation is similar when, in connection with the presentation of a living organism different from our own, another ego is "appresented," with this important difference, however, that here it is impossible that, in the development of our perception of the object, its appresented back can be transformed into a fully presented front. What is supposed to take place in the case of the other ego is that, by a kind of "analogizing transposition" or "interpretation" (*Auffassung*), also called, to be sure in a new sense, "association," first a foreign organism (*Leib*) similar to my own is coupled with my own (*Paarung*), and that then the other ego is coupled with this foreign organism. All this is supposed to happen by a kind of passive constitution, not by any active and deliberate procedure. In addition to this new type of association, we also hear the older term empathy, used here in the sense of a process by which we invest the other organism with mental acts similar to our own. Verification and falsification of these constitutions take place on the basis of the consistency (*Einstimmigkeit*) and inconsistency of the appresentations of the other ego and his world, as our experience of him expands.

We need not examine these ingenious descriptions in detail for their clearness and adequacy.[10] For us the decisive point is how far Husserl's approach can give us direct access to the other and his world. Is this still phenomenology in the strict sense? On this point Husserl's position seems to waver curiously. On the one hand he asserts that in our experience of the other he stands before us in person (*leibhaft*). "What we really see is not a sign nor a mere analogon or in any ordinary sense a likeness. . . . The other is seized in real originality." [11] On the other hand, Husserl frankly admits that, in spite of the experience of givenness in person, "it must be conceded that, properly speaking, it is not the other ego, his experiences and his phenomena which we are given originally, and that the given-

---

[10] For detailed and penetrating criticisms see Alfred Schutz, 'Das Problem der transzendentalen Intersubjektivität bei Husserl,' *Philosophische Rundschau*, V, (1957), pp. 81-107, see also *Collected Papers* III (The Hague: Nijhoff, 1966, pp. 51-83).

[11] *Husserliana* I, p. 153; English translation by Dorion Cairns (The Hague: Nijhoff, 1960, p. 124).

ness of the other in our intentional acts has a certain indirectness"
(*ibid.*, p. 139; Engl. p. 108f.). He also freely admits that what is
appresented by analogical appresentation is never really present (p.
142; Engl. p. 112), and that the fulfillment of appresentative givenness by full presence is impossible in principle (p. 148; Engl. p. 119).

Thus, Husserl never fully made up his mind about the question
whether phenomenology has direct access to the other and his world
or whether they are only indirectly presented by what is directly
given. To put it bluntly: he wanted to stick ascetically to pure and
absolute certainty, represented here by the primordial world, and
yet to enjoy the forbidden fruit of real access to the transcendent
other. Thus it is really impossible to tell with certainty whether
Husserl's phenomenology of the other is still direct phenomenology
or an expansion of it.

A final appraisal depends on a much more basic issue in Husserl's
mature phenomenology, namely the nature and the function of the
so-called phenomenological constitution. It would lead too far to
discuss this conception in all its intricacies and ambiguities as it
unfolded during Husserl's later philosophizing. In this context the
decisive question is whether and how far what is constituted *in* consciousness is also constituted *by* consciousness, in the sense that it
forms what Husserl calls an achievement (*Leistung*) of consciousness. If it is, then what is of consciousness' own making is of course
also directly accessible to it. This would then also be true of the
other and his world, whom Husserl very often characterized as
constituted in and by the primordial consciousness (*ibid.*, p. 152f;
Engl. p. 124), only that this constitution is of a higher level and in
this sense a secondary achievement. Nevertheless, the other ego as
constituted should be accessible to a direct phenomenology. Yet, we
must not overlook the fact that most of this constitution is supposed
to be passive, i.e., that it takes place by a process in which the object
"constitutes itself" in a way that is clearly not under our direct control. This introduces an alien ingredient into the constitutive process
which makes the constituted object less directly accessible.

Thus far it may seem that Husserl's solution applies, if at all, only
to the problems of access to the normal other and his world. How
about the abnormal other? The phenomenological psychopathologist
might be interested in a highly condensed paragraph of the *Cartesian
Meditations* in which Husserl pays passing attention to the problem

of abnormality (*ibid.*, p. 154; Engl. p. 125f.). He mentions first the case of "abnormalities such as blindness, deafness, and the like," which means that our normal systems of perspectives are not shared by some other egos. Husserl thinks that such abnormality can constitute itself in our consciousness only against the background of antecedent normality. Both normality and abnormality are, however, to be considered as modifications of the constitution of our own egos and our own worlds. These considerations are followed by the following remarkable passage:

To the problem of anomalies belongs also the problem of animal nature and of its order of higher and lower animals. Relative to the animal, man, under the aspect of constitution, is the normal case, just as I myself am the prime norm for all men, as far as constitution is concerned. Animals are constituted for myself essentially as anomalous variations of my humanity, even though we can distinguish among them according to normality and anomalousness.

But no matter what one thinks of these suggestions for a method by which phenomenology could approach the problem of the abnormal and its constitution, the decisive question remains whether this entire attempt offers us the hoped-for direct approach to the phenomena of the other and his world. I am prepared to admit that Husserl made it indeed possible to expand the range of phenomenology beyond the narrow confines of a solipsistic primordial world. His conception of constitution, no matter how ambiguous and problematic it may be, allows us at least to approach the other and his world phenomenologically by converting them into higher levels of the constituted world. As such they would be secondary phenomena. Nevertheless they would be accessible to direct investigation without any inferences or constructive hypotheses. Great as this achievement would be, I believe it has remained incomplete. As a matter of fact, I see little likelihood that it will be completed. If not, then there is no chance that the other and his world can be explored by direct phenomenology. Does this mean that we are forced to return to the old methods of inference and constructive hypothesis as supported by analogies and similar symbolic clues?

VI. THE IDEA OF A PHENOMENOLOGY THROUGH
VICARIOUS EXPERIENCE

In the remainder of this essay I want to suggest an alternative which would allow us to speak of a genuine phenomenology even in the case of phenomena which are not given first hand. Its main promise would be that it could justify the concrete achievements of the phenomenological psychopathologists.

Obviously, all indirect phenomenology will have to be built on a solid foundation in direct or first-hand phenomenology. By this I do not mean merely the first-hand knowledge of one's own self and of one's private world. I also assume the possibility and actuality of a direct perception of the other person as person, at least in some rudimentary form. Such a minimum perception of the other may be considered as phenomenologically established. I also believe that the alternatives of the analogy theory and the empathy theory are in-adequate as psychological explanations. They can supply at best some kind of supplementary justification for our epistemological claims. This does not mean that our perception of other selves is infallible. It may be subject to the usual, plus some unusual, illusions to which all uncritical, and perhaps even some critical, perception is exposed. All the same, here is the only possible gateway to all knowl-edge of others, sane or insane.

Speaking more concretely: I believe that, at least in *some* normal cases we can see eagerness or anger in the face of another person and, through such emotion, also this person as one of a certain emotiveness and irritability. In other cases of ambiguous expression we may only be able to *infer* the eagerness or the anger. I am not sure that a non-psychiatrist can see with equal clearness the "madness" in the look of a psychotic, his panic or his schizophrenic aloofness. But I con-sider it highly probable that, with sufficient experience and proper training, most people can develop a direct perception of abnormality.

Yet, even seeing the other as a person, normal or abnormal, does not give us direct access to his world. We may see his eyes as seeing but we cannot see what it is that he sees through these eyes. And without knowing this we really cannot understand him as the global system of this person and his world. It is at this point that for every-one, trained or untrained, the need for an expansion of firsthand phenomenology arises.

The first and most radical method of expanding our phenomeno-logical grasp would consist in the actual conversion of the phe-nomenologist into the other or at least in his adoption of the other's frame of mind. To take an extreme case: Cannot the phenomeno-logist share in parallel experience the condition of insanity, if only temporarily and experimentally? I understand that there was at least one psychiatrist (Franz Fischer) who developed schizophrenia and reported on the transformation of his personality and his world during a period of remission. But my psychiatrist friends tell me that his reports proved of very dubious value. Apparently the illness had sapped even his phenomenological powers.

Of greater validity might be the experimental studies with normal people who subject themselves to the influence of hallucinogenic drugs, such as mescaline or lysergic acid. These stimuli seem to pro-duce experiences of a very special variety and have considerable value in widening our normal range of firsthand phenomena. But here again, friends who have taken part in such experiments and are phenome-nologically oriented tell me that what is thus induced is anything but a "model psychosis." It differs from an actual psychosis both in quantity and quality. Certainly the known artificiality or escapability of such experiences makes them different and is apt to throw con-siderable doubt on the epistemological value of such excursions into territory which is merely adjacent to, but not identical with, the pathological domain.

Thus, the attempt to enter the world of the other by force, as it were, and then see it with our own eyes, is anything but a clear suc-cess. How, then, and how far, is it possible for the phenomenologist to see it through the eyes of others, using them as reflectors, at it were? Now, we know very well that such an expansion of our range is impossible, and even impossible in principle. How far can we at least approximate this impossible ideal?

I see at least two avenues for some progress in this direction. I shall call them here the avenue of imaginative self-transposal and that of cooperative encounter.

The avenue of imaginative self-transposal is one which would depend entirely on the investigating phenomenologist who can initiate and control it. This is its great asset. But this method is also apt to arouse grave suspicions. Since when is the imagination a genuine tool of authentic knowledge? Isn't this simply an appeal to something like Bergson's celebrated metaphysical intuition – that "intellectual sympathy by which one places oneself within an object in order to coincide with what is unique in it and consequently inexpressible"? [12] No doubt this was a brilliant suggestion for metaphysics, but one, nevertheless, which should make the conscientious phenomenologist shudder. What else could this mean, particularly in the realm of psychopathology, but fooling oneself deliberately?

It would take considerable time and apologetics to make even my more modest conception of imaginative self-transposal epistemologically defensible and science-proof. My only goal here is to give it at least the looks of sanity and practicability.

First, it should be made clear that what is involved is not simply the appeal to wild fiction or even science fiction after the manner of H. G. Wells, Aldous Huxley, or even B. F. Skinner (*Walden II*). Just to imagine, without sufficient background in experience, what it would be like to be "mad" or "crazy," as only too many people do in their fears and superstitions about insanity, would clearly be courting scientific *and* phenomenological disaster. We should remember from the very start that there are different kinds of imagination, not only the freely roaming variety but also the disciplined one of which the scientific as well as the artistic imagination provide prime examples. Such disciplined imagination uses clues and is limited by rules. It is obvious that our new kind of phenomenological imagination subjects itself to this kind of controls. In another context I have attempted a first sketch of what seems to me involved in imaginative self-transposal.[13] Here I would like to point out merely some of the features of this operation which are pertinent to our present concern:

1. Imaginative self-transposal requires that the investigator imagine himself as occupying the real place of the other and view from there the world as it would present itself in this new perspective.

2. It requires more than merely the transposal of his actual self into this new location: A mere local transposal could lead only to the kind of grotesque misunderstanding which arises from seeing the other's world through one's own eyes, resulting in silly meddling and

[12] Introduction à la métaphysique 1903.
[13] 'Toward a Phenomenology of Imaginative Understanding of Others,' *Proceedings of the XIth International Congress of Philosophy* (Brussels: 1955) VII, pp. 235-39.

irreverent fault-finding ("if I were in your place" or even "if I were you"). The point is that the transposing self has to submit to a transformation in which it not only divests itself of its congenital and historically acquired peculiarities, but adopts imaginatively as much as it can of the frame of mind of the other person. Clues for this adoption are to be derived from firsthand perception of the other and from facts of his available biography. This is clearly no small assignment. But the ability to vary oneself in imagination in easily one of the most remarkable capacities of the human self, which deserves a full and differentiated study. I would like to point out only one dimension of such self-variation, which may be of particular significance for the understanding of abnormalities. In the negative direction it consists in the partial and even total removal of some of our present qualities and capacities. This is the imaginative modification which allows us, to some extent, to share the situation of the blind, the deaf, or other handicapped persons in their respective worlds. In contrast to such restrictive imagination the one which tries to add to our actual equipment may be much more difficult and problematic. But there seems to be no reason to question it in principle. For instance, such imagination might enable us to understand what it would be like to be subjected to the compulsive ideas of a persecution complex.

3. Imaginative self-transposal requires a peculiar style of occupying the place of the other by our transformed self, not a complete fusion for good, but one which allows us to shuttle back and forth between our own understanding self and that of the other who is to be understood. If we lost ourselves head over heels in his place we should no longer be expanding our phenomenological grasp. We would be cutting ourselves off from our base of operation.

4. At this point begins the actual work of constructing the other and his world on the basis of the clues which we find in the situation into which we have put ourselves imaginatively. Now we have to try to build, from these elements, his self and the world as he is likely to see it.[14] In other words, we are to project the world as it would

---

[14] The expression used for this operation by Hans Kunz, 'imaginatively thinking projection' (*phantasierend-denkendes Entwerfen*) seems particularly appropriate (*Uber den Sinn und die Grenzen psychologischer Erkenntnis*. (Stuttgart: Ernst Klett, 1957, p. 150 ff.)).

appear through his eyes, although we cannot use his eyes, but merely our own.

5. At the same time we shall have to mobilize our critical faculties in order to avoid the pitfalls of imaginative license. This critical operation does not differ in principle from what we do in the case of any critical perception. It means the constant test of our anticipations as based on imaginative construction in relation to new clues and other new evidence which may either confirm them or clash with them. In the latter case we shall of course have to revise and rearrange our construction so that it fits in with the new data. I am indebted to my colleague Carl Wellman of Washington University for suggesting the following more specific tests:

(1) additional items which come to mind as we put ourselves into the other person's shoes;

(2) perceptions arising from observing the actual behavior of the other person or by looking at the objective situation in which he finds himself.

All this does not alter the fact that the result of imaginative self-transposal will be vicarious imagination, not perception. There can be a phenomenology of this peculiar operation, but this is no direct phenomenology of the objects which are made accessible by means of it. All the more reason is there to remain cautious and critical in hitching the wild horses of the imagination to the wagon of phenomenology. But we should also recall that from the very start the imagination has played an important part in the framework of Husserl's phenomenology. Especially in his phenomenology of essences (eidetic phenomenology), the so-called "free variation in the imagination" – really a rather methodically controlled imagination – always appeared as a legitimate, in fact even as a privileged, method for obtaining and securing essential insights. The use of the imagination which I am suggesting here is actually a more modest one, since it deals primarily with concrete cases, not with general essences. All the less reason is there to outlaw it from the outset.

Next, I would like to clarify what I named the method of cooperative encounter, and might also be called "cooperative exploration."

Freud's psychoanalysis has opened up the road for exploring the mind and the world of his neurotic patients by techniques which make use of their more or less spontaneous contributions. By virtue of "transference" his patient enters a specific cooperative relationship with his analyst in which they embark on a joint exploration of phenomena which only the patient experiences directly, while the analyst can do so only through him. Now to adopt such a method does not mean subscribing to any of Freud's special techniques, such as free association or symbolic interpretation, and even less to his theory of the subconscious and its dynamics. What is significant here is what Ludwig Binswanger and Medard Boss have pointed out, that psychoanalysis provided the basis for a new relationship between patient and psychiatrist, one of mutual trust, respect, and participation in a joint enterprise of exploration and understanding. This is what is involved in the new emphasis on loving encounter as the basis of the therapeutic relationship.

What can these possibilities add to the limited and problematic powers of an imaginative phenomenology? First of all, the patient, by putting his own perspective – to the best of his communicative ability – at the disposal of the phenomenological analyst, provides him with a unique extension of his operating base. Now the analyst can really use the eyes of the patient. Yet he must not be under the illusion that these eyes are his own eyes. They remain at best new mirrors, and by no means undistorting mirrors. They provide some fresh and even unique new material, but, coming from a source which is clearly troubled, it cannot be accepted at face value.

What, then, is the phenomenologist to do with this additional raw material? Certainly he is not to interpret it in the light of more or less precarious hypotheses about its symbolic meaning. All he can and must do, is to explore the material as deeply and as cautiously as possible through the opening which the patient has provided for him. Imaginative self-transposal may help again. But what is clearly more important is the cooperation of the patient on which the phenomenologist may now count and which he may develop and reinforce by that accepting and loving attitude which is at the heart of any genuine encounter. True, he can only imagine the other's world, but he can now do so with the constant help of and check by his client. Some of Binswanger's case studies are instructive models of such cooperation.

What does this method actually involve? Suppose a patient with hallucinations has confided in his psychiatrist to the extent of telling him spontaneously about his frightening or enrapturing phenomena. Suppose the psychiatrist has listened patiently and acceptingly to these reports and then expressed the desire to share the patient's viewpoint vicariously. Will this not increase the patient's wish to clarify his own perspective and to make it communicable? Does this not offer a chance for joint efforts in the expansion of a phenomenology at first hand? All this does not imply that the phenomenologist has to accept the account of the patient uncritically. He may combine with his explorations a sympathetic probing, a probing which might eventually lead the patient to compare his hallucinations with ordinary perceptions. He may then be able to modify and even to discredit some of the patient's particularly flighty and self-contradictory accounts. But all that matters in the present context is that the psychiatrist has enlarged his range of phenomena in live interchange with the patient who alone has direct access to them.

Obviously, this is merely a beginning of what has to be done in order to clarify this method phenomenologically. Nor do I intend to give a conspectus of all the possible techniques of a phenomenology through vicarious experience. Enough has been said if it has become clear that between firsthand phenomenology and merely hypothetical construction there is a middle ground which calls for cautious and critical cultivation. Clearly, vicarious phenomenology is even less foolproof than firsthand phenomenology. But fools or not, in an area like this the psychiatrist cannot afford to wait until the angel, in this case the rigorous firsthand phenomenologist, no longer fears to tread on the new ground.

I would like to close with a tribute to the man who, more than any other known to me, has helped to develop the road toward a phenomenology and psychiatry of encounter, for whom being a psychiatrist actually depends upon "encounter and communication with the fellow man (note: *not* the patient) as a whole and is aimed at the understanding of man in his entirety": Ludwig Binswanger.[15]

In 1962 I had the privilege of encountering this unique octogenarian, more youthful in spirit and more outgoing than most members of my generation. Toward the end of the nearly three hours in which he allowed me to explore his amazing treasure of live memories of the phenomenological past, he also invited me to ask him the sort of questions which still puzzled me about the phenomenology of the psychiatrists. So I broached to him the quandary from which I started

---

[15] *Ausgewählte Vorträge und Aufsätze* (Bern: Francke, 1955, p. 278).

here, i.e., whether phenomenological psychopathology in view of its indirectness could really be claimed as phenomenology. Binswanger listened with a warm smile and replied genially: "There, one can see that you are little acquainted with the actual practice of the psychiatrist." And then he proceeded to tell me how the real psychiatrist lives with his patient in his world and shares it, for instance the volatile world of the manic, or the viscous world of the melancholic.

I am afraid that even now I have not been able to overcome my basic handicap. But I have at least begun to understand the truth and the profundity of Binswanger's reply about the sharing between doctor and patient, between man and fellowman that can take place in genuine encounter. What is more, I have come to see that this is also an opening for an enlarged phenomenology which need not be a diluted phenomenology. There is every reason not to embark on it rashly and to keep up one's guard. But there is also no good reason for being a phenomenological purist and for barring the road to a genuine phenomenology with a wider and richer scope.

5. EXISTENTIAL USES OF PHENOMENOLOGY*

Is it at all legitimate to subject phenomenology to questions of such a pragmatic, if not utilitarian, nature as that of its human uses? Isn't it below the dignity of a true science and particularly of a philosophy which started out with the ambition of being a rigorous science to submit to this kind of a cross examination? In fact, Edmund Husserl in his historic manifesto article on "Philosophy as a Rigorous Science" solemnly disclaimed all pretensions that it could bring aid and comfort to modern man in his dire need for a philosophy of life (*Weltanschauung*).

But even so, it must not be overlooked that Husserl himself, during the later parts of his career, could not escape the challenge to his enterprise and to his very existence that came from the political and moral crises of the twentieth century and particularly from Nazi totalitarianism. He answered it by the plea that philosophy and specifically his own transcendental phenomenology had a mission in the service of mankind and that this mission was the defense of a phenomenologically reconstituted reason against the rampant ir-rationalism of the time.

I shall not attempt to defend phenomenology on such lofty grounds; nor shall I try to give here the kind of merely theoretical justification which might show the usefulness of the phenomeno-logical approach in the framework of the total intellectual enterprise or in the treatment of specific philosophical problems. Thus I shall forego the justification on such grounds as the claim that phenome-nology, being itself free from all unexamined presuppositions, can supply firm foundations for all other scientific and philosophical

* From F. J. Smith, ed., *Perspectives in Phenomenology* (The Hague: Martinus Nijhoff, 1970, pp. 16-31). The original title was 'On Some Human Uses of Phenomenology'.

knowledge. This is more or less an internal affair of philosophy and philosophy of science. It is by no means an easy assignment. And personally I have considerable doubts that phenomenology, especially in its present shape, is in the position to carry it out.

My concern here is more restricted. But it is all the more basic in its practical significance. I would like to tackle the question of whether phenomenology can make any direct contributions to human existence. It is all very well to show that phenomenology is a necessary or even a sufficient presupposition to knowledge. But even if it is, what would be the concrete use of such knowledge? What I would like to show within the limits of this essay is that practicing the phenomenological approach can affect one's concrete living, not only one's thinking about life. To my knowledge such an attempt has not yet been undertaken explicitly. I shall call this the question of the *human uses* of phenomenology. In posing it I do not want to set human uses against other non-human, or possibly even inhuman, uses. I merely want to focus on the question of what difference to man's living in his total world it could make if at least once in a while he would adopt the phenomenological stance. I am under no illusion that one can do this all the time. I certainly would not claim that *I* can. I am not even sure that this would be a good thing. Nevertheless, what I would like to show is that adopting this attitude explicitly, if only intermittently and partially, can change one's whole style of living.

Let me confess that until some ten years ago I too have never bothered much about any non-technical uses of phenomenology. At that time Douglas V. Steere, a genuine friend of phenomenology, in the presence of some non-philosophers, dropped the fateful question: "What can the ordinary man expect from your phenomenological enterprise?" This finally hit my conscience. How to justify the phenomenological way of life, if there is such a thing, before oneself as well as before one's tolerant and possibly even tax-supporting fellow-beings? I am not thinking so much of the all too familiar, if not vulgar questions: "What is the use of all your talk? Where does it get you? Does it pay?" I am concerned about Socratic self-examination and existential justification, which even the philosopher cannot shirk.

How can I meet this challenge? Certainly the answer presupposes some acquaintance with, if not complete knowledge of, what phenomenology is all about. I am fully aware that in the present context I have no right to assume this. All I can do is to supply a first taste of the dish or, for some, a few reminders of previous tastes, although I cannot guarantee that what I can offer will taste exactly the same. For here I have to face an even more serious hurdle: Is it possible at all to present a unified conception of phenomenology? There are those who believe that a closer inspection reveals not only *one* phenomenology but as many of them as there are phenomenologists. Personally I am not that despondent. I believe, and I hope I have been able to show, that there is at least a common core and enough connection between the various versions of phenomenology to allow for a comprehensive account even on an introductory level. What I shall attempt, then, is to present these varieties as additions to the common core around which they can be arranged like concentric shells.

Concretely, my plan is the following: I shall first try to give a preliminary survey of these phenomenologies. I shall then discuss in greater detail for each of them at least some of their human uses. It would of course be in order to discuss also their misuses. But here I shall have to be even more selective. For their name is legion. Any instrument, say a knife, lends itself to infinite misuses, from shoving to poking, from digging to impaling. A word is enough for the wise, and many words won't do any good to the inrushing fools or the "lotus-eaters," who have begun to invade the scene. As examples of more general misuses I shall mention only two. The first I shall call "jargonism": the tendency to use technical terms needlessly, especially when they are not properly introduced by definition or illustration. Terms such as "transcendental," or "noetic" lend themselves too easily to window-dressing, if not to browbeating. But I am at least equally concerned about a more pretentious second misuse, the tendency to recommend phenomenology as a royal road to a new system of metaphysics. It is exactly this kind of irresponsible philosophy which Husserl wanted to stop once and for all.

First, then, for a preview of phenomenology in its varieties and its underlying unity: Here I shall draw on the conception of the phenomenological approach which I have developed at the end of my historical introduction to phenomenology, where I tried to distinguish between several steps or phases of the method, arranged largely according to the degree to which they were common ground among all those who identified with the phenomenological movement.[1] Let me call this the staggered approach. Its steps are:

1. Direct exploration, analysis, and description of particular phenomena, as free as possible from unexamined presuppositions, aiming at maximum intuitive presentation; I shall call this "descriptive phenomenology."

2. Probing of these phenomena for typical structures or "essences" and for the essential relations within and among them; this can be called *phenomenology of essences,* or, even shorter, but perhaps more riskily, *essential ("eidetic") phenomenology.*[2]

3. Giving attention to the ways in which such phenomena appear, e.g., in different perspectives or modes of clarity, to be called here *phenomenology of appearances.*

4. Studying the processes in which such phenomena become established ("constituted") in our consciousness, often labeled as *constitutive phenomenology.*

5. Suspending belief in the reality or validity of the phenomena, a process which may be considered as implicit in the preceding phases, though later Husserl insisted on its explicit performance as basic for phenomenology; in short, *reductive phenomenology.*

6. Finally, as introduced by Heidegger, and to some extent Sartre, a special kind of phenomenological interpretation, designed to unveil otherwise concealed meanings in the phenomena, which he called *hermeneutic phenomenology.*

In distinguishing these six types of phenomenology and arranging them in a sequence I would like to point out that there are essential connections between them. These do not prevent one's adopting only some, and particularly the earlier ones, without their successors. However, the relative independence of some of these steps does not prevent their basic unity of purpose; they all are aimed at giving us a fuller and deeper grasp of the phenomena.

On the basis of this preview I shall now try to give a more concrete picture of each of these steps and combine it with the promised discussion of their human uses.

---

[1] *The Phenomenological Movement,* 2nd Edition (The Hague: Nijhoff, 1965); also separate edition under the title *The Essentials of the Phenomenological Method.*

[2] At this point I have simplified the account of my book by not distinguishing between the closely related steps of 'investigating essences' and 'apprehending essential relationships.'

I. DESCRIPTIVE PHENOMENOLOGY

The watchword of phenomenology from its Husserlian beginnings to Heidegger and beyond has always been "To the things!" (*Zu den Sachen*). What does it mean? The German "*Sache*" has the connotation of "subject matter." Thus, "*Zur Sache!*" is simply a summons to come to the point of the discussion; to "get down to brass tacks." In the context of the philosophical discussion of the day the meaning of *Zu den Sachen* was negative as well as positive. It meant on the one hand a turning away from preoccupation with concepts, symbols, theories, and hypotheses. But it also meant a turn toward their concrete referents in experience, i.e., to the uncensored phenomena. In thus deëmphasizing symbols, phenomenology paralleled Bergson's attack on symbolism. This does not mean that phenomenology denies man's distinction as the symbolic animal (Ernst Cassirer). However, it is wary of the mere substitution of symbols for what is symbolized without returning to the full intuitive presentation of the phenomena thus symbolized. Clearly, to explore what is immediately given as it is given in its pure shape is no simple assignment. Husserl was fully aware of this difficulty. In fact, it was in the attempt to get at these pure phenomena that he developed the procedure of the so-called phenomenological reduction, the suspension of our beliefs in the existence of the phenomena.

Such a return to the phenomena had its primary use in technical philosophy, beginning with mathematics, where Husserl's search had started. One of the main functions of this return was to counteract the over-simplifications which, in the name of Occam's razor, had distorted and impoverished the picture of our experienced world. A prime example would be the sensationalist reduction of material bodies to mere aggregates of sense data in Bertrand Russell's classic analysis of our perception of a table in the first chapter of his *Problems of Philosophy*, an analysis for which what is given of the table is really nothing but the sense data of its slanted and discolored perspective appearances. By contrast, for phenomenology what is actually given through these variable and seemingly contradictory appearances is the table itself in its identical squareness. However, phenomenology does not confine itself to a new account of such stock in trade of traditional epistemology. Its main ambition is the exploring and describing of phenomena which have been neglected or completely overlooked. Its main contributions to technical philosophy thus far are in the field of perception; but they range all the way to the phenomena of value.

In the present context my main concern is to show how descriptive phenomenology can affect man's dealings with his everyday life. In the first place, I submit that the adoption of the phenomenological attitude can heighten our perceptiveness for the richness of our experience. By challenging the dogmatic restriction of our experience to the supposed data of our sense organs, phenomenology readmits us to a world in which everything has a claim to recognition, as long as it presents itself in concrete experience. What phenomenology opposes is the attempt to debunk this experience as expressed in the typical reductive phrase "nothing but." The principle of the "economy of thought," if it means the suppression of phenomena in the interest of greater simplicity of operation, can easily become the pretext for a philosophical and human waste that may be irreparable.

Let me, however, use this occasion for a general and emphatic disclaimer: I am not asserting that phenomenology has a monopoly on this use or even on many of the subsequent human uses which I am going to distinguish. While it may still be true that at the turn of the century phenomenology was the most prominent defender of a rehabilitation of immediate experience, it has been preceded and joined in this respect by other philosophies. I should like to mention specifically Bergson's defense of the immediate data of consciousness, Peirce's phaneroscopy, William James's radical empiricism, John Dewey's "experimentalism," and Whitehead's critique of classical science. In this sense phenomenology is only one more wave superimposed on the groundswell of a much vaster historical movement. Its distinctive contribution may be merely that it has made a more detailed and more effective use of these motifs.

Now I would like to show some specific areas of our world of human living which such a training in perceptivity can rehabilitate:

1. There is the range of what is all too often condemned without fair trial as the world of the "merely subjective." It includes not only the so-called "subjective" colors, sounds or smells, but also more complex characters for which no such intersubjective criteria as direct or indirect measurement can be specified, for instance emotive characters. As a consequence they are either denied all existence or simply relegated to the limbo of unredeemable private data. In other

words, public verifiability becomes the entrance ticket to the world of facts. Phenomenology does not know of any such restrictive credentials. Whatever presents itself to anyone's careful and discriminating observation has prima facie equal rights. If, in the process of intersubjective comparing of notes with others and of patient efforts to lead others to similar experiences, no confirmation should be forthcoming from their side, this may be good reason for putting such phenomena under scientific quarantine. Nevertheless, they have a right to exist and be recognized as belonging to our world of lived experience. Even science has to start from this basis, although it may decide not to use all of it in its attempt to limit itself to those parts of experience which are public and measurable. In any case, there is a primary first need for a conscientious inventory of all our immediate experience in all its richness, as it presents itself.

2. An even more significant area for reclamation by descriptive phenomenology is the world of meanings and values. The precarious status of values and value judgments under a narrowly scientific dispensation, according to which merely empirical facts given to sense perception have any claim to be recognized, does not need elaboration. What can phenomenology do about it? First of all, it can lead us back to concrete experiences in which meanings and values are experienced as phenomena. This is what especially Max Scheler attempted to do. But I would like to make an even more specific suggestion. Rather than using such threadbare and colorless terms as "value" and pale general predicates as "good" and "bad" we should begin with the concrete experiences of our delights and disgusts, admirations and indignations. The phenomena which give rise to these experiences are the delightful and the disgusting, the admirable and the outrageous. These are the concrete bases for our experiences of value and disvalue. At this stage there is no need to claim for them more than personal significance. The important thing is that the descriptive approach can salvage and reveal a richness of qualities which the impoverished talk about values as merely a matter of likes or dislikes misses completely. We live in a world of concrete meanings. Their readmission to our consciousness, philosophical and extra-philosophical, is bound to make a vast, if not decisive difference in our outlook. No matter what the final status of these subjective meanings may be, phenomenology should put an end to the tired and blasé despair about the meaninglessness of this universe.

3. Lastly, I should like to outline what is possibly an even more momentous use of descriptive phenomenology. I submit that it can enlarge our existence in the direction of both a widened sense of the world and a deepened sense of ourselves. Of these two dimensions the enlarged awareness of the world has been called the discovery of the life world. Much has still to be done to fathom the dimensions of this world of our experience in lived space and time. A full realization of the range and richness of this world is bound to lead to a new sense of the wonder and dignity of the microcosm which is man. In our superficial everyday and scientific view of man we are only too apt to look upon him as a self-enclosed physico-chemical system occupying a volume of space, for instance in a public conveyance with a "capacity" for accommodating so many "persons." And we believe that his pictorial likeness includes all there is to him. How far are we awake to the fact that each such organism is the center of a world, and that he would not be a human being without this world of his? Moreover, not only does he include his own world. In including other people as parts of his world, he also includes their worlds as worlds at first remove, as it were. In turn, these worlds of his fellowbeings include third persons with their respective worlds, which form worlds at second remove in relation to him. Obviously there is no end in this series of inclusion of worlds within worlds. How much could a live awareness of this situation add to our respect, if not reverence for man? How much more could it add to our realization that in destroying one human life we destroy his world along with him and at the same time all those worlds which he embraces vicariously in this awareness of others. What shocking light does this cast on the inhumanity of a "war" whose successes are measured primarily in body counts!

But what is ultimately even more important is the fuller realization of the depth of the self at the center of these worlds. One of the strangest documents of phenomenological insensitivity was Ernst Mach's facetious drawing of what he saw when he looked at himself lying on his couch: namely his foreshortened trunk and legs framed by the outcroppings of his flourishing whiskers and eyebrows. This was surely an excellent representation of the perspective visual appearance of his own body, but a weird caricature of his own observing, perceiving, drawing, and amused self. How was it possible that so careful an observer got so diverted from the phenomenon of his own selfhood? Equally, if not more puzzling, is David Hume's dis-arming confession about the outcome of his search for his own self as consisting of nothing but a bundle of perceptions. Yet the very accounts of Mach and Hume show the irrepressibleness of the first person singular pronoun in their reports about the failure of their search. All the more impressive is the story of Husserl's discovery of the ego after his initial failure to see it. It shows not only the difficulty of this discovery but also the need for proper focusing and training. Here is another task for descriptive phenomenology which is far from accomplished.

And what about the human uses of such an enriched picture of the self? I submit that a full realization of the self in its depth can revive and deepen our sense of wonder at the mystery which we are and of reverence for the potentialities which it includes. How much more reason for reverence for the mystery of the other! In this sense the phenomenological approach, in making us more keenly aware of the task of understanding others and their worlds, is a new incentive for increased efforts and increased humility in our social relations. Finally, this deepened sense of selfhood should add to our reverence for the sanctity of all life as the basis for the emergence of such selves as world centers.

II. ESSENTIAL PHENOMENOLOGY (EIDETIC PHENOMENOLOGY)

The second step in the phenomenological approach is the attempt to grasp the essential structures of the phenomena and the essential relationships within and among them. Such essential intuition or insight is still under suspicion, even among sincere friends of phe-nomenology. And it is true that it has at times been invoked without paying due attention to the prerequisites which Husserl himself had specified repeatedly. For essential intuition does not consist in any unprepared staring at a peculiar entity confronting our inner eyes. I should like to spell out two such prerequisites: (1) No adequate essential insight into general essences is possible without backing by specific examples as their intuitive foundation; this was the sense of Husserl's insistence on the need for small change (*Kleingeld*) in phenomenological research. (2) Every assertion about essential re-lations within or among such essences presupposes the kind of free variation in the imagination which has often been called an experiment in thought. Only if such variation reveals that its variables cannot be separated even in imagination, can any necessary essential connection be asserted; only if they cannot be forced together, can an essential impossibility be claimed; only if they may or may not be brought together, is there room for an essential possibility. Thus variation in the imagination is the necessary condition for determining what is or is not of the essence of a phenomenon. Perhaps the best illustration for such variation in the imagination can be found in the area where Husserl made his first contribution to mathematics, combinatorial analysis, and particularly in the area of what is called "permutations." In establishing its permutative formulae we can run, especially for purposes of initial instruction, through all possible combinations, changing them one at a time. Such variation can be practiced also in other fields, for instance by varying the consciousness of our own body in the imagination, imagining what it would be like to have only one eye or none at all, or perhaps even additional eyes in the back of our heads.

How, then, can the proper pursuit of essential insights add to human existence in general, in a similar way as descriptive phenomenology did by its training of our perceptiveness? To begin with, if intuiting essences requires constant reference to concrete examples, then essential thinking is anything but a flight from concreteness. It calls for a constant mobilization of our imagination. Thus, contrary to common belief, essential insight will not lead us to indulging in empty abstractions but to shuttling back and forth between the concrete and the abstract. Essential insight in this sense should develop the sense for responsible generalization.

But even more significant are the demands that essential insights make on our imaginativeness by asking us to vary freely but systematically the ingredients of the essential insights. I am not implying that only essential insights require such imagination. But I think that phenomenology in its appeal to imaginative variation is one more incentive for the training of the imagination. There is little need to emphasize this need. As a witness, let me simply quote George Brock Chisholm, the Canadian psychiatrist and former Director General of the World Health Organization:

What we, the people of the world, need, perhaps, most is to exercise our imaginations, to develop our ability to look at things from outside our accidental area of being.[3]

[3] *Prescription for Survival* (New York: 1957, p. 76).

Finally, essential insight requires that on the basis of such variation we determine what is essential or necessary and what is merely accidental or contingent. I submit that the development of the sense for the essential and for the contingent are major needs of human existence. To see what is essential, not to be diverted and detained by inconsequential features, and to keep one's eyes on the central features is clearly involved in "seeing life steadily and seeing it whole." But it is no less important to develop the sense for the accidental and the contingent. This sense can effectively counteract our tendency to take things for granted, that mark of philistine complacency. It should increase our awareness of the ultimate contingency in our own existence and condition, as expressed in the pregnant phrase "the accident of birth." This can add to the feeling of existential humility which is one of the better uses one can make of recent existentialism. Let me also quote a passage from what I consider one of the really profound and farsighted books of our time, which in the eleventh hour tries to shake the arrogance of our power-drugged national egocentricity:

> It seems obvious that almost all of us acquire our ideological beliefs not principally as the result of an independent intellectual process but largely as the result of an accident of birth. If you happen to be born in the U.S., the chances are overwhelming that you will grow up believing in democracy; if you happen to be born in Russia or China, the chances are just as great that you will grow up believing in communism.[4]

But what is so obvious to Senator Fulbright seems to be anything but obvious to the average respondent to the public opinion polls. How can we reach him and cope with his unwillingness or incapability of imaginative self-transposal? At least one way might be to awaken his imaginativeness about himself, his sense of the accidental character of his being – and his sense of undeserved privilege if he should insist on his dogmatic self-righteousness.

III. PHENOMENOLOGY OF APPEARANCES

Phenomenology pays attention not only to the *what* but also to the *how*, to the ways or modes in which the phenomena appear. In so doing, it watches particularly the different aspects under which an

---

[4] J. William Fulbright, *The Arrogance of Power* (New York: 1967, p. 171).

object with its many sides presents itself, i.e., its perspective shadings (*Abschattungen*), its degrees of clearness, its illumination, etc. All this is being studied in connection with the analysis of the so-called "intentional" structure of the conscious acts, as they are directed to their "intended" objects. In most cases we pay little, if any, attention to the mediating appearances through which the object appears, as if they were transparent. We become aware of them only as this transparency decreases.

In the visual field those most keenly aware of and interested in these appearances are the painters, in particular those making use of perspective, and, as far as such features as contours and illumination are concerned, the impressionist painters. In many ways they are the pioneers of this aspect of phenomenological seeing. As a particularly striking example of focusing on the appearances, I nominate Monet's eighteen versions of one slanted view of the facade of the Cathedral of Rouen, as seen at different times of the day. One of the lessons of this remarkable series is that it shows how completely different "pigments" can reveal the same *side* of the same *object* through an amazing variety of its appearances.

Now what could be the human use of attending to such mere appearances? Did not Plato frown on the painters precisely for this kind of "deception"? But *is* it *really* deception? Is not the variety of the perspectives the means for showing us the identity of the "truth"?

However, this is not the use of the appearance in which I am interested here. There is a line in Goethe's *Faust* at the end of his introductory monologue to Part II, where, after a striking description of the play of the early sunlight on the foam rising from a cascade, he concludes: "Colorful reflection is what gives us real life." [5] No matter what the full connotation of this ambiguously rich line may be – there is also an agnostic touch to it [6] – it also makes it clear that for Goethe one of the major delights of life was to watch the varying perspective appearances of the world. In fact, it would seem to have been one of the fascinations behind his preoccupation with the phe-

[5] '*Am farbigen Abglanz haben wir das Leben.*'
[6] See, for example, a similar passage in Goethe's essay '*Versuch einer Witterungslehre*' (1825) to the effect that 'we can never know the true directly; we intuit only in the reflection (*Abglanz*), in the example, in the symbol, in single and related appearances. We become aware of it as incomprehensible life and yet we cannot abandon the wish to comprehend it.' (my translation from *Jubiläumsausgabe*, vol. 40, p. 53).

nomena of color and his opposition to Newton's optical theory, which make him one of the ancestors of the contemporary phenomenology of color.

However, the main lesson of this example in the present context is that it demonstrates the infinite possibilities of enjoyment which we can derive from giving our attention to the play of perspectives surrounding each object as we approach it, walk around it, and, after having become acquainted with it, re-see it, now no longer with the pleasures of surprise but of recognition and confirmation of our memories. True enough, every day we see "the same old things," but we never see them in the same way, in the same perspective, illumination, and atmosphere, with the same history and in the same context. Even if the world should remain unchanged – which, as we know only too well, it does not – its perspectives are inexhaustible and only partially predictable. Phenomenology, in cultivating such attention to the ways and modes of appearance, can be one of the best antidotes to staleness and boredom, without the artificial, and in a deeper sense undignified, stimulants of hallucinatory drugs. Aldous Huxley's "doors of perception" are always open to the open-eyed and open-minded. Chemical keys may open some side-doors. And they certainly have to be opened by qualified and critical viewers. But thus far their reports do not indicate that these side-doors are worth opening to the general public, quite apart from the risks which "trips" without proper safeguards involve. Meanwhile the world of drugless perception is rich enough for the adventurous delights of really perceptive perceivers.

IV. CONSTITUTIVE PHENOMENOLOGY

Another feature of the phenomenological approach, developed especially by the later Husserl under the title of "genetic phenomenology," is the study of the constitution of the phenomena in our consciousness. Disregarding the various possible meanings of the ambiguous term "constitution," I shall confine myself to the interpretation according to which it means the process in which the phenomena "take shape" in our consciousness, as we advance from first impressions to a full "picture" of their structure. In this sense constitutive phenomenology explores the dynamic, as compared with the static, aspect of our experience. Actually Husserl distinguished between a *passive* constitution, concerned with the way in which, especially in perception, our impressions crystallize into full intuitive givenness without our doing, and *active* constitution, exemplified chiefly by our productive thought in logic or mathematics. One of the best examples may be watching the way in which for a newcomer a new location constitutes itself, as he becomes oriented in it, or the way in which we become acquainted with other people as we form our views of their personalities.

What difference can our attention to these processes make for our human existence? It can certainly add to our sense of drama in the development of our "image" of the world, make us aware of our expectations, their fulfillments, or surprised disappointments. In passive constitution we may be watching with amazement the self-organizing processes in which the chaos of data takes shape against the background of disjointed impressions with which merely inattentive gaping or staring would confront us. Active constitution in which we try to put together the pieces of the puzzle by way of constitutive effort can add to our sense of power and achievement. What all this amounts to is that there is nothing dead or restive about our relations to the world of our knowing. There is something dynamic in the way in which the knower and the known are interrelated. Cognition becomes a progressive adventure. At least in English the principal meaning of the word "knowledge" is in this sense too static, signifying primarily the state in which we are already "in the know." But this state is based on a dynamic process of *getting* to know, of *becoming* acquainted with the known. The real center of the drama is *cognition* (the equivalent of the German *Erkenntnis*, as opposed to *Wissen*).

V. REDUCTIVE PHENOMENOLOGY

Finally something should be said about the non-technical uses of the operation which has perhaps attracted most attention in phenomenology, at least of the Husserlian variety: the bracketing of the natural world, also known as the phenomenological reduction or *epoché*. In mentioning it last, I do not mean to imply that it is not implicitly present in all other steps of the phenomenological approach. It is certainly implied in our concentration on the pure phenomena as such. But at times even those who do not attribute to the explicit act of suspension of judgment the importance that Husserl did may see a special aid in an act which makes us stand back from the natural involvement in our everyday world. For Husserl this was to give us access to entirely new "horizons" of phenomena and ultimately to the foundations of science, and prepare the ground for a new science which would be free from the presuppositions of the dogmatic sciences and lead to the ultimate checking of their foundations. Later on, Husserl hinted that such an operation might also lead to a radical "conversion" of our entire existence.[7] However, considering not only the lack of ultimate clarification of this operation, but also the lack of agreement on its indispensability for all phenomenology, I would like to point out only some of its humbler uses.

Suspending our belief in the reality of the outside world on the ground of its dubitability is an act of intellectual self-discipline. In a sense it is an attempt to push skepticism to its utmost limits. But it does not write off the world by the kind of denial of existence, however temporary, implied in Descartes' doubt. Thus the phenomenological attitude can be an expression of simple intellectual humility, admitting the ultimate precariousness of knowledge, especially of the external, but also of our internal world beyond our immediate horizon of the indubitable present. It can help to undermine the dogmatic arrogance of naive realism, without committing us to an equally pretentious idealism. It should protect us particularly from rash claims to knowledge of other people, other groups, and other nations with their different worlds, about which we tend to be so naively dogmatic. Suspension of judgment is closely related to the attitude of open-minded social skepticism, which is one of the chief needs, in fact a desperate need, of our time.

Or to put it even more pointedly: What right have we, each one of us, to claim that his beliefs are true, that he is born with the "silver spoon" of truth as his birthright, and that it has been staying with him throughout his life? Once one comes to realize that not only for theoretical reasons can we have no ultimate assurance of "being right," what moral right do we have to claim this privilege, considering how many people are born and have to live without it? [8] "Taking things for granted" is a phrase which, taken literally, would be moral-

[7] *Husserliana* VI, 140. 2nd edition (The Hague: Nijhoff, 1962); Engl. p. 137.
[8] "Is the Reduction Necessary for Phenomenology? Husserl's and Pfänder's Replies," *Journal of the Britisch Society for Phenomenology* IV (1973), 14-15.

ly legitimate if we realized that this is really a "grant," an un-earned gift. The indefensible use of this grant is if we "take it" thoughtlessly rather than receive it with the sense of something that we must not take without realizing our privilege.

Seen in this perspective the suspension of existential belief may have an additional function: to make us aware that truth as well as anything that is given or granted us is ultimately unearned, that there is no moral right to such a grant as truth, and that at best we can earn it through an apprenticeship of doubt or suspension of belief and empathic understanding for those deprived of it. Such a tempo-rary alienation may be one of the most effective ways for making us realize and re-appropriate our possession as something merely granted and to be earned.

VI. HERMENEUTIC PHENOMENOLOGY

When in the introductory section of *Being and Time* Heidegger proclaimed the need for an interpretation of the phenomena as a way of bringing out their hidden meanings, he seemed to be violating the spirit of a descriptive phenomenology which would abide by what was immediately given. However, one might argue that even Husserl admitted increasingly the need for uncovering the hidden achieve-ments of intentional consciousness in constituting our world, only that in his case such a function was to be uncovered by means of what he called the transcendental reduction. Now this is not the place to clarify Heidegger's hermeneutic method and to discuss its problems and limitations. Suffice it to point out that there is at least a possi-bility of extending the conception of phenomenology in such a way that it can give us access to meanings of the phenomena which are not directly perceived. Such an extension would clearly make a sig-nificant addition to our insight.

What could such an interpretation add to the human uses of phe-nomenology? Hermeneutic phenomenology, insofar as it should be really in the position to interpret for us the meaning of human ex-istence (*existenzielle Analytik*), could clearly change not only our outlook upon life but our actual living. Even if it should end up with Heidegger's seemingly so gloomy interpretation of human existence as being-toward-death, it could give us a sense of direction which a merely descriptive account may not be able to supply. And if beyond this hermeneutics of human existence it could even interpret the universal sense of the Being of all beings, not only of human being (hermeneutic ontology), this would give to this limited human existence a cosmic meaning. Only I am far from convinced that Heidegger's interpretation of human existence as being-toward-death is the only valid one. To interpret its meaning as death almost seems to confuse the terminus with the goal, and make existence a dead-end street.

This is as far as I am prepared to go at this stage in my claims for the human uses of the phenomenological approach. To summarize them: I suggested that phenomenology in its descriptive stage can stimulate our perceptiveness for the richness of our experience in breadth and in depth; that in its search for essences it can develop imaginativeness and the sense for both what is essential and what is accidental; that, in its attention to ways of appearance, it can heighten the sense for the inexhaustibility of the perspectives through which our world is given; that, in its study of their constitution in consciousness it can develop the sense for the dynamic adventure in our relationship with the world; that by the suspending of existential judgment it can make us more aware of the precariousness of all our trans-subjective claims to knowledge, a ground for epistemological humility; and that in its hermeneutic phase it can keep us open for concealed meanings in the phenomena.

Is there any unity to these functions? It would not be too difficult to bring them under the common hat of an enveloping formula, e.g., to the effect that all these uses serve to widen and deepen human existence. But such words as "widen" and "deepen" are so vague and general that, short of a repetition of the specific uses pointed out before, they would add little and detract much.

Before I close my apologia for phenomenology, I would like to issue a final challenge to the court. Thus far, I have played the game of accepting the demand for a special justification of phenomenology. But is this a fair demand? Why must everything have uses? Aren't some things to be done for their own sake, if only for the fun of it?

However, I am not going to argue the case of truth for truth's sake, phenomenology for phenomenology's sake. I am actually thinking of a much more fundamental challenge, that of the justification of man himself at the center of all these human uses. Compared with this existential challenge an apologia of phenomenology is only a secondary issue. Who will speak for man? Chances are that philosophy, and more specifically philosophical anthropology, will have something to do with it. If so, I submit that phenomenology will be one of the witnesses for the "phenomenon of man."

B. ON THE RIGHTS OF PHENOMENOLOGY

6. HOW SUBJECTIVE IS PHENOMENOLOGY?*

There is no better way to honor Husserl than to obey his most advertised if not quite authentic motto: *"Zu den Sachen,"* i.e., "Go to the things." But what are "the things" in Husserl's sense? Right here seems to be one of the paradoxes about his present fame. For in his final interpretation these "things" led him not to the "objects," but toward "subjectivity" as the ultimate foundation for the new scientific rigor which he wanted to bring to philosophy. Just how subjective is phenomenology? There is no sense in tackling this question before there is some measure of agreement about the meaning of the almost hopelessly ambiguous terms "subjective," and "objective." Even if we disregard here the scholastic meaning, which our modern usage has reversed, so many uses of the terms remain that an initial clarification is imperative.

Among the many meanings that can be attached to the term "subjective" I find the following relevant and helpful in disentangling the issues:

1. Subjective in the sense of *merely personal,* hence varying from person to person and from case to case, according to purely empirical circumstances: Any idiosyncrasy, any preference for what we call "merely personal reasons," is subjective in this sense. By the same token, "objective" is what is not subject to such personal variation.

2. Subjective in the sense of *dependent upon a subject* regardless of his personal, his typical or atypical constitution: Here the decisive fact is that in this case the subjective is dependent upon the subject, like a dependent upon an independent variable. A goal of action or a stipulated meaning is in this sense subjective. Correspondingly, "ob-

* *Proceedings of the American Catholic Philosophical Association* 33 (1959), pp. 28-36; also, abridged, in Natanson, Maurice, ed., *Essays in Phenomenology* (The Hague: Nijhoff, 1966, pp. 137-143).

jective" means here anything that has no possible connection with a subject, and is therefore independent of it.

3. Subjective in the sense of *subject-related*: To justify this distinction, which English usage may not fully sanction, I should like to point out the fact that not every dependence upon a subject in sense (2) need be complete dependence. Even a partially subject-dependent object is essentially related to the subject. A reflection on a smooth surface is not completely dependent on the viewer, but it can occur only in relation to him. Subject-relatedness thus appears to be a wider concept, which includes total subject-dependence (sense 2) as a special case.

I now want to put these distinctions to use by applying them to two different kinds of phenomenology whose diversity is usually, if not ignored, at least underestimated. The name for the one is obvious in view of the fact that Husserl, its founder and possibly its only consistent representative, labeled it as *transcendental phenomenology*, a phenomenology which also implied for him what he called *transcendental idealism*. To be sure it is less obvious what "transcendental" stands for in this context. I will have to presuppose some familiarity with Husserl's use of the term, which differs basically from the original scholastic and even from Kant's later use.[1] Merely as an installment for those who want at least a first indication, let me state that Husserl's adjective "transcendental" is used to characterize a stratum of consciousness in which the phenomena that are not part of consciousness, hence are "transcendent" to it, are intended or meant. Thus transcendental phenomenology studies the strata of consciousness in which the transcendent phenomena are constituted together with the phenomena so constituted.

The other phenomenology includes a vast variety of conceptions which have hardly more in common than their non-acceptance of Husserl's transcendental idealism, as he had developed it gradually, especially during his Freiburg period. Hence I shall call it here simply *non-transcendental phenomenology*; but more positive designations such as *purely descriptive phenomenology* or *direct phenomenology* might also be worth considering. This group includes the Older Phenomenological Movement (*"Altphänomenologie"*) of the interlocking

---

[1] For fuller discussion see Iso Kern, *Husserl und Kant* (Den Haag: Nijhoff, 1964) and Ludwig Landgrebe, 'La phénoménologie de Husserl est-elle transcendentale?' *Etudes philosophiques* 9 (1959), pp. 315-323.

Göttingen and Munich Circles with Alexander Pfänder, Adolf Reinach, and Moritz Geiger as the leading names, followed by Dietrich von Hildebrand, Jean Hering, Roman Ingarden, Hedwig Conrad-Martius, and Edith Stein. Max Scheler belonged for some time to the outskirts of these Circles but outshone them by his creative originality. All of them subscribed more or less explicitly to a peculiar phenomenological realism. Martin Heidegger, who appeared on the scene only after World War I, shared with this group the rejection of Husserl's transcendentalism. It is less easy to tell exactly where the French supporters of phenomenology pitch their tents.

I shall begin with Husserl's *transcendental* phenomenology. In his *Logische Untersuchungen* of 1900-01 Husserl had developed a descriptive phenomenology of intentional consciousness in which the parallel structures of intentionality, i.e., of the intending acts and the intended objects, were studied without any pronounced preference for either side. Husserl came to the conclusion that the subject pole of this relation was the decisive one. An adequate understanding and justification of our knowledge required, so he believed, a deeper exploration of the subject, in which he came to see the source or origin of all object knowledge. For this purpose he devised a special method, the phenomenological reduction. In his *Ideen* he had introduced it as an operation of "bracketing" or suspending our belief in the existence of the phenomena under investigation. But almost unnoticeably it became an elaborate procedure by which Husserl tried to trace all phenomena back to subjectivity, to an irreducible core of absolute consciousness, a transcendental subject. Here Husserl believed he could uncover the intentional acts by which the whole objective world was constituted. Thus reductive phenomenology led to constitutive phenomenology, which was to demonstrate that not only all meanings but all being was due to the constitutive functions of intentionality. It was also to provide proof for Husserl's transcendental idealism. There can therefore be little question that for Husserl's phenomenology all phenomena were subjective in the sense of dependence, a dependence to be sure upon a special subject, the transcendental subject which he tried to keep apart from the empirical subject. It can be left undecided here whether and how far the appearance of the so-called transcendental *hyle* (stuff) justifies a modification of this conclusion; for the *hyle* is certainly not dependent on the subject. More significant may be certain ambiguities in

Husserl's use of the term "constitution," which does not always imply an "active" constitution of the object by the subject, but has also a "passive" or receptive form.

It hardly needs pointing out that the situation differs considerably for the non-transcendental phenomenologies. Husserl had attracted his first following on the basis of his classic critique of psychologism in the interest of a new pure logic free from psychology. His subsequent program of a descriptive study of the phenomena in their essential structures was therefore widely understood as a "turn to the object," and a turning away from the subject. In retrospect this may appear as a strange misunderstanding. But it was a creative misunderstanding which produced some of the finest concrete descriptive studies in all phenomenology. These were based on intuitive analysis of intentional phenomena, describing equally both the intending acts and the intended objects. This led to a universal phenomenology of essences, not restricted to consciousness, including phenomenological psychology as well as phenomenological ontology. Such phenomenology revealed no evidence for the universal dependence of all phenomena upon a constituting subject. In fact it produced considerable evidence for the independence of the perceptual phenomena of the subject, thus giving support to the realist position.

But the fact that the phenomena of the non-transcendental phenomenology are not subjective in the sense of subject-dependent does not yet rule out the possibility that they are essentially subject-related. All phenomenology takes its start from the phenomena. A phenomenon is essentially whatever appears to someone, that is to a subject. Such subject-relatedness does not involve the dependence of the phenomenon upon the subject. But it does indicate that even non-transcendental phenomenology cannot simply ignore the subject. In fact the non-transcendental phenomenologists may have been too naive in taking a shortcut from the phenomena to a reality entirely independent of the subject. Thus Husserl's liberation from psychologism and from the straitjacket of a reductionist positivism has often been misused as an ontological license, and at times it even led to a metaphysical licentiousness to which Husserl had wanted to set a permanent stop. A more critical version of non-transcendental phenomenology cannot altogether overlook the subjective ingredient in the phenomenological approach.

But if thus both phenomenologies imply a subjective factor, does this commit them to subjectivism, the view that everything is personal and that there is no objective common world, but only more or less unrelated private worlds?

In trying to answer this question I shall again begin with transcendental phenomenology. The "triumph of subjectivity" would be a Pyrrhic victory if it achieved scientific rigor only at the price of dissolving all objectivity in a chaos of subjectivities, possibly even in one all-comprehensive solipsism. Husserl's late but important idea of a personal life-world (*Lebenswelt*) as a new point of departure for transcendental phenomenology, a conception which not only Merleau-Ponty but, more recently, John Wild has taken up for its own sake, makes this question even more urgent. It was clearly one of Husserl's major ambitions to establish a valid foundation for objectivity, in the sense of belief in a common world of life and science. His critique of objectivism, e.g., in his last work, *The Crisis of the European Sciences,* applies merely to the physicalistic science of Galileo, which ignores all the features of the life world except the mathematical ones. Seen from this angle, Husserl's enterprise may well be characterized as the triumph of objectivity over subjectivity, or better as the establishment of objectivity in the very heart of subjectivity.

How could Husserl hope to achieve it on the assumption that it was the subject that constituted the world of objects? The main key to his solution has to be sought in his conception of a priori essences. For phenomenology is not the study of consciousness in all its empirical varieties, but that of the essence of consciousness, or of its essential structure. Insofar as this essential structure is the same for all consciousness, it seemed possible to Husserl to eliminate all the personal varieties of the subjects as accidental. Based on this identical essential consciousness, even the world constituted by several transcendental subjects could not fail to be identical. It will be apparent that this conception resembles closely that of Kant with his transcendental a priori of human reason and its a priori forms. It is therefore not surprising that Husserl felt more and more attracted by Kant's transcendentalism along with his prior and more conspicuous attachment to Descartes.

How far did Husserl exhibit such common essential structures within constituting subjectivity? Husserl's programs always outstripped his concrete achievements. But it may be maintained that at least in such works as his *Ideen* he exemplified some of the essential laws of consciousness, for instance in the field of perception or judgment. But nothing like a systematic science of consciousness after the model of the mathematical sciences was built. Whether this can be done sufficiently to demonstrate the necessity of an identical world for all transcendental consciousnesses must therefore still remain an open question.

How safe, then, is *non-transcendental* phenomenology from subjectivism? At first sight there would seem to be less reason to fear that mere subject-relatedness, specifically the necessary relatedness between phenomenon and subject, should result in a subjectivism where each phenomenon would have to reflect the personal differences of the individual subjects. But unfortunately this reduced danger does not guarantee objectivity. What is much more serious, there seem to be concrete reasons for worrying about the fact that phenomenologists, non-transcendental as well as transcendental, all too often do not agree in their verdicts about essences. And all of them seem to base their claims on self-evident intuition of the phenomena. Thus it would seem that the subjective factor in the phenomenological approach lays it wide open to subjectivism.

What can phenomenology do to meet this threat?

The first thing is to point out that not everybody's claims to self-evidence need be taken at face value. There is no bureau that grants phenomenological licenses, not even to self-declared phenomenologists. And it is obvious that any intuitive method has a fatal attraction for lazy thinkers. There is no foolproof safeguard against this pitfall other than increased self-discipline and vigilance. But there can be some protective aid from a critical phenomenology of self-evidence, which should at least be able to narrow the margin of unsafety. For there is self-evidence and self-evidence. Specifically, there is pseudo-self-evidence. There is, for instance, the pseudo-self-evidence of the first impression or the self-evidence of the blinker-mind with its narrowed perspectives. Not until the claimant to self-evidence can give himself and others proof that he has made every effort to deactivate his personal and institutional biases, and to fill out with intuitive content ("fulfillment") all the empty or signitive anticipations of his thought, has he the right to claim anything approaching self-evidence. There is every reason to hope that a self-critical phenomenology of the varieties of self-evidence can dispose of at least a good many rival claims to genuine self-evidence. There is unfortunately reason to suspect that a good many claims even in the phenomenological literature have not undergone such tests and re-tests. But there is no reason to despair of self-evidence and of objectivity via self-evidence because of this remaining unsafety factor.[2]

I would like to make one more suggestion to bolster the confidence in the subjective approach of phenomenology. The alternative would seem to be an objective approach of the type which is usually associated with the scientific method and its concentration on objective data or public facts. But the question may be asked: How can we know that a certain datum is objective in the sense of "public"? What else can we do but first record our direct experiences as completely as possible and then see what others in the face of the same phenomena have to report? Only as the result of such comparing of notes (not an easy matter anyway) of these full experiences can we even think of selecting what is public. In fact, before this is done we cannot even say what is merely private. In this sense all objective experience is really intersubjective experience, i.e., a selection from subjective experiences. This makes subjective experience even more indispensable.

There is then no escape from subjectivity. The only cure for subjectivistic subjectivity is more and better subjectivity, more discriminating subjectivity, and more self-critical subjectivity, which will show the very limits of subjectivity.

I conclude that all phenomenology as a study of the phenomena is subjective in the sense that its objects are subject-related, but not in the sense that it makes them completely subject-dependent. And there is no compelling reason why phenomenology should end in subjectivism. There is merely a risk which, with adequate care, can be reduced to proper proportions.

One final remark: It will be apparent that the few hints I give here are only the outlines of a full answer. Especially today when there is a tendency to refer to phenomenology as a complete philosophy, it needs saying that phenomenology is at best unfinished business. No one has stressed this more than Husserl himself did. There is no good reason for either triumph or defeatism. But there is certainly no reason for complacency. In fact phenomenology is under-

[2] See my article on 'Phenomenology of Direct Evidence' in *Philosophy and Phenomenological Research*, II (1942), pp. 427-456, and below pp. 80-109.

going a crisis, especially as far as transcendental phenomenology is concerned. Under these circumstances phenomenology is in no shape to tackle all the unsolved problems of philosophy. I am saying this advisedly because the failure of other methods to do so presents a temptation for outsiders to call in phenomenology as a panacaea, and for insiders to let themselves be drafted for irresponsible assignments. Husserl always had the ascetic courage to resist these temptations.

Contrary to Scheler's bold offer phenomenology is not a maid of all work. Least of all is it a handmaiden for enterprises as ambitious as metaphysics and metaphysical theology. Whoever thinks of hiring her for such a job should be warned that he will find her a highly unsatisfactory maid, perhaps even a rebellious one. It may be the necessary condition for a new and better metaphysics. But thus far it is certainly not a sufficient one. Phenomenology follows its own laws. Whoever embarks on it has to follow it wherever it leads. It makes no promises of safe and easy solutions. But it may at least be a help in facing the data of our world squarely and honestly, without deflation or inflation, without the impoverishment of a reductionist positivism or the self-deceptive constructions of a merely conceptual metaphysics.

7. PHENOMENOLOGY OF DIRECT EVIDENCE
(SELF-EVIDENCE)

I. PHENOMENOLOGY AND THE UNTRUSTWORTHINESS
OF SELF-EVIDENCE

One of the none too numerous tenets shared by all phenomenologists is the principle that intuitive experience (*Anschauung*) constitutes the ultimate basis for the justification of all our concepts and beliefs. As the editorial preface to the first volume of the phenomenological yearbook put it in 1913: "It is not a system that the editors have in common. ... What unites them is rather the common conviction that only by a return to the primal sources of intuitive experiences and to the insights into essential structures ("Wesenseinsichten") which can be derived from it shall we be able to utilize the great traditions of philosophy with their concepts and problems, and that only in this way will it be possible to clarify the concepts intuitively, to reformulate the problems on an intuitive basis and thus, ultimately, to solve them, at least in principle." [1] Thus, as do other forms of intuitionism, phenomenology adopts as its final test of truth the direct evidence or self-evidence of the intuitive data.

Consequently, phenomenology must face all the objections which

---

* From *Philosophy and Phenomenological Research* II (1942, pp. 427-452. Part of this paper was read at the Meeting of the American Philosophical Association, Eastern Division, in Philadelphia (December 27, 1940). The original title of this essay, as the text itself still reveals, used only the term "self-evidence." If I have not restored it in this volume, adding "self-evidence" merely in parentheses, the reason is less for purposes of identification than because the term "self-evidence" seems to be due for a critical reappraisal and is anything but "self-evident." It is worth pointing out that it is peculiar to the English language since the days of John Locke, who used it first in his *Essay Concerning Human Understanding* Book IV, Ch. VII, pp. 1 ff. More serious objections will emerge from the text of this article.

[1] Cf. *Jahrbuch für Philosophie und phänomenologische Forschung*, ed. by E. Husserl (Halle: Max Niemeyer Verlag, vol. I, 1, 1913).

have been levelled at self-evidence as a reliable criterion of truth. Is it in a position to put up a better defense than other intuitionists have been able to give? I shall argue that it is. A phenomenology of self-evidence offers not only an illustration of phenomenological method; it is at the same time an indispensable buttress of its methodological principles.

In pursuing this double purpose, I do not propose to examine all the arguments which have been brought forward against self-evidence as a test of truth. I shall concentrate on the most current and most influential one, taken over, e.g., by Morris R. Cohen and Ernest Nagel,[2] to the effect that self-evidence changes from period to period. Stock examples in support of this claim are drawn from the fact that at one time it appeared self-evident that the sun revolves around the earth, that heavy bodies fall faster than light ones, that there can be no antipodes, and the like, whereas nowadays all these beliefs have lost their self-evidence. Now, the argument runs, since truth is something unchangeable, its changing criterion, i.e., self-evidence, must be fallible.

This line of argument has been attacked by Hastings Rashdall and others who have pointed out that what is self-evident need not be self-evident to everybody,[3] and even judicious opponents of self-evidence as a criterion of truth, such as Brand Blanshard, admit this.[4] In the case of self-evidence as in any other case, whether it is a question of truth or values or whatever else, the fact of disagreement has as little significance as the fact of agreement.

However, it seems to me that such a defense of self-evidence is far from sufficient. It shows only that changes in our assertions about self-evidence are compatible with objective self-evidence. It fails to explain why it is that sometimes this self-evidence does *not* appear self-evident to everybody. Also, it does not indicate how we can continue to use self-evidence as a criterion. For how can we determine what is *really* self-evident, if the self-evident is not necessarily self-evident to *us* and if what is self-evident to us may not be *really* self-evident? To raise self-evidence above the level of human

[2] *Introduction to Logic and Scientific Method* (New York: Harcourt, 1934, p. 131). Cf. also Morris R. Cohen, *Reason and Nature* (1932, p. 139).

[3] *The Theory of Good and Evil*, 2nd ed. (Oxford University Press, 1924), vol. 1, p. 85).

[4] *The Nature of Thought* (London and New York: Macmillan, 1939, vol. II, p. 239). For a detailed discussion of his specific arguments can be found in an Appendix here omitted; see he Introduction, p. XVII.

dispute is likely to make it a sword without a handle, unfit to serve as a criterion for our guidance in concrete situations.

How can phenomenology meet this dilemma? One of the main assets of the phenomenological method consists in the careful observation and description of the phenomena in their irreducible nature and in their full variety. If this method is applied to the phenomenon of self-evidence, it seems to offer one important help which other kinds of intuitionism have not been able to provide. There are phenomenal differences between one self-evidence and another self-evidence. Such differences may serve to reduce, if not to remove, the seeming contradictions between the conflicting phenomena which all aspire to be genuinely self-evident. More specifically, they may allow us to separate genuine self-evidence from pseudo-self-evidence.

In Husserl's writings we occasionally find the distinction between *adequate* and *inadequate* self-evidence. A "thing in the real world," for instance a three-dimensional object, can appear only with inadequate self-evidence.[5] Such inadequate self-evidence, as distinguished from adequate self-evidence, is capable of increase and decrease.[6] Besides, Husserl stresses the difference between *assertoric* self-evidence, referring to empirical individual objects or states of things, and *apodictic* self-evidence or insight into general essences and essential relationships, which apodictically excludes any alternatives; as a rule only the latter is considered to be really adequate.[7] He also distinguishes between *pure* and *impure* self-evidence, according to whether or not such self-evidence includes an element of matter of fact,[8] between *purely formal* ("analytic," "logical") and *material* ("synthetic a-priori") self-evidence,[9] between *theoretic, axiological,* and *practical* self-evidence,[10] and even between *immediate* and *mediate* self-evidence.[11] In the *Formal and Transcendental Logic* Husserl contrasts, moreover, *self-evidence of distinctness* ("Evidenz der Deut-

[5] *Ideas: General Introduction to Pure Phenomenology*, translated by W. R. Boyce Gibson (New York: Macmillan, 1931, § 138). In *Formale und tranzendentale Logik* there is only one passing reference to 'imperfect' and 'perfect,' 'possibly spurious' and 'genuine' self-evidence (p. 179): translation by Dorion Cairns (The Hague: Martinus Nijhoff, 1969, p. 201).

[6] *Ideas*, p. 386.

[7] *Ibid.*, § 137.

[8] *Ibid.*, pp. 383 f.

[9] *Ibid.*, p. 383; cf. also pp. 68, 78.

[10] *Ibid.*, p. 389.

[11] *Ibid.*, § 141. What is self-evident in such a mediate sense, however, should, properly, hardly be called *self*-evident but at best simply 'evident.'

lichkeit"), which is supposed to occur in a judgment that is explicitly performed and is not passed merely in the vague and confused way of a casual idea or of a sentence which is merely read or faithfully taken over, and *self-evidence of clearness* ("Evidenz der Klarheit"), which, in addition to being distinct, presents even the object to which the judgment refers.[12] Of particular significance is, moreover, Husserl's scale ("Stufenfolge") of self-evidences, as introduced here, in which the self-evidence referring to particulars stands out as primal and basic.[13] The *Cartesian Meditations* add distinctions between *predicative* and *pre-predicative* self-evidence,[14] between *absolute* or *perfect* and *relative* or *imperfect* self-evidence, a distinction which probably coincides with that between *adequate* and *inadequate* self-evidence. There is again the distinction of *apodictic* self-evidence, characterized by an absolute indubitability "in a quite definite and peculiar sense" (*ibid.* I, 55), and a non-apodictic, or merely *assertoric* self-evidence. Finally, in the *Crisis of the European Science and Transcendental Phenomenology* there is a "*phenomenological* self-evidence," which in its apodicticity is distinguished from everyday self-evidence in daily life and science.[15] A fully developed phenomenology of self-evidence would have to investigate these distinctions in detail and determine how far they point to completely different or overlapping differences in the phenomena. In some cases the difference may not be one in the quality of the self-evidence but in the carriers to which it attaches.

Valuable as all these distinctions may be, Husserl did not attempt to utilize them in order to meet the objections against the trustworthiness of self-evidence as a criterion of truth. At the stage of the *Logische Untersuchungen* and the *Ideen* his defense is much simpler. Here, he makes self-evidence simply a correlate of actual self-givenness, as it occurs particularly in the processes of the intuitive fulfillment of our unverified "signitive" meanings (anticipations, mere thought of, etc.).[16] In fact, self-evidence has been identified even

---

[12] *Formale und transzendentale Logik,* (Halle: Max Niemeyer, 1929, § 16, especially p. 53).

[13] *Ibid.,* § 84.

[14] *Husserliana* I, 52.

[15] *Husserliana* VI, 192-93; tr. Carr p. 189.

[16] 'In view of the strict interpretation of the concept of self-evidence which we have here taken as our basis, it is obvious that such doubts as have occasion-

with self-givenness, e.g., by Ludwig Landgrebe.[17] Now, it seems to me begging the question if we grant to a phenomenon the title *self-givenness* (*leibhaftige Selbstgegebenheit*). For the problem is precisely whether what is given to us is really the object itself or only a misleading pretender. To be sure, the self-evident phenomenon pretends to be the object in person. But it would not be in accordance with the attitude of phenomenological "suspension of judgment" (*epoché*), to accept such a claim at its face value without further examination. All the more would it involve a *petitio principii* if we should use such an account of self-evidence as proof that self-evidence always implies actual self-givenness of the object and that it can never be misleading. A cautious account of the phenomenon does not allow us to say more than that a particular "given" makes the impression, has the appearance or look of *self*-givenness of the object which it pretends to be.

Besides, to fuse self-evidence and self-givenness would be to imply that the term self-evidence could legitimately be used only where it is absolutely certain that the self-evident object is actually, and not only apparently, given in person. In thus taking self-evidence out of the actual argument, such a procedure disqualifies it as a usable

---

ally been brought out in recent time are absurd: namely, whether with one and the same datum A there might not be connected in one person the experience of self-evidence and in another that of absurdity. Doubts of this kind were possible only as long as self-evidence and absurdity were interpreted as peculiar (positive or negative) feelings which, attached to the act of judgment by accident, allot it that peculiar distinction which we evaluate logically as truth or falsehood respectively.' 'If somebody experiences the self-evidence A, it is self-evident that nobody else can experience the absurdity of the same A; for the fact that A is self-evident means: A is not only referred to, but it is also actually given exactly as what is referred to; it is in the strictest sense itself present. Now, how shall it be possible that for a second person this same A is referred to, but that by an actually given non-A the view is genuinely ruled out that it is A? We realize that we are here concerned with a situation based on essential structures (*Wesens-Sachlagen*), the same situation which is expressed by the principle of contradiction.' (Translated from *Logische Untersuchungen,* 2nd ed., Halle, Max Niemeyer, 1921, vol. II, 2, p. 127.) Cf. also *Log. Unters,* vol. I, pp. 190 f.: and *Ideas,* § 145, p. 400, against the interpretation of self-evidence as a 'mystical voice' indicating truth. Justified as the protest against a psychologistic interpretation of self-evidence as a feeling may be, it seems doubtful whether the assertion that self-evidence differs in different observers depends upon the view that it is a feeling. Even if self-evidence should be a character of the object, like familiarity or strangeness, the objection could still hold.

[17] Cf. his *Einleitung* (p. 11) to Husserl's posthumous, but highly important book on *Erfahrung und Urteil,* which had at least Husserl's general approval.

criterion of truth. For how shall we make sure that the speaker really has the self-evidence he claims and that the matter is really self-given to him, and not merely one that purports to be self-evident? Can we establish this directly without any further criteria? If Husserl's defense were accepted, we should not be entitled to speak of A's being self-evident to anybody before we have made absolutely sure that what appears to be self-evident exists exactly in accordance with such appearance – a fact which a cognitive subject can never establish in a more direct manner than by self-evidence. Until this fact has been ascertained, we could at best speak of A's *appearing* to be self-evident.

It is, therefore, all the more remarkable that in the *Formal and Transcendental Logic* Husserl reverses his earlier stand almost completely. Here it seems a foregone conclusion that self-evidence by its very nature includes the possibility of illusion; and this concession is supposed to apply even to *apodictic* self-evidence. To be sure, self-evidence can be refuted only by better self-evidence. But never does it hold out an absolute guarantee which would enable us to use it as an infallible criterion of truth.[18]

There is no explicit statement of the reasons for this striking shift. It may be suspected, however, that it took place as a consequence of the more radical interpretation of the phenomenological reduction which was bound to affect even the interpretation of the phenomenon of self-evidence.[19] Such a reflective critique is supposed to show

[18] *Formale und transzendentale Logik*, §§ 58, 59, especially pp. 139 ff. transl. p. 156.

[19] *Ibid.*, § 69, pp. 156 f; § 107, p. 255. In the *Cartesian Meditations* Husserl points out that self-evidence 'does not exclude the possibility that what is evident can become subsequently dubious, that what is *(Sein)* can turn out to be a semblance *(Schein)* ... This open possibility of becoming dubious ... *in spite of self-evidence* can be anticipated at any time by critical reflection'. Nevertheless he claims for apodictic self-evidence the absolute inconceivability of its misleadingness. It seems remarkable that in the slightly earlier *Formal and Transcendental Logic* even self-evidence in the apodictic sense is not claimed as beyond possible illusion and error. (§ 59, p. 140) The problem posed by this seeming contradiction is confronted conscientiously though not yet conclusively by David M. Levin in *Reason and Evidence in Husserl's Phenomenology* (Northwestern University Press, 1970, pp. 107-113). This book contains a provocative attempt to show that Husserl's objective of achieving apodicticity and not merely relative adequacy is doomed to failure. Levine's ultimate argument to the effect that the 'eidetic variation' required to establish eidetic insights even in fields like mathematics remains essentially incomplete because it can never exhaust all possible variants, is debatable. It would not

"straight" self-evidence (*gerade Evidenz, Evidenz geradehin*) as a secondary achievement (*Leistung*) of constitutive intentionality; the adequate evaluation of such a view would require a much more detailed examination of the concept of intentionality in Husserl's later philosophy.

It may be asked, however, whether in the light of a closer observation of the phenomena this complete reversal in Husserl's appraisal of the reliability of self-evidence is not somewhat too sweeping. At any rate, it seems as if some of the difficulties in the doctrine of self-evidence might be overcome by a development and application of Husserl's earlier distinctions. Not all of them are significant for our problem. Only the relevant ones, such as that between adequate and inadequate self-evidence, will be taken up. But we shall also have to draw further distinctions with a view to separating authentic and inauthentic self-evidence.

II. ON AUTHENTIC SELF-EVIDENCE

It would be out of the question to give here a full analysis and description of the whole phenomenon of self-evidence. Besides, much as further investigation is still needed, it should be acknowledged that most valuable pioneer work has already been done, not only by Husserl's analyses but by medieval and modern scholastic thinkers as well.[20] For, though the term '*evidentia*' (and its equivalents in other languages) is comparatively recent in its epistemological application – it occurs only occasionally in Thomas Aquinas and in the later great classical systems – the phenomenon referred to under different names has long been known.

a. Subjective Self-evidence

One of the most significant distinctions brought out by the modern scholastics is that between subjective and objective self-evidence. Objective self-evidence is supposed to appear in the object of our cognition. It contrasts with subjective self-evidence, which is said to

---

affect the apodicticity of insights about lowest species, where no variation is possible, and likewise that of the *ego-cogito-cogitata mea,* which is not an eidetic insight.

[20] Cf., e.g., Caspar Isenkrahe, *Zum Problem der Evidenz,* (1917).

inhere in the act of cognition itself.[21] In using the terms "objective" and "subjective" in this context, we should, of course, be on our guard against including any connotation of objective epistemological stability and reliability or subjective instability and untrustworthiness respectively.

Subjective self-evidence is clearly the secondary phenomenon. From the point of view of ordinary language the subjective use of the term self-evidence is entirely unnatural.[22] Unfortunately, however, this subjective self-evidence has so far been the center of interest in the phenomenological investigation of self-evidence. To be sure, Husserl does emphasize the double-meaning of self-evidence as "noetic" and as "noematic" in accordance with the essential parallelism in the structure of consciousness.[23] Nevertheless, his main accounts are concerned with the self-evident *acts*, not with the self-evident objects or states of things (*Sachverhalte*). In fact, in these cases he does not even describe self-evidence as a special character *in* the act, as the scholastics did, but he identifies it with the complete acts of cognition (*Erkenntnis*), insight (*Einsicht*), experience (*Erfahrung*), and the like.[24] On the other hand, it should be noted that

[21] 'Self-evidence (*in abstracto*) is that very visibility or perspicuity of a thing thanks to which the thing is clearly seen. Self-evidence is to the intellect what the lucidity of external things is to the eyes. But from this objective meaning the word is also extended to a subjective meaning. Self-evidence, as seen from the point of view of the subject, is the perspicuity of knowledge which removes all uneasiness or, it is the clarity of perception in the one who, as it were, 'sees' the thing. Self-evidence, therefore, is twofold, one of the object, the other of knowledge...' (Translated from the Latin of Tilman Pesch, *Philosophia Lacensis*, vol. I, L. II, cap. V, § 3.)

[22] One is hardly inclined to speak of an act of judging as being self-evident, if its object is self-evident. Even in German the extension of the use of the word 'evident' to experiences (*Erfahrung, Wahrnehmung* etc.), seems to be somewhat artificial. That applies to Franz Brentano's 'mit Evidenz wahrnehmen' as well as to Husserl's use of the phrase 'ich habe eine Evidenz.' English is apparently much stricter in this respect. It seems to me significant that, in a very important passage of the *Ideas*, W. R. Boyce Gibson had to translate 'Evidenz,' as equivalent to 'Einsicht,' by 'evidential vision' (p. 383).

[23] *Ideas*, § 136, p. 382; *Formale und transz. Logik*, § 46, p. 113 transl. p. 128. In *Ideas*, (§ 145, p. 401) self-evidence is even described as belonging primarily to the 'noema'; still immediately afterward this 'peculiar way of positing' ('Setzungsmodus') seems to be ascribed primarily to the act as a whole, not to its object.

[24] Cf. *Logische Untersuchungen*, vol. II, 2 (translated) 'self-evidence as the experience of truth' (p. 122) or as total coincidence between the acts of merely empty 'intention' and those of intuitive 'fulfillment'; similarly in *Ideas*: 'evidential vision (*Evidenz*) as 'apodeictic in-seeing' (*apodiktisches Einsehen*); also

Husserl is very anxious to keep this experience apart from anything like a feeling, for instance, from the blind feeling of certainty or conviction. In fact, he considers a feeling of self-evidence as a mere fiction.[25]

Still, this self-evidence of our cognitive acts, according to its structural meaning, seems to refer to the self-evidence of the experienced object as its basis. The permeation of an act with the illuminating character of self-evidence has its apparent foundation in the self-evidence which appears in the object of the cognitive act.[26] It is, therefore, this objective self-evidence upon which I propose to concentrate.

b. The Carriers of Objective Self-evidence

Before discussing the *nature* of objective self-evidence we must make a full survey of its *field*. At first sight, there seem to be two chief classes of objects to which we ascribe self-evidence in this sense: namely propositions, or more specifically, asserting propositions (e.g., S is P), and the states of affairs (*Sachverhalte*) to which these propositions refer (the fact that S is P, the being-P of S). Now it seems to me that the meaning of the term self-evidence is slightly different in these two cases. Can we properly say that a proposition, conceived of as a meaningful combination of subject, predicate, copula, and other elements, is self-evident, i.e., evident by itself? Do its terms in their juxtaposition tell us anything about its truth? I should hardly think so. Not unless we consider the state of things delineated by such a proposition can a judgment become evident.

Formale und transz. Logik, pp. 143 ff. (transl. 159 ff.), pp. 245 ff. tr. 277 ff; self-evidence as an active achievement ('*Leistung*'), p. 251: as the experience of self-presentation (*Selbstgebung*). In Landgrebe's Einleitung to *Erfahrung und Urteil* self-evidence appears at first as the subjective characteristic of intelligibility ('Einsichtigkeit,' p. 8), and every consciousness which is selfpresenting is characterized as evident (p. 12). Later on, however, self-evidence is identified with self-giveness (*Selbstgegebenheit*). In this kind of account of self-evidence Husserl is followed even by neo-scholastics such as Joseph Geyser in his *Erkenntnistheorie* (Paderborn, 1922): "Self-evidence, to put it briefly, is intuition of states of things (*Sachverhaltsschauen*)" (p. 194).

[25] *Ideas,* § 21.

[26] The prerogative of objective self-evidence ('*gegenständliche Evidenz*') over the subjective self-evidence of our judgement ('Urteilsevidenz'), as presupposing the former, is now brought out with gratifying explicitness in *Erfahrung und Urteil* (p. 14) by Landgrebe, as it seems, with Husserl's personal approval.

Strictly speaking, then, propositions are never self-evident; at best they may possess indirect self-evidence. This may seem to be a rather hair-splitting distinction. Its serious background is, however, that all too often we call propositions self-evident without examining the things and states of affairs to which they refer; in other words, we fail to inspect the phenomena which are the real basis of the alleged self-evidence of the proposition.

Ultimately then the only legitimate claimant to objective self-evidence is the self-evident state of affairs. We say: it is self-evident *that* the whole is bigger than its parts, etc. Everywhere it is such a "that"-combination to which we ultimately ascribe self-evidence. We cannot meaningfully say that a thing, for instance a stone, or a relation, for example equality, or anything perceived is self-evident. On the other hand, we should be well aware that the basis of the self-evidence of states of affairs, e.g., of the one that snow is white, is the perception of the concrete object with its concrete properties, e.g., of the white substance snow. And there is something in this supporting perception which makes us sure that it is the real thing we face. However, in common usage this criterion of veridical perception is not called self-evidence. If we name it at all, we might call it *apparent* self-givenness, (or self-presence, or self-presentation; *anscheinende Selbstgegebenheit, Selbstgegenwart;* cf. p. 84). But although we do not ordinarily call such a character 'self-evidence', it is certainly closely related to what we mean by that term. Actually, it is even the more fundamental phenomenon. I should, therefore, like to include it in this discussion of self-evidence. The following analyses will, then, under the name of self-evidence refer to "apparent self-givenness" regardless of whether it occurs in states of affairs (objective self-evidence in the strict sense) or in concrete perceived objects (objective self-evidence in the wider sense).

c. The Characteristics of Objective Self-evidence

At first sight it seems rather doubtful whether a rigorous definition of such a simple phenomenon as self-evidence can be given at all. But that is not even the most important task of a real phenomenological account. The first and essential thing is that we determine the generic structure of a phenomenon and that we describe it with all of its basic properties in such a way that it can be identified unfailingly among all related phenomena. In the case of objective self-

evidence this task has been neglected thus far, even in phenomenological analyses.

But before attacking it we shall have to eliminate one particularly
dangerous source of confusion. Self-evidence has often been characterized, to be sure mostly by its opponents, as a mere feeling. Husserl
has made it plain that such a characterization is completely misleading. It confuses self-evidence, which always appears on the side of
the object, with the feeling of certainty, i.e., with a merely subjective
state of mind. The two are independent of each other. There may be
self-evidence without the feeling of certainty, e.g., in the case of the
overscrupulous skeptic, and there occurs certainty without the presence of self-evidence, as in the case of the gullible person, although
in the ideal case the two would go together. For this reason the fickle-
ness of our feeling of certainty is no valid argument against the
reliability of self-evidence, whether subjective or objective.

Objective self-evidence, then, is primarily a property which resides
in self-evident objects. This property, however, is not to be compared
with shape or size which, it is generally assumed, belong to the intrinsic make-up, the inner structure, of the object without reference
to any other object outside. Nor is it a relation, such as equality or
difference in size. Self-evidence is not located "between" objects, as
a relation is. It attaches in a peculiar way to the object. Yet at the
same time it refers to the subject to whom the matter appears self-
evident. Thus, in its generic structure, objective self-evidence seems
to form a relational property of certain states of affairs (in a wider
sense also of concrete objects), inherent in them but referring somehow to a subject beyond.

What is the peculiar nature of this relational property? It is always
instructive to investigate the literal meaning of such a term as evidence, although we must never rely exclusively on an etymological
interpretation. The Latin verb "e-videri" seems to suggest something
which moves out of the background to the fore, which puts in an
appearance. This would imply the idea of a somehow intensified
phenomenon stepping out of its environment and, as it were, introducing itself personally. Forced though this interpretation may appear, it indicates the spontaneous appeal, i.e., the capacity of pro-
ducing immediate assent, which seems to distinguish any self-evident
phenomenon.

Yet, we must not be misled by such first indications as language can give us, however suggestive they may be. Rather we must try to penetrate into the thing meant by the linguistic symbols. Such an attempt should be based on the examination of a case of unquestioned self-evidence. Of the many examples suitable for examination I suggest the following: "I am now seeing something white with small black marks on it"; or, "Of two contradictory propositions one must be false."

What we mean to assert in claiming self-evidence of such states of affairs or "truths," as they are often termed, can be partly indicated by a number of more telling synonyms. "Manifest," "obvious," "patent," "plain" are perhaps the most fitting and telling ones.[27] What they all express is the fact that the object lies open to our view, is freely accessible. Or, to put it negatively, their meaning is that there are no dark corners left, that every aspect of the object is so clearly presented that it could not possibly hold any further surprises.

In fact, "clearness" is the expression most frequently used in the characterization of objective self-evidence, especially among the scholastics.[28] Clearness is certainly very closely related to self-evidence, even though it is perhaps not fully identical with it, since even illusions and dreams may be clear in certain respects.

Thus the characterization as unobstructed cognitive accessibility or plain "visibility" is the best approximation to an adequate account of objective self-evidence which I can suggest.

d. The Subjective Factor in Objective Self-evidence

All these synonymous terms, including even "plain" and "clear" if taken in their epistemological meaning (as distinguished from their ontological meaning, as in "clear water," "plain dress," etc.), have some reference to a cognitive subject. To be sure, obviousness, accessibility, etc., have their ultimate foundation in certain structural

---

[27] G. F. Stout ('Self-evidence and Matter of Fact' in *Philosophy,* vol. IX, p. 392) points out that 'What is self-evident need not be obvious.' Apparently, he takes 'obviousness' in a more restricted sense and the same may happen with the other terms mentioned above. It is certainly not essential to self-evidence that it strike one at first sight, that 'cela saute aux yeux.'

[28] Cf., e.g., Josef Gredt, *Elementa philosophiae Aristotelico-Thomisticae* (Freiburg, Herder, 2nd ed. 1932, vol. II, p. 596): 'Self-evidence (*enargeia*) in general is the clarity of the object by which it manifests itself actually (*actualiter*) to the cognitive faculty.' (Translated from the Latin original')

properties of objects which facilitate cognitive access, particularly if their structure is simple and transparent. Still, self-evidence itself is a relational property based on the relation between the lucid object and the subject who faces it.

But what kind of a subject is meant in this case? Certainly not the empirical subject, the real man in the street. Primarily we think of an "ideal," normally equipped, unprejudiced observer with sound judgment. For self-evidence it is not necessary that every actual subject see the self-evident object. As Rashdall put it: Self-evident truths are not truths which are evident to everybody.

This seems to imply a serious danger: On the one hand, to detach self-evidence from the empirical subject would seem to make it more objective. On the other hand, the question will at once arise: How can we know what would be self-evident to such an ideal subject except from our own experience, i.e., from what is self-evident to us? Thus, self-evidence would again become highly subjective. Complete relativism would be inescapable, and that for reasons contained in the very nature of self-evidence. The reference to an ideal normal subject would involve us again in the old dilemma of saving objectivity at the price of isolating self-evidence from the subject, or of sacrificing its objectivity to its applicability. At any rate, in the former case such a criterion, by implying that self-evidence refers to a subject which is not ourselves, would appear to require an additional criterion, allowing us to see what would be self-evident to such a subject.

I shall maintain, however, that every individual has a very clear sense of what is self-evident only to him, because of his special sensitivity and position, and what is unqualifiedly self-evident, i.e., self-evident to every normal observer, such as the principle of contradiction. Besides, the objection involves a considerable misunderstanding of the conception of normal subject as here applied, which does by no means imply the idea of a subject which would be permanently different from ourselves. What we have in mind, is rather ourselves in a state of normalcy. By normalcy I refer, then, to a state in ourselves which we can identify as such not only when we have attained it, but also when it is affected by circumstances such as exhaustion. Whenever we know that our understanding is *not* hampered by these purely subjective factors, such as our not being sufficiently equipped or adequately trained to perform a certain mental operation, we are clearly and immediately aware of fulfilling the requirements of normalcy in this sense.

Very often, in this context, we hear the phrase: "This is self-evident to me." Does this not clearly imply a reference to our actual empirical selves regardless of the consciousness of normalcy? But we have to consider that this phrase is highly ambiguous. The following meanings may be distinguished: 1. The phrase may refer to what is plain to me or to some other subject, while implying that only he or I have immediate access to it: it is true, but it is self-evident only to somebody in our peculiar position. Thus, the fact of a certain crime may be self-evident to the eyewitness but not to the judge whose evidence can only be mediate. One might call this sort of self-evidence to me "objective self-evidence as restricted to subjects in a peculiar position." 2. If I say: "It is self-evident to you that all red-haired people are inferior to brunettes," I imply that I consider this generalization as by no means valid. In fact, I do not even admit that it is really self-evident to the other person: he only believes it is. So, this usage is slightly ironical and will generally be applied only to judgments of other people whose assertions we doubt. One might call this "purely subjective self-evidence." 3. Suppose I say: "This mathematical axiom is self-evident even to me, a non-mathematician," I imply that it is *not only* self-evident in itself, but, besides, that it has penetrated into my understanding. "Self-evidence to me" in this sense includes unqualified self-evidence. Whatever is self-evident in this sense is certainly also self-evident in itself for any normal observer, the converse, however, not being necessarily true. One might call this "objective self-evidence, subjectively realized."

Only "self-evidence to me" in this third sense, which implies self-evidence to any reasonable observer, can be taken as a sufficient criterion of unqualified objective self-evidence and, ultimately, of truth.

e. The Cognitive Actualization of Objective Self-evidence. Apparent Self-givenness

Self-evidence has been described here as unobstructed cognitive accessibility or plain "visibility." This implies that it constitutes not only a relational property but also a potential property of an object, i.e., a latent possibility capable of being actualized.

This realization suggests the question of how such a potentiality can possibly serve as a criterion independent of any actualization. Can we know directly about possibilities of access to objects without actually having approached them? How can we verify possibilities at all? Is there any other way except by actualizing them, either in perceptual experience or in testing imagination?

Indeed, there seems to me no other method of verifying potentialities in general, and in particular the cognitive potentiality contained in self-evidence. Unobstructed accessibility is given to us only by actual approach, i.e., by the actualization of the possibility which self-evidence indicates. In using the immediate access to the object which self-evidence supplies and in bringing the object into full focus we realize at the same time the potentiality in the object for affording such access and allowing such presentation. In principle the situation is similar to the case of elasticity which is revealed to us by its characteristic resistance to pressure. Likewise, we cannot appraise self-evidence clearly unless we have tested it by cognitive actualization.

Does this not imply that self-evidence is not the real criterion of truth which it pretends to be? Yes and no. Certainly we have no direct access to a potentiality except by its actualization. On the other hand, in this actual presentedness we are given more than an indirect criterion from which we may infer the potentiality. In the plain presentedness we are at the same time immediately aware of the lasting potentiality of presentation which a self-evident object contains. Full presentedness alone, if not at the same time seen as an expression of such a potentiality, would not be able to function as a criterion of truth. Still, I should not hesitate to admit that the real ultimate test of truth is not the potentiality of full presentedness, which we literally mean by self-evidence, but the actualized form of such potentiality in actual presentedness, in which the self-evident is apparently self-present.[29]

---

[29] As to the reasons why it seems to me necessary to speak of *apparent* self-givenness and not of self-givenness and self-presence unqualifiedly, I refer to the discussion on pp. 84. Moreover, it seems to me desirable to speak of self-presence, instead of self-givenness, in view of the fact, to be discussed later, that self-evidence may be given more or less adequately. And it would certainly sound odd to say that self-giveness is given inadequately.

f. The Degrees of Self-evidence

The prevailing view seems to be that there can be no degrees of self-evidence.[30] Self-evidence is supposed to be something absolute. Either a state of affairs is self-evident or it is not. *Tertium non datur.*

On the basis of the preceding account of self-evidence, both objective and subjective, I cannot see any good reason for accepting such a view without proof. Quite apart from the gradation which may occur in the presentational modi of self-evidence, the nature of self-evidence itself as free cognitive accessibility by no means excludes degrees. States of affairs and objects may be more or less complicated and, accordingly, more or less plainly visible. Thus, although self-evident, they may be more or less accessible to our understanding. For instance, the axiom that two points determine a straight line seems to me to be much less complicated, clearer, and, to that extent more self-evident than the one that in a plane through one point there can be only one parallel to a given line, a circumstance which was so important in the controversy over the parallel axiom.

III. SELF-EVIDENCE AND NECESSITY OF THOUGHT

Self-evidence is often identified with, or at least treated as an equivalent of, necessity of thinking (*Denknotwendigkeit*).[31] Actually such necessity is frequently interpreted as psychological compulsion. By such an account, our awareness of self-evidence would be reduced to a mere subjective feeling. And such a feeling can naturally have as little claim to objectivity as any other mere feeling.

It is not only self-evidence which seems to be in this plight. The connections between premises and conclusions likewise involve a certain logical necessity. And this necessity is again manifested

[30] Notable exceptions are Bertrand Russell (*Problems of Philosophy,* Home University Library, pp. 182 ff). and Brand Blanshard, *The Nature of Thought* (New York: Macmillan, 1940, vol. II, pp. 246 ff.).

[31] Cf. e.g., Christoph Sigwart (*Logik,* 2nd ed., vol. I, General Introduction, § 6), who, however, tries to draw a distinction between a mere psychological and a 'logical' necessity of thought, the latter being based in the nature of the object of our thought. Cf. also A. K. Rogers, *The Nature of Truth,* 1923, p. 32: "And what I mean by self-evidence ... is this: I find it impossible, even in imagination, to think of myself as conceivably in a state of mind where I should consider the proposition open to doubt, the ground of my assurance lying within the content of the proposition itself."

psychologically by experiences which have been described as feelings of compulsion. The question therefore seems urgent: Is there really no way of distinguishing between the necessity of thinking, corresponding to logical necessity and self-evidence, on the one hand, and mere psychological compulsion on the other? Only a phenomenological examination of the case can decide this.

There are, as far as we can see, cases where the course of our thinking is subjected, if not to inescapable compulsion, at least to a pressure which comes very close to it. The plainest case is perhaps represented by pathological obsessions (*Zwangsvorstellungen*), as occurring in a persecution complex. However, to most of us such abnormal states are accessible and understandable only to a very limited degree. For this reason the case of posthypnotic suggestion has certain advantages over that of obsessions, but again it cannot be sufficiently reproduced and inspected at will for purposes of phenomenological analysis. Perhaps the closest we can come in normal awareness to an experience of absolute psychological compulsion is in the case of certain popular tunes, which seem to pursue us against the most determined efforts to shake them off. Of course, as soon as the normal resistance against the usual stream of ideas ceases, nearly all of our thinking takes a rather automatic course. Dream is the extreme example of such a condition. However, in such states there is hardly any awareness of being forcibly compelled to think along definite lines. The real experience of psychological compulsion implies that the subject is the powerless victim of a pressure from without, suffering more or less painfully from an overpowering flood of ideas.[32] In everyday life, we seem to have this experience only

[32] Cf. the phenomenological descriptions of abnormal process given by Karl Jaspers (*Allgemeine Psychopathologie*, 2nd ed., Berlin, 1920) who, in summing up, gives the following account of 'Zwangsideen': "The thoughts of the patients all center around a basic idea which, against the will of the patient, recurs unceasingly in his consciousness ('Denkzwang,' compulsion of thought) and the 'correctness' of which thrusts itself upon the patient with overwhelming persuasiveness ('Geltungszwang,' compulsion of validity; a more adequate term might be 'persuasive compulsion': 'Ueberredungszwang,' p. 65)." Particularly noteworthy is the following general remark on 'the consciousness of psychological compulsion as an ultimate fact: "[In abnormal life] all the psychological processes may occur with the characteristic of psychical compulsion" (p. 66); observe also Jaspers' distinction between different types of such compulsion. Experiences of compulsion may, besides, occur in 'Ideenflucht' (flight of ideas) as described by a patient of Forel's (*Ibid.*, p. 99): "In my head, like a clockwork, a compulsory, uninterrupted chain of ideas ran its inevitable course."

exceptionally and scarcely in pure form and full intensity. But that does not preclude that we have a perfectly clear idea of what such compulsion would mean.

Is there any element of such compulsion in the case of our drawing conclusions from given premises, e.g., "S is P, therefore some P's are S"; or in the case of our hitting upon a necessary solution of a mathematical problem, or in that of our being won over by the self-evident impression that "this paper is white" or that "the straight line is the shortest distance between two points"? Is it really "physically impossible" for us to deny such assertions and to conceive of their opposites? Certainly, nothing forbids us to say it. It is not only in a freakish mood that we do assert it; every lie is a flat contradiction of the self-evident. But even our abstract (pre-intuitive) thought (*"signitives"* or *"symbolisches Denken"* in Husserl's terms) and our rudimentary imagination, as we ordinarily practice them, may easily contradict material "necessities." Although we are unable to visualize a regular polyhedron of a thousand faces, we may conceive of it in the same way in which we may conceive of parallels which intersect; in fact, this latter possibility forms the basis of all non-Euclidian geometry.

Yet, it cannot be reasonably denied that for anybody who looks carefully at the facts themselves there is, in these cases, a kind of compulsion to acknowledge the actual structures and relations of the objects. However, such pressure compels only those who want to know, who are willing to accept the verdict of the facts themselves and to follow their structure and relations as guides in their thinking. In this purely phenomenological discussion the metaphysical issue of free will and thought has, of course, to be disregarded. But it can hardly be denied that, phenomenally at least, we are free to go our own way as soon as we abandon our cognitive objective. There is no more compulsion for the thinker to follow truth than for the engineer to make correct calculations, for the musician to play according to the score, or for the driver to follow the road sign. Only as long as he wants to get ahead, is he compelled to keep to it. At any moment he is at liberty to run off the road onto soft shoulders or into a telegraph pole.

It appears from the above discussion that the necessity implied in our logical thinking is never absolute or categorical, but only hypothetical, conditioned by our will to know. Only as long as this will remains alive is there any compulsion or even directing resistance on the part of the object of our thought and, consequently, any necessity of our thinking along certain lines. In other words, necessity leads our thinking only in so far as thinking is prepared to follow it. So ultimately the necessity of thought derives its compulsory influence from the subject himself who submits to this objective necessity. The object of our thought does nothing but indicate the direction in which correct thinking would have to move. The compelling object can at most be likened to a signpost in the manner it influences the person who consults it.

In this free and always revocable subjection to "compulsion," necessity of logical thinking differs even from such cases of hypothetical compulsion in which the hypothetical necessity cannot be interrupted, once it has been released; this applies to the cases where the necessity of thinking depends upon the realization of certain external conditions, as taking a hallucinogenic drug or being hypnotized, either voluntarily or involuntarily; as soon as we are under its influence, the course of our ideas is irrevocably determined and in fact compulsory, although we may not experience the compulsion as such.

But there is another and perhaps more significant phenomenological difference between mere psychological necessity and logically determined necessity of thinking. In the case of self-evidence as well as in that of logical deduction, the experience of "compulsion" is by no means that of a blind, and, in that sense, of a mechanical compulsion by some brute force which we cannot recognize directly. Here we are influenced and guided by the clear and direct insight into the subject that confronts us and into its nature and relations. (In speaking of insight I do not mean to say that a full understanding of the object, of its structure and of its relations is required; I refer only to insight into its phenomenal givenness.) In the light of this insight we can even understand why there is such a (hypothetical) necessity. It is not a case of a "vis a tergo," overpowering us from behind but that of a frontal appeal to the self-determination of free minds.

For the same reason we can also recognize that such a logical necessity exists not only for ourselves personally but for any reasonable person who has access to the matter under consideration. Such necessity has nothing to do with the individual person but is derived solely from the nature of the object. In principle even God, conceived as the perfect knowing being, would be subject to this necessity.

The case of compulsory ideas is entirely different. Such ideas are not accompanied by any insight, nor by the awareness that the compulsion is a function only of full insight into the matter before us. Here, without any cooperation on our part, we succumb blindly to the sheer force of the compulsory ideas. In the case of posthypnotic suggestion we may try subsequently to rationalize our way of thinking and acting under the compulsion of the hypnotic instruction; but even phenomenologically such behavior seems to have a character quite different from thought and action if guided by free and full insight. In the case of blind psychological compulsion there are certainly causes why one idea calls forth another in our mind. But they are of an entirely factual, non-intelligible character.

We may say, then, that logical necessity of thinking is an hypothetical insight-necessity, whereas mere psychological necessity is absolute, blind compulsion. There is a distinct phenomenological difference between the two. Regardless of whether or not self-evidence and mediate evidence are identical with, or are only closely related to, necessity of thinking, they are clearly different from a mere subjective feeling of momentary compulsion that cannot claim any objective validity.

IV. ON INAUTHENTIC SELF-EVIDENCE

However, there are other adjacent phenomena which are much more easily confused with genuine self-evidence and which constitute an immediate threat to our confidence in self-evidence as a criterion of truth. It is one of the tasks and practical services of phenomenology to identify these phenomena and thus to make us safe against confusing them with the genuine types.

a. Speciousness

I shall here omit criteria so closely related to, and partly identical with, self-evidence as "clearness and distinctness," which are hardly likely to create any confusion. There is, however, one particularly dangerous phenomenon which we shall have to investigate, namely speciousness (*Trug*). As here used, the term "speciousness" is not meant to imply at once an unfavorable connotation. Certainly I shall have to give an unprejudiced account of what is phenomenally present wherever one speaks of speciousness as something fully and adequately given. For speciousness has a clear and definite nature of its own, which phenomenology has to unfold. As an example I might take a specious argument, represented by a fallacy like the fallacy of the undistributed middle term, or a specious phenomenon, such as a perceptual illusion.

However, the view about the nature of speciousness as here presented implies a certain conception of knowledge in general, which needs brief statement.[33] It maintains that every aspect of an object is closely connected with other aspects of it. Aspects contain anticipating references to one another which may be either fulfilled or foiled. Thus the aspect of a cube from a certain angle implies the anticipating reference to the aspect which it would present after a change of the observational angle. These anticipating references need by no means always be fulfilled. The frustration of these anticipations is the basic feature of all our illusions and of the speciousness which they contain.

Any kind of illusion, if there is such a phenomenon at all, could illustrate this point. As an example I choose the familiar Mueller-Lyer illusion, where one of the two equal sections of a line is bounded by lines pointing inward, the other by lines pointing outward. Unless we are already warned against this illusion and have trained ourselves to eliminate it, our impression is here that the two sections are definitely unequal. And the implied anticipation is that the removal of the surrounding pattern would not make any difference to that impression. It is the frustration of this anticipatory reference which is responsible for the speciousness of these phenomena. Once we analyze more closely and check on the anticipatory references, notably by testing with a measuring tape and, possibly, even by eliminating in imagination the pointing lines, we discover that our anticipatory reference was misleading, that, after the removal of the lines, the structure of the objects does not agree with what we were made to expect. Thus our anticipatory references cannot make any ultimate claim to be veridical. In passing from an anticipatory reference to its fulfillment we hit in such cases upon a discontinuity, a

---

[33] Cf. 'Critical Phenomenological Realism' in *Philosophy and Phenomenological Research*, vol. 1, p. 160, see now below in essay 9 p. 155.

break in the structure of the phenomenon which is incompatible with the pervading lucidity of genuine self-evidence.

Speciousness, by its very nature, has a certain superficial appeal. At first sight it lends to the subject under consideration a peculiar clearness, obviousness, transparency which makes us expect that it pervades the whole object. Without further examination we are therefore bound to fall victims to this surface impression. Only if we penetrate more deeply and see where the structure of the object deviates from this superficial pre-delineation, are we able to discover the deception and to unmask the speciousness as such.

Likewise, in the specious argument there is an apparent continuity of argument between premises and conclusions. Take, for instance, the following syllogism: "White is a color; snow is white; therefore, snow is a color"; or "Chicago is west of Moscow; Moscow is west of Tokyo; therefore, Chicago is west of Tokyo." On the surface, the logical connection between the parts of these arguments seems to be unbroken. It is only if we penetrate into their meanings, into the ambiguities and implications of the middle terms that the fallaciousness of such arguments is manifested.

Speciousness, thus, may be described as the epistemological property of a phenomenon which contains superficial traces of pervading self-evidence, while its deeper structures belie the anticipatory references to its deeper structure. In other words, speciousness is incomplete, superficial self-evidence combined with hidden self-evidence to the contrary, where this hidden self-evidence at the same time possesses superior veridical dignity. It implies both the promise of full self-evidence extending to all the aspects of the phenomenon and the non-fulfillment of that promise.

Speciousness once it is unmasked and identified no longer presents any real danger of confusion with genuine self-evidence. This danger exists only as long as we stick to the superficial strata of the objects under consideration, without following up the anticipatory references which they imply. Until then we shall, indeed, easily fall prey to the trap which the surface of speciousness presents.

b. Semblance. The "First Impression"

As a rule self-evidence and speciousness are not given in full adequacy. They appear in various "modes" of givenness, are more or less fully, completely, adequately presented. Here, according to the letter at least, I shall have to depart from one of Husserl's distinctions. I do not think there is such a thing as adequate or inadequate self-evidence as special types of self-evidence. There is only more or less adequate or inadequate givenness of self-evidence. According to our distinction between various degrees of self-evidence as corresponding to specific objects, a state of affairs may have more or less self-evidence dependent upon whether it has a more or less complicated structure. Thus to each object corresponds its specific type of self-evidence which, however, is always a full and adequate self-evidence, whatever degree it may have. But such full self-evidence may be more or less adequately *presented*. There are, in other words, degrees in the adequacy of *givenness*. We therefore have to distinguish between degrees of full self-evidence as based on the nature of the object, and degrees of adequacy in the presentation of such self-evidence as based on the varying completeness with which the self-presence of the self-evident is actually exhibited to the cognitive subject.

To investigate the various types and degrees of such givenness is the task of a special type of phenomenology which is concerned exclusively with the modes of presentation of phenomenal objects (*Gegebenheitsweisen*). One may call this the phenomenology of presentational modes (*Phänomenologie der Erscheinungsweisen*). It contrasts with the phenomenology of the phenomenal objects as given through such modes. The latter type of phenomenology, because of its prevalent interest in the object and its characteristics, may be called "ontological phenomenology." These objective characteristics would *in a wider sense* include not only the immediate ontic properties of objects, such as round or black, but even such secondary characteristics as occur only in relation to a subject, for instance, epistemological characteristics like clearness and distinctness, or all that is implied in Husserl's account of the noematic object as "*Sinn im Modus seiner Fülle*," "*im Wie seiner Gegebenheit*." [34] In this extended sense even the preceding analysis of speciousness would be a specimen of ontological phenomenology. The analysis of the various forms of *givenness* of such characteristics, however, would be an example of a phenomenology of presentational modes.

Even self-evidence then may be given with varying degrees of

[34] *Ideas,* § 132.

adequacy. Very rarely do we take the trouble to bring the free visibility of the self-evident, as revealed by its apparent self-presence, to full presentation and examine it calmly and thoroughly. Generally we are satisfied (and, as far as practical matters are concerned, even legitimately satisfied) when something "looks evident," i.e., gives a general or first impression of self-evidence. In that case, the self-presence of the self-evident appears as if given only through a veil. Nevertheless, even this "first impression" or "semblance" of an object, as I suggest to call it, this givenness in an indistinct and largely anticipatory way is an authentic phenomenon of its own. One may think here of the first impression of self-evidence in a mathematical theorem or in an introspective insight before they have undergone thorough examination.

There are any number of degrees and types of such inadequate givenness of self-evidence, depending partly upon the specific nature of the object under consideration and ranging from a faint and sketchy idea through first indications or impressions up to a fully adequate presentation.

Incomplete givenness of self-evidence often betrays itself by the conspicuous use of certain phrases or by suspicious intonations. Thus the indiscriminate adverbial application of such words as "evidently," "undoubtedly," "naturally," or of phrases like "without doubt," "of course," if uttered in a sweeping and pontifical way, may raise a doubt as to whether the speaker has not failed to bring self-evidence to a fully adequate presentation.[35] Likewise, excessively emphatic assertions are all too often the sign of a scientifically bad conscience. Besides, even honest formulations, such as "it seems to me," if not mere expression of modesty, may indicate that self-evidence has not yet been fully and adequately attained.

c. The Significance of Speciousness and Semblance

Semblance is, however, not only the forerunner of self-evidence. It may just as well precede speciousness, the intrinsically discordant counterpart of real self-evidence. It is this fact which seems to me largely responsible for the alleged contradictoriness and fallibility of self-evidence. As long as we do not pass on to adequate givenness, we cannot possibly determine whether semblance heralds self-evidence

---

[35] Cf. also B. Russell's remark in *Analysis of Mind*, p. 263.

or speciousness. To decide this with adequate safety requires a much more thorough examination than we are generally prepared to give to the matter. In the twilight of first impressions, self-evidence and speciousness are actually indistinguishable.

Phenomenology forbids us to take the easy-going claims of semblance at their face value. It is wary of the trap of speciousness behind every semblance. And it should enable us to separate genuine self-evidence from its misleading substitutes such as speciousness and semblance.

V. A DISCUSSION OF SPECIFIC CASES

It remains to be shown how this distinction would work in cases of alleged changeability and misleadingness of self-evidence. Is it safe to say that in all of them people have been the victims of semblances which had not been explored with sufficient care?

There is a sense in which even today the refuted "self-evidences" have kept some plausibility. That the sun revolves around the earth, that there can be no antipodes, are beliefs which have a certain indestructible appeal to us if we are not sufficiently on our guard; we easily relapse into them, for instance, in the aesthetic attitude. From this instinctive understanding of the earlier so-called self-evidences we shall have to start.

a. The "Self-evidence" of the Geocentric View

How are we to decide whether the semblance of truth in the geocentric view is the precursor of self-evidence or of speciousness? The most obvious way of doing this would be to cross-examine our supposed self-evidence and to ask ourselves: Do we really see directly how the sun revolves around the earth? Once we are self-critical, I do not think we can seriously uphold this interpretation. Even if we disregard the fact that we do not see the earth as such, i.e., as a cosmic body (something which, however, has become possible now for space travellers), we could never claim more than that we see how the sun moves across the sky from one side of the horizon to the other. But do we even see how it *moves*? I cannot convince myself that there is any sound basis for claiming direct observation of any such motion. At best we notice, after certain intervals, a discontinuous change in the position of the sun in relation to the horizon. From this we infer that it must have moved. In so doing we simply assume that the horizon is stationary. But is this assumption supported by phenomenal evidence? It is at this point that self-evidence ends and speciousness enters. Once we disregard this habitual prejudice, nothing is plainly given to us but the relative change of position or, at best, the relative motion. Without delving into the vast but fascinating phenomenology and psychology of motion,[36] I would maintain that, if we are really critical, even phenomenally we do not have any self-evident perception of absolute motion in relation to absolute space. At best there may be the semblance of such motion. If we look critically at all the parts and at all the aspects of the situation, the speciousness of the geocentric view is apparent even without any additional knowledge about the heliocentric or other systems.

The difference between such alleged self-evidence and genuine self-evidence becomes even clearer if we contrast this case with instances of self-evidence as expressed by such propositions as, "I am now seeing black signs on a white background" or "Purple is between red and blue." Here all the aspects of the situation are equally and fully presented. No obscurity remains, as in the case of the alleged revolving motion of the sun around the earth. No new experience may possibly interrupt this closely knit connection, no hidden assumptions may suddenly be exposed. And our assertions do not go beyond what is actually and, with proper scrutiny, adequately given.

b. The "Self-evidence" of the Impossibility of Antipodes

The situation is slightly different in another familiar example, that of the alleged impossibility of the existence of antipodes. The real reason for this belief seems to have been the assumption that all heavy bodies must fall "downwards" i.e., in a direction parallel to that of bodies at our present location. And so the antipodes would of necessity fall off from any place opposite us.

Now, in examining a proposition such as "All bodies must fall downwards," we must consider that the type of fact referred to would be a necessity. In order to ascertain necessity we have not only to

---

[36] Cf. Husserl's stimulating, if not fully convincing sketches about the constitution of spatial experience and motion in his 'Notizen zur Raumkonstitution,' *Phenomenology and Phenomenological Research*, vol. I, pp. 21 ff. and 217 ff. As to the psychological side of the problems cf. K. Duncker, 'Über induzierte Bewegung,' *Psychologische Forschung*. vol. XII, pp. 180 ff., and E. Oppenheimer, 'Optische Versuche über Ruhe und Bewegung,' I, c., vol. XX, pp. 1 ff.

make sure that bodies actually do fall as asserted but even that there is no alternative to this kind of a fall. In other words, this is a case where we need, in Husserl's terms, not only assertoric but also apodictic self-evidence.

What, then, is the evidence for claiming that all bodies must fall downwards in the way just described? [37] That, other things being equal, bodies in our immediate neighborhood do fall approximately in this way may be obvious. But does this entitle us to generalize and to infer that the same is true of freely falling bodies everywhere? Do we derive any real understanding at all of falling and of its causes from simply watching falling bodies? To assume that bodies have a natural tendency to fall "downwards" and parallel to each other is nothing but a habit of thought. Once we know that the earth is a sphere, would it not be rather strange to expect that it should possess one preferential direction in relation to the entire cosmos, as believed by the Epicureans, and that bodies should fall everywhere exactly parallel to this direction and away from the opposite side of our plate? If we were to make this assumption, we should have no real understanding of the downward fall and its causes. Nothing is, in fact, self-evident in this case but the simple observation that in our position heavy bodies tend to fall "downward." Beyond that, the primary situation is far from clear and lucid but rather full of obscurities and puzzles. Only the hypothesis of the mutual attraction of masses throws some light on the matter. In view of this lack of intelligibility of free fall there is certainly no basis for any predictions or general assertions about necessity, impossibility, or the like. There is at most the semblance of the alleged direction of a general "downward" fall, but this, on careful examination, turns out to be specious, especially once we become aware of the true situation and, thus, can unmask the former "self-evidence."

This becomes particularly plain once we compare such a case with one of really self-evident necessity, as exemplified by the laws of contradiction. As soon as we have fully grasped the meaning of these laws, we see that there is no alternative to an object's either having or not having a certain property, to its either accepting or repudiating its ascription and that, consequently, one of these alternatives cannot possibly apply. Nothing in this case remains hidden. Everything

[37] Cf. the concise discussion of this example by G. F. Stout in 'Self-evidence and Matter of Fact' in *Philosophy*, vol. IX, pp. 393 f.

is plainly presented without any "dark corners." Whenever we take the trouble to examine the situation thoroughly, such necessity will therefore appear to be genuinely self-evident.

VI. CONCLUSION

The primary purpose of these analyses was a phenomenological one. Regardless of whether self-evidence is ultimately trustworthy or not, my concern was to exhibit the phenomenal characteristics of self-evidence as they occur in our actual cognitive life. If there is anything to my account, it may be at least maintained that there are such differences among our self-evidences; they may or may not have epistemological significance.

I think however that beyond this there is in fact good reason to believe that these differences have some bearing on the question of the trustworthiness of self-evidence in epistemology. Wherever self-evidences seem to clash, one of them, upon careful analysis, turns out not to be genuinely self-evident; it represents a case of semblance as a forerunner of speciousness. By thorough examination of alleged self-evidences we are generally in a position to distinguish between such cases without going beyond the phenomena. Thus, self-evidence, if only we take the trouble to bring it to full presentation, need not cease to be a criterion of truth because of superficial contradictions among the claimants to it. A careful phenomenology of self-evidence allows us to eliminate the false pretenders and to separate authentic self-evidence from the various forms of inauthentic self-evidence.

On the other hand these distinctions make it necessary to practice utmost caution in the application of our criterion. In fact, they often require us to refrain from asserting the self-evidence of a proposition which is not within the range of reasonably safe judgment, and to content ourselves with claiming merely plausibility, which only gives the *impression* of truth or falsehood, or with asserting a certain objective probability of such truth or falsehood (verisimilitude). It cannot be denied that even so-called phenomenologists have not always observed this point. But the phenomenological method is as little foolproof as any other, once it falls into the hands of uncritical enthusiasts.

Nevertheless, once we do use such critical care in examining concrete situations, self-evidence will not lose its significance for epistemology nor for our concrete tasks. Between the Scylla of complete subjectivity, which would follow from the uncritical acceptance of all claims to self-evidence at their face value, and the Charybdis of inaccessible transcendence, which we would have to face once we reserve the title of self-evidence only for those cases where we already know that the object is actually, and not only supposedly, self-present, there is a middle course safe enough for our practical and theoretical needs.

I do not claim that this analysis disposes of all possible objections against the trustworthiness of self-evidence as a test of truth. The most radical objection left would be: Suppose there is such a *phenomenon* as that of authentic self-evidence in the sense of unimpeded accessibility and apparent self-presence; what guarantee is there that it is supported by real self-evidence, that what is supposedly accessible and self-present is actually in our grasp? To answer this most sweeping objection would require a comprehensive defense of the phenomenological method in its application to epistemological issues, it would have to clarify the whole relation between phenomenon of reality and reality itself. Elsewhere I have tried to face this problem; here I can only refer the reader to this full-scale discussion.[38]

On the basis of the preceding considerations I maintain: Only subjectival phenomena of reality, i.e., phenomena belonging to our immediate consciousness, have a self-evidence which is absolutely infallible. As to phenomena of reality which exceed this narrowest circle, it always remains "logically" possible that their self-evidence, even if it should be full and authentic self-evidence, is eventually misleading. In fact, we observe here frictions between the anticipations which certain of these phenomena of reality contain and others which seem to refute them (e.g., in the case of the notorious stick with one end dipped into the water). However, no isolated non-subjectival phenomenon of reality is ever the carrier of full, authentic self-evidence. It can only give partial self-evidence, which is necessarily inadequate as long as not all the other aspects of the phenomenon have been checked. In practically all cases of illusions, whether of the type of the Mueller-Lyer illusion or of a more tenacious kind, the "self-evidence" involved is never authentic as long as not all the

[38] 'The Reality-Phenomenon and Reality' in *Philosophical Essays in Memory of Edmund Husserl,* (Harvard University Press, 1940, pp. 84 ff.); See below pp. 130-172.

anticipatory references have been followed up. Wherever self-evidence has been verified in this way (inasmuch as this can be done at all) there seems no longer to be any sound reason to reject it. If, in the course of such verification, one self-evidence supplants another whose references could not be confirmed, that does not yet disqualify self-evidence as such. It only means that one inauthentic self-evidence in its incompleteness has been unmasked as specious. But it does not mean that an authentic self-evidence has been exploded. Thus, the distinction between authentic and inauthentic self-evidence seems to be sufficient to meet the theoretical difficulties. However, I am prepared to admit that this does not constitute any absolute guarantee with regard to the world of "non-subjectival" phenomena of reality.

Dwelling on phenomena such as speciousness and semblance as inauthentic phenomena of self-evidence may appear like telling an old and trite story. In order to see them we do not have to resort to any special method. But phenomenology does not claim to tell only completely new stories. It does not want to invent or to construct but to find. Nor does it claim to make sensational new discoveries. Its main office is to keep phenomena in sight which all too easily drift beyond the beam of our attention. In so doing it implies that to see the phenomena in their full and irreducible variety is an indispensable preparation for a full discussion of philosophical problems. Only such descriptive preparations can prevent dogmatic over-simplifications and disastrous generalizations, regardless of whether they come from the speculative or from the negativistic wing of philosophy. To skip this stage runs counter to the ideal of philosophy as a universal and, at the same time, as a rigorous science, which was Husserl's deepest concern.

8. CRITERIA IN PHENOMENOLOGY*

"What can phenomenologists do if they disagree in their descriptions of their 'intuitions'? Do they have any criteria by which they can settle their disputes?"

These kinds of questions can often be heard from outsiders, both philosophical and non-philosophical, with the implication that they are unanswerable and that they doom phenomenology to helpless and hopeless subjectivity. I remember in particular an incident at the recent International Congress of Philosophy in Vienna, where this situation came to a head. Roderick Chisholm had reported on Franz Brentano's unpublished "Descriptive Psychology," introducing his example that "the color violet involves as its components the experience of red and the experience of blue." [1] In the discussion J. N. Findlay had called this "a veritable paradigm of malobservation and bad analysis, inspired by a theory that can only understand graduated affinities in terms of variously combined elements." [2] At this point in the actual symposium, Chisholm issued a dramatic appeal to the audience to face up to this stalemate in which two philosophers equally appealing to experience come up with contradictory findings. ("Phenomenologists, think of it.") I have tried to face it, and the result is this paper.

Unfortunately, there are thus far few, if any, explicit answers by phenomenologists to this challenge.[3] In particular, no such explicit

* First read at a Colloquium of the Department of Philosophy of Washington University in 1969.

[1] *Akten des XIV. Internationalen Kongresses für Philosophie* (Wien, 1968, vol. II, 166).

[2] *Ibid.* II, p. 201.

[3] A notable exception is Max Scheler, who in a posthumously published paper on phenomenology and epistemology of 1913 (*Gesammelte Schriften* X, 377-430) discussed the subject of 'phenomenological controversy' (*phänomeno-*

answer can be culled from the published writings of Edmund Husserl and other phenomenologists who had a sterner epistemological conscience than most of their more adventurous colleagues and successors. In many ways this situation is surprising, if not an outright scandal. For it must never be forgotten that Husserl's enterprise was and remained fundamentally an attempt to raise philosophy to the level of a rigorous science, more rigorous even than the mathematical and exact sciences in which he had grown up and whose lack of ultimate foundations had driven him into philosophy. Besides, he cherished and never abandoned the ideal of a cooperative philosophy in which a community of researchers would "philosophize together." The fact that in the process of radicalizing his own demands for rigor he had isolated himself more and more from his erstwhile collaborators, ending up in practical, if not theoretical, solipsism, is a kind of tragic irony. His later writings, with his ever repeated attempts to prepare introductions to his transcendental phenomenology can be interpreted as a more or less desperate attempt to break out of an isolation which was anything but splendid.

It should also not be overlooked that Martin Heidegger, while rejecting the idea of philosophy as a science, claimed that his philosophy had its own standards of rigor which were in a sense even higher than those of science.

A. INITIAL ASSUMPTIONS

But before tackling the main issue I had better mention some of the presuppositions for the following discussions. Thus I have obviously to presuppose a certain operating acquaintance with what the

---

logischer Streit) (p. 391 ff.; see also my The *Phenomenological Movement,* p. 242 f.) in the following terms:
    What if B after A has tried to show him something he has sighted (*erschaut*) asserts that he does not see it? This can have the most diversified reasons: A believes to have sighted something which actually he has observed merely in himself, he is deceived in the phenomenological sense, he believes to have insight where he does not. His method of showing can also be bad and insufficient. He may not have understood. B himself can 'deceive' himself phenomenologically. There is here no so-called 'general criterion.' It has to be decided from case to case. (My translation.)
Sketchy as these hints are, they indicate at least awareness of the concrete problems. Scheler's paper has now been translated by David R. Lachterman in *Selected Philosophical Essays* (Evanston: Northwestern University Press, 1973) pp. 136-201.

forbidding label 'phenomenology' stands for. In the present context all I can do is to offer the following capsule definition:

Phenomenology in the sense of this paper is a cognitive approach to any field of studies which aims at being rigorously scientific, i.e., to achieve systematic and intersubjective knowledge; it does so by (a) describing first what is subjectively experienced ("intuited") insofar as it is experienced, whether real or not (the "pure phenomenon") in its typical structure and relations ("essences" and "essential relations"), and by (b) paying special attention to its modes of appearance and the ways in which it constitutes itself in consciousness.

How to bring this dehydrated formula to at least a rudimentary life? Clearly by an example; theoretically any experience would do, even that of the phenomenon of a colloquium (a social phenomenon). I suggest one equally close at hand (or "at ear"), that of the experience you are undergoing right now in listening to this paper. Let me point out parts of its phenomenology by mentioning some of its relevant features:

1. "describing what is subjectively experienced":
Concretely this means describing both your experiencing of the paper and that *of which* it is an experiencing, i.e., the *experienced*. (This polar structure is what phenomenologists call, none too felicitously, the intentional structure [intentionality] of consciousness.) As to the former, the experiencing, this means describing the event in you with its fluctuations, e.g., in attention and feeling reactions; as far as the latter, the experienced, is concerned, it means the description of what is present by way of sounds, given as words in the context of phrases expressing thoughts which belong to the pattern called 'paper.' "Typical structure and relations" in the experienced are that it deals with a limited theme and is to be read to a group for consideration and discussion.

2. "paying special attention to its modes of appearance":
There are characteristic ways in which such a paper will appear to you at first hearing, at reading and at re-reading it (given a chance), or when you have trouble in hearing because of noises, etc.

3. "ways in which it constitutes itself in consciousness":
Gradually, as you are now undergoing the experience, the paper takes shape (or loses it) as you try to follow it, aided by memories and guided by more or less vague anticipations.

It is also important that I discuss some assumptions behind the original challenge which seem to me in need of airing. For it is far from clear that they are correct. Specifically, what is the state of disagreements among phenomenologists? Is it any worse than within other schools or movements? By asking this latter question, I do not mean to appeal to the "you too" argument to the effect that other schools too have their disagreements and that in any attempt to settle them there ultimately comes the point where they can only appeal to premises that have to be taken for granted. What I have in mind are the following questions:

1. How far is the protasis of the conditional clause "What can phenomenologists do if they disagree?" actually fulfilled? This is by no means clear, and even the objectors rarely, if ever, introduce conclusive examples. Actually there is remarkably and perhaps deplorably little open dissent among those who give sustained accounts of their phenomenological findings. They mostly talk about disparate, though related phenomena. And when they seem to disagree, there is a good chance that these disagreements are merely verbal. Before drawing any conclusions from a merely hypothetical situation, which may very well be contrary to fact, one certainly has to make sure that the dissent is real.

By stressing the need for a careful check on the alleged evidence, I do not mean to deny that there are serious disagreements among those who identify with, or are at least grouped by others with, the Phenomenological Movement. There is, for instance, the basic division between the idealistic phenomenology of the later Husserl, the more or less realistic phenomenologies of his earlier students, and the anti-idealism of the existentialist phenomenologists. And there is the glaring contrast between the objectivist position on value questions of Max Scheler and Jean-Paul Sartre's seemingly total value subjectivism. But here the question may be asked whether these contradictions are actually phenomenological, based on a careful study of the phenomenological evidence rather than on certain non-phenomenological assumptions and decisions. It is certainly open to doubt whether and how far Sartre has ever made a serious study of Scheler's concrete phenomenological work. Only insofar as there is sufficient evidence for the belief that both sides claim their supposed insights as phenomenologically supported and are ready to show their evidence can they be accepted on an equal level.

However, if only for the sake of the argument, I shall concede that phenomenologists, even as phenomenologists, do at times seriously disagree. In fact, I shall even go one step further, a step which eventually may prove helpful for breaking the supposed stalemate among several phenomenologists, by suggesting and admitting that a phenomenologist may and does differ with himself at different times. As an example I would like to introduce Husserl himself, who at different times held seemingly contradictory beliefs about a number of questions.

To mention only some of the most striking changes:

a. In the first edition of his *Logical Investigations* Husserl denied the givenness of an identical I or self over and above the acts of consciousness. But in his *Ideas* and his later writings the ego, as described by an "egology," became the absolute or "apodictic" foundation of phenomenology.

b. In *Ideas* Husserl claimed that, in contrast to objects in space, acts of consciousness do not appear in perspective (*Abschattung*). In his later writings he amended this view, admitting that consciousness too could appear in different perspectives.

c. In Husserl's *Logical Investigations* universals or essences seem to have an ideal being independent of our thinking. In his later philosophy even such ideal entities are constituted by transcendental consciousness.

On the whole, Husserl never claimed to be infallible, and the history of his development may well be interpreted as a constant revision of his previous claims in the direction of a more and more rigorous application of his own standards.

Now the obvious question is: for what reasons did Husserl make these revisions? He himself mentioned some reasons explicitly, e.g., by pointing out that in the case of the ego he had been misled by certain metaphysical misinterpretations, and that since then he had learned to see phenomena which he had previously overlooked. In other words, he offered reasons why he considered his later views to be superior to his earlier ones. An examination of such reasons may yield clues for appraising the claims of several phenomenologists who actually, and not merely verbally, dissent.

2. The second part of the initial challenge to phenomenology ("Do phenomenologists have any criteria by which they can settle their disagreement?") contains an additional assumption, namely

that all knowledge must include criteria, and that this need applies particularly to intersubjective knowledge. Now this assumption raises the question of the meaning of and the justification for the universal demand for criteria. As to the question of meaning I shall merely point out that, as the result of Ludwig Wittgenstein's philosophizing, the whole concept has become problematic. Certainly this meaning calls for differentiations and refinements. This uncertainty affects also the legitimacy of the demand for criteria in specific situations.[4] I am afraid the major dictionary definitions, using such terms as 'rules,' 'standards,' or 'signs,' would get me tangled up in additional troubles. I therefore have improvised a working definition which I consider sufficiently safe:

A criterion is a clearly given or accessible characteristic in its capacity of allowing us to tell reliably whether some less clearly given or accessible characteristic (the 'indicated') is present.

Not all criteria in this sense are immediately criteria of knowledge. There can be criteria for ontic properties in the way in which the rise of the mercury column or the movements of the pointer of a Geiger counter are criteria for a rise in temperature or radioactivity. But indirectly even such criteria indicate the truth of the *statement* that the temperature has risen. In any case, in epistemology the function of the term is that of specifying signs for the truth of certain beliefs which claim to be knowledge. By knowledge in this sense I shall understand any kind of belief which is true and supported by adequate evidence.

Now it is far from obvious that all types of knowledge need or possess criteria in this sense. As far as the general concept of criterion is concerned, its applicability depends on certain antecedent conditions:

a. It does not make sense to ask for criteria for something if it is directly and fully given. Thus there is no point in asking for a criterion for the presence of noises you are now hearing as you are hearing them or for the black marks on white you now see as you see them. Otherwise we would have to ask for criteria for the criteria and thus

---

[4] For a first orientation see A. C. Kenny's article 'Criterion' in Paul Edward's *Encyclopedia of Philosophy* and the literature listed in his bibliography.

end up with an infinite regress. The very concept of criterion implies thus that there are some items which do not need criteria.

b. The use of criteria for something only indirectly or incompletely given presupposes that there is an essential connection between the criterion and that for which it is a criterion (the indicated). A perfect criterion must provide sufficient conditions for believing in the presence of the indicated. There may be such a thing as an imperfect criterion which makes this presence only probable or possible, as is the case with certain inconclusive symptoms, such as fever.

c. In order to know whether and how far the criterion in question is reliable we must have some antecedent knowledge about the relation between the criterion and what it is the criterion *for*, including knowledge about both. This implies that at least at some time we must have had some knowledge of the indicated. In this sense all knowledge through criteria is derivative.

B. THESES

I shall now begin the actual discussion of the place of criteria in phenomenology by presenting and discussing a number of theses:

Thesis 1: Phenomenology is in need of criteria of knowledge and has supplied some, at least implicitly.

It is true that in general phenomenology is not in the habit of using the language of criteria.[5] But this does not mean that in its actual practice it has neglected them. This is true particularly of Husserl in his phenomenology of self-evidence.[6] What he makes plain here, at least implicitly, is that knowledge has to be supported by the kind of intuitive evidence which "fulfills" our anticipatory or "empty" meanings or "intentions." Take as an example our knowledge of this building in which we probably have only vague anticipations of what is on the upper floor. Only by checking upstairs can we verify them.

---

[5] Offhand I can only think of my article on " 'Reality-Phenomenon' and Reality" in Farber, Marvin, ed., *Philosophical Essays in Memory of Edmund Husserl* (Harvard U.P.) pp. 84, 105, esp. 102 ff ("Reality-Criteria"). See now in this volume, pp. 146.

[6] See especially the last of the *Logische Untersuchungen* (VI) on "Elements of a Phenomenological Elucidation of Knowledge" and Chapter II in Part IV of the *Ideen I* on "Phenomenology of Reason," especially par. 137 and 138, which develop Husserl's conception of "self-evidence."

But how far is phenomenology under any obligation to supply such criteria? At first sight one may think that a philosophy which concentrates on the description of what is immediately given does not need, and even spurns any appeal to, criteria *qua* indirect indications for something not directly or fully given. And it is true that phenomenology will never be satisfied with relying on criteria alone without ultimately going to the intuitively given "things" (*Sachen*) whose presence the criteria signal.

But phenomenology is more than phenomena and their direct inspection. It is a systematic account of these phenomena. As such it is expressed in descriptive statements which claim to be true. And the truth of statements *qua* propositions composed of concepts is never directly given by mere inspection of the statements themselves. Their claim to truth has always to be checked against the facts, if only the facts of the phenomena. At least to this extent all phenomenology has to be concerned about verification, although this term too (*Verifizierung*) is little used by phenomenologists. They do talk, however, about *Ausweisung*, (best rendered perhaps as "showing forth"), a slightly neologistic term even in German, equivalent to the act of showing one's credentials. In this sense and to this extent all phenomenological statements are in need of the fulfillment (*Erfüllung*) of their empty meanings ("*Intentionen*") by intuitive phenomena.

Moreover, there is good reason to ask also for special criteria allowing us to tell when these meanings are intuitively fulfilled. The truth claimed by phenomenological statements is a relation between them and the facts which pretends to be more than merely a phenomenon, i.e., a *real* relation. Now this transphenomenal relation can never be fully and directly given. At best we can establish the truth relation between our statement and the *phenomenon* of the facts in succession. This raises the question of what signs there are for the presence of the actual relation. In short, the demand for a criterion for the truth of phenomenological statements cannot be evaded.

Thesis 2: Criteria may be divided into intra-subjective (private) and intersubjective (public) ones. Thus far phenomenology has concentrated on the intra-subjective ones.

The usual demand for criteria, especially as found among positivist philosophers, seems to imply that all criteria must be intersubjective or publically accessible in the way a public yardstick is as a criterion for length. But this assumption seems to me by no means obvious. For it hardly applies to such criteria as clearness and distinctness as used and publicized by Descartes. This suggests to me that there are basically two types of criteria, which I would like to label as "intra-subjective" (or private) and "intersubjective" (or public) respectively. It is by no means true that criteria have a place only in intersubjective or social situations. Even one subject by himself in his attempt to reach certainty and insight is in need of criteria that can help him to decide which of several possible views deserves preference. In any case these are the kinds of criteria which make it possible for a phenomenologist to judge critically his own knowledge of the phenomena and to develop it progressively.

Thesis 3: The primary criterion for phenomenological knowledge is critical self-evidence understood as apparent intuitive self-presentation.

There can be little doubt that for Husserl, and implicitly for most, if not for all, who claim to be phenomenologists, the basic criterion of phenomenological knowledge is what in English [7] is called 'self-evidence.' But it is important to point out that the evidence to which phenomenology appeals is not self-evidence in the naive sense in which it is generally understood, especially by the Anglo-American critics of self-evidence, i.e., as a mere feeling of comfortable subjective assurance. Compared with this naive self-evidence, the self-evidence to which phenomenology refers had better be termed '*critical self-evidence*,' meaning that it is a self-evidence which has to be criticized and tested. This raises the question of what is meant by such criticizing or testing beyond the obvious fact that such self-evidence does not mean a merely passive falling for first impressions, but presupposes careful and unbiased inspection and scrutiny.

In my earlier paper on the "Phenomenology of Direct Evidence"

---

[7] "In English" – because it is not unimportant to note that there is no equivalent to the term in German ("Selbst-evidenz"), nor, to my knowledge, in any other language. This term, which seems to go back to John Locke, is anything but "self-evident." Certainly it does not apply to any statement as such, since a statement, as composed of concepts, cannot be evident in any customary sense by the statement alone. At best the evidence can come from the facts to which it refers.

I tried to give a phenomenological analysis of such self-evidence.[8] In the present context I shall not repeat the argument of that paper. I shall merely point out that I suggested as the least misleading description of the phenomenon of self-evidence "unobstructed cognitive accessibility." I shall characterize it here as apparent intuitive self-presentation, which allows the self-evident object or state of affairs to "shine forth." I also tried to point out descriptive phenomenal differences between genuine self-evidence and spurious or pseudo-self-evidence, as in the case of semblance and speciousness. Preliminary and in need of revision though these characterizations may be, in the present context and at the present moment I see no opportunity of improving on them significantly.

Instead I would like to show more concretely than by a prestige-laden term such as "critical" what it means to criticize and test self-evidence as it occurs in everyday contexts. In the following subsections I shall try to identify some of the procedures which are involved in criticizing and testing the uncritical or pre-critical forms of self-evidence.

Thesis 3.1: Self-evidence may be divided into adequate self-evidence (in the case of phenomena which are directly and fully given at once) and inadequate self-evidence (in the case of phenomena which are given only indirectly and incompletely in succession). In the case of inadequate self-evidence the fulfillment of the open anticipations ("intentions") by intuitive experience may be either exhaustible ("terminating") or inexhaustible ("non-terminating").

Among the many differentiations within the phenomena of self-evidence to be found in Husserl's repeated treatment of the subject [9] the one of special interest in the present context is that between "adequate" and "inadequate" self-evidence (*Evidenz*), the former being one which cannot be refuted, whereas the second is capable of refutation and also of increase and decrease. In the former case the phenomenon is so fully exposed to view that we cannot even conceive of other exposures, and consequently there is no room for anticipations or empty "intentions" which can be confirmed or refuted.

---

[8] "Phenomenology of Direct Evidence," PPR II (1942), 427-458. See now this volume, pp. 80-109.

[9] See *Ibid*. II. pp. 429-432; see above pp. 82-86.

This is, however, always possible in the case of inadequate self-evidence, where our anticipations outrun what is immediately given. In this latter case there is room for a further meaningful distinction based on the chances for checking on these anticipations subsequently. At this point I shall make use of a distinction introduced by C. I. Lewis under the name of "terminating" and "non-terminating judgments." In the former case it is possible to exhaust the anticipations by a *finite number* of steps, in the latter it is *not*. This seems to me to have considerable bearing on the question of how and how *far* self-evidence is capable of critical re-examination.

Thesis 3.2: In the case of adequate self-evidence, critical self-evidence requires the probing of the phenomena by questioning doubt.

How can I tell that I am in pain, that I think, that I am? Do I need any criteria for these statements? Is it even conceivable that there are any criteria for them?

Surely in a sense these phenomena are so directly and fully given that any demands for additional criteria seem to be absurd. But even in such cases the determined sceptic may raise meaningful questions about the possibility of being mistaken. At least some schizophrenics voice doubts about their own existence. Lots of people claim that they are thinking, when they are actually only talking about it. And I may not be really in pain when I have merely a fleeting twinge or am merely in fear of pain which has not yet materialized. But more important, all statements about immediate and seemingly fully given experiences are at least by one step removed from the actual experience. This time lag allows for additional errors. In this sense no statement about experience can be self-verifying. Thus it does make sense to ask for criteria even in the case of knowledge of direct experience ("knowledge by acquaintance"). And if critical self-evidence is this criterion, how can we test such self-evidence?

The traditional testing hammer or probe in such cases is doubt. Its main function is the attempt to shake the evidence with a view to replacing it by some alternative possibility. This may well be done by some kind of experiment of reinterpretative imagination. If and when the phenomenon proves to be unshakable by such measures, i.e., doubt-proof, we may consider it sufficiently established for meeting the demands of critical self-evidence.

Thesis 3.3: In the case of inadequate self-evidence with exhaustible fulfillment critical self-evidence demands the successive exploration of all the unfulfilled anticipations.

Suppose I assert that the number of people in this room is x. Experimental psychologists will tell us that above a certain number, depending also on the configuration of its constituents, we cannot perceive this without counting. This means that the "tellers" successively look, however, briefly, at each counted member. But in cases like these it is possible to run through the members in a finite number of steps. This seems to me the model case for what I understand by exhaustible fulfillment. Whenever we are unable to grasp a phenomenon at one stroke, we may still be able to run over all its constituent parts in succession. And this allows us to fulfill the empty anticipations of our claims at least one at a time and recall the results of the preceding intuitive fulfillments.

For practical purposes and in most cases this may well be the equivalent of adequate self-evidence. But there are exceptions. When we cannot freeze people in their places they may well play us the trick of returning to the stage of our counting with or without disguises, in which case we would count them double. More seriously, most of the evidence in this case is available only through memory, with all the practical and theoretical pitfalls which this involves. It would therefore go too far to claim for *this* kind of self-evidence the adequacy which can be found in the case of *complete* fulfillment at one stroke. Nevertheless, once we have carefully gone over all the anticipating intentions, fulfilling them one by one intuitively, we may feel reasonably assured that our self-evidence meets critical standards.

Thesis 3.4: In the case of inadequate self-evidence with inexhaustible fulfillment critical self-evidence requires the successive exploration of a representative sample of fulfillments, with corresponding loss in degree of self-evidence.

The inexhaustibility of the anticipations in this case may actually be of two kinds: 1. While all the features of the phenomenon are given in some fashion, as are the sides of a transparent cube, it is impossible in principle to run through all its aspects from all the possible perspectives. 2. Not only the perspectives but even the sides of the phenomenon are inexhaustible, as is the case with a non-transparent three-dimensional cube, particularly as far as its interior is concerned.

In the case of the inexhaustibility of possible perspectives it is of course possible to anticipate more or less clearly what the object would look like from another angle, most clearly in the case of a sphere, as far as its front is concerned, but only very inadequately in the case of a human face, where for purposes of criminal identification not only the full-face but the profile view is practically indispensable. As long as we can predict, as it were, how the object will look from another angle on the basis of an intuitive or theoretical grasp of the structural or essential relationships between these perspectives, there is at worst merely a theoretical danger of trickery by an evil genius.

The situation is clearly different where features or facets of the phenomenon are not given at all and at the most all we know is that there must be such features, as is the case with the inside or the microstructure of a material object. Here it is impossible even in principle to intuit the object exhaustively. At best we can take samples. And while in some cases within a certain range we can anticipate some of the sides not yet given, we are in for surprises and shocks once new dimensions are opened up as in the case of the microscopic aspects of a substance. In such cases certain sides of the object are given with some adequacy, but the total object is given only with double inadequacy, due to the infinity of its sides and to the infinity of their possible perspectives. This does not mean that there is no self-evidence whatsoever; only that its claims have to be trimmed down in proportion to the inadequacies mentioned. In other words, this self-evidence is indeed a matter of degrees.

Thesis 3.5: In the case of general insight critical self-evidence demands the methodical variation in the imagination of the variables within the range of the general essence under investigation.

Before claiming self-evidence in the case of general insights it is particularly important to resist the temptation of falling for uncriticized mere impressions of self-evidence. This has been one of the main pitfalls of the phenomenological enterprise.

Essential insights concern the essential relationships, necessary, possible or impossible, among entities, usually universal, based not on empirical induction but on an insightful grasp of their structures. How can such relationships be established? One technique suggested by Husserl is that of "free variation in the imagination." Perhaps it would be more appropriate to speak of "methodical" variation. For the point of this operation is systematically to run through all possible combinations of the ingredients of such relationships, and to determine which of them exclude, permit or demand one another. Thus, in testing an insight such as "no color without extension," we must try to drop extension in varying the colors, with the result that extension turns out to be an invariant. However "no extension without color" will reveal that we can indeed drop color and still retain extension, which goes to show that color is not an essentially necessary companion for extension, but merely an essentially possible one. It is only when we have run through all possible variations within the range covered by an essential insight that we can claim necessity, impossibility or possibility.

Thesis 4: On the intersubjective level a first way of dealing with other subjects' possibly divergent intuitings is to look for criteria indicating whether or not their self-evidences are genuine (authentic).

Suppose phenomenology can develop explicit criteria enabling the phenomenologist to distinguish within himself between genuine and spurious insight, tested and untested self-evidence: How can this help him in coming to terms with the claims of other subjects to equal, if not to better, insight into the same phenomena?

One way of trying to find such help could be to decide within oneself whether to accept such claims as equal and possibly superior to one's own. In order to do so one would have to determine whether his competitor is really, and not merely by his own word, in the presence of critical self-evidence. And for this there may be secondary criteria: Have we good reasons to believe that he has used the necessary self-critical caution before making his claim? There are usually indications in his behavior such as the kind of meditative delay in his responses which suggest such caution. Also, there are certain impulsive and emotional responses which make one suspicious of the other's real insight. In fact, the ready and excessive use of such expressions as "obviously," "of course," "naturally" are pretty clear indicators that he has *not* looked closely and is trying to suppress his own rising doubts.

But while such uses of criteria for the presence of the original criterion 'self-evidence' in others may be a help in appeasing one's uneasiness, and a very dubious help at that, they are also apt to lead to a pharisaical self-righteousness which will do little to promote common and especially scientific knowledge.

Thesis 4.1: In addition to this approach, phenomenology attempts by means of "showing" and describing to communicate and correlate merely subjective insights and self-evidences.

It is often believed that in the case of actual disagreements phenomenology is not only helpless but also is really not interested in attempts to reach the public level of knowledge. However understandable, this belief is completely mistaken. Phenomenology, and in particular Husserl's phenomenology, is at least as much interested in intersubjectivity as it is in subjectivity.[10] In fact, it can be shown that from the very start the phenomenological enterprise was an attempt not only to enlarge and deepen the range of private experience but also to communicate it in the sense of making it common knowledge. In support of this assertion I would like to point out the fact that phenomenology stresses not only intuiting but also describing. Intuiting itself may at first seem to be a completely self-centered enterprise. But in a social context a need to share such intuiting is apt to develop, a wish to make others see as one oneself sees, in other words, to show.[11]

However, the case is much clearer as far as the phenomenological

---

[10] A closer study of the role of this concept in Husserl's development seems to reveal, however, that, while in *Ideen* when using this term he was primarily interested in the problem of common knowledge, later on, and particularly in his *Cartesian Meditations,* his main concern was with the evidence for the belief in the existence of subjects other than ourselves and in the establishment of an intersubjective community. See, e.g., *Ideas* §§ 29, 151 in contrast to *Cartestan Meditations V.*

[11] The most telling expression of this tendency seems to be the etymology of the English word "showing," (old English *"sceavian")* whose root was "seeing," corresponding to German *schauen.* While, according to C. T. Onions, ed., *The Oxford Dictionary of English Etymology* (1966), "the reversal of meaning from "see" to "cause to be seen" ... is unexplained, all the continental German languages retaining the original sense' (p. 823), one might point out that there are similar changes, at least in colloquial English and German, e.g., in the case of the transition from "to learn" to "making learn," whereas in French *"apprendre"* has always the double meaning of "perceiving" and "teaching." One may suspect as a reason that such experiences as seeing entail an urge to share.

program of *description* is concerned. For a phenomenological analysis of the act of description, which to my knowledge is still strangely neglected, can show that description is essentially part of an intersubjective enterprise. This is not the place for a full-fledged investigation of the subject. But one of the questions which would have to be raised is not only that of the structure of description but that of its essential function. At first sight one may well wonder what is the point in merely describing an object which is actually present before one's eyes. What else could a description achieve but to give us a duplicate of what we already know, and a much poorer one at that? Clearly, in order to be meaningful, a description must be something quite different from a mere repetition in words of what we already know in perceptual experience. But if it makes little sense to describe something to oneself, this does not mean that it does not make a lot of sense to describe something to others. In fact, what I would like to suggest here is that the primary function of a description is to do something for others, to write ('scribe') something off ("de-") the phenomena which they can then "read" off.[12]

Now if we want to convey some of our own experience or insight to others, our first and most sensible attempt would be to make them experience or see our own experience, in other words, to *show* them. But obviously what we can show them either directly or by "audio-visual" aids is limited from the very start. For instance, we can show them only *what* we experience but never our experienc*ing*. Also, as Ludwig Wittgenstein has insisted, we can never show them such private experiences as our toothaches. But if "showing," an act which also is still in need of much more thorough phenomenological exploration, has not only factual but essential limits, this does not mean that we are utterly helpless in conveying to others what is unshowable, such as our private experiencing. Thus we can "show" our feelings in ways other than by exhibiting them on a platter, as it were,

---

[12] See also the article by S. E. Toulmin and K. Baier "On Describing," (*Mind*, 61 [1952], 13-38), which is unusually suggestive even from the phenomenological point of view. Among other important things they point out that a meaningful description is essentially addressed to an audience: "One never says 'that he is describing the mountain, for to do that immediately gives rise to the question, 'To whom?'" The clear implication is not only that this is what we ordinarily *say*, but that description itself is essentially addressed to an audience or at least to a potential audience.

i.e., by "expressing them." We can also use devices which allow others to construct or reconstruct an analogon of our experience in themselves. One of these devices is precisely the description of our private phenomena. What it does, among other things, is to identify the kind of conceptual coordinates with reference to which the described object can be located in ourselves. More accurately, by supplying our partner in the proper manner with the most essential ingredients of our experience, we allow him to construct an analogon of our own experience sufficient, if not for complete duplication, at least for making a rough picture for himself.

Thus if it is true that one of phenomenology's prime objectives is to describe phenomena, this in itself is a clear indication that it wants to describe to others, that its basic intention is intersubjective. The only question is how far is it and, more important, how far can it be successful in this attempt? More specifically, how far do the results of our descriptions jibe? If so, how far can we trust such agreement as evidence of concordant experiences? If not, how far do divergent descriptions prove that the actual experiences are discordant?

There is no obvious answer to all these questions. Neither does agreement in description prove agreement in experience nor does disagreement in description prove that the describers actually disagree. But particularly disagreement is a serious indication that even the phenomena to which these descriptions refer differ in the observers. So we had better be prepared for this situation. What can be done about it?

Thesis 4.2: Among the techniques available for achieving an attunement of the perspectives of several phenomenologists are (1) mutual exploration with a view to entering into one another's perspectives and (2) mutual pointing out of evidence possibly overlooked.

It is now in order to return to our initial quandary about what to do if and when two phenomenologists confront each other with real and not only verbal disagreements in their accounts of the phenomena. At this point most people, including phenomenologists, are apt to throw up their hands in despair and take the line of no resistance: This is the end of the argument and nothing can be done about it. I dissent. And even if no one has the right to promise that it will be possible, let alone easy, to remove such differences, I see no reason why we cannot at least reduce them. What this means is to develop and to apply techniques which will guide the participants in examining and re-examining their own claims in the light of additional evidence in a way which will make them more appreciative of the position of their dissenting partners. I may as well add that this is one of the goals of what a group of us has tried to practice in several workshops in phenomenology at Washington University since 1965.

In the present context I shall merely try to sketch some of the techniques which seemed to us most helpful in reaching an attunement of dissonant views. But before doing so I would also like to point out that the basis for these attempts is the mutual recognition that none of the partners has the right to assume that his own perspective is superior, that even if it were so, this would be an undeserved privilege which he has to earn by an increased readiness to understand his partner, and that he cannot expect the other to understand him unless he himself has made a maximum effort to understand the other, whose position he does not occupy merely by an undeserved accident of birth. In this spirit the following moves should be taken as attempts to revise one's own perspective as well as to make the other re-examine his.

1. Starting from the account of the phenomena as given by our partner's description we can make an effort to penetrate further into it by exploring his perspective through appropriate questions, indicating the areas in which his account does not or not yet jibe with our own. There is even a good chance that such questions will help him to clear up relatively obscure areas in his own perspective, as well as to express it more effectively.

2. It is equally important that we subject ourselves to similar exploration by our partner in an attempt to help him to see as far as possible through our own eyes. Chances are that his questions and our answers will not only give him better access to our perspectives but will make us ourselves aware of "weak spots" in our own accounts, if not vaguenesses in our own perspective of which we were not aware before. In other words, the attempt to show can make us see better ourselves.

3. On the basis of our better empathic understanding of our partner's perspective and his evidence we may now be able to point out to him new evidence which he may have overlooked or not paid attention to ("May I draw your attention to . . ." "Have you con-

sidered the fact that . . ."). This is the sort of thing which has been done, and can be done perhaps even more effectively, in the context of art education.

4. We must also invite him to do the same thing in our own case. We might encourage this by pointing out cases where such additional evidence pointed out by others has helped us in the past in revising our own perspective.

In recent days there has been an increasing stress on the need for dialogue as the cure for our divided world in its desperate need for understanding and conciliation. There is no question that the first prerequisite of any meaningful understanding is the attempt to talk to one another on equal terms. But there is dialogue and dialogue. We still lack an adequate theory, let alone a phenomenology, of the dialogue in its multiple perspectives. Simply talking with each other may still be talking past one another. And the Platonic dialogue as such, in a sense the model of them all, is hardly the means for bringing about genuine understanding and attunement.

What I would like to suggest here is that the type of dialogue represented by group phenomenology may be one of the means to achieve fuller and more sympathetic understanding of opposite viewpoints, together with a chance of modifying them by promoting the attempt to exchange one another's perspectives as a preparation for introducing new evidence which may lead to better attunement. If not, it may at least help us to the kind of tolerance based on the insight that each one of us occupies his own perspective through no fault or merit of his own, that we are all victims of the "accident of birth" and in this sense are all fellows in fate who should have patience with, or at least mercy on, one another.

In conclusion I would like to raise a question which might help toward a realization that phenomenology, in pressing the priority of subjectivity and intra-subjective criteria, really is not so far apart from philosophies such as positivism which put the primary emphasis on intersubjective or public criteria. My question is this: Does not the search for so-called intersubjective criteria such as public observability, verifiability or measurement presuppose a stage of private observation and verification before intersubjective publicity can be ascertained? Here is what I have in mind: Before we can assert public observability we have to establish:

1. that we ourselves observe the phenomenon and have sufficient

(subjective) criteria for the reliability of our observation to exclude the possibility of illusion;

2. that we have (subjective) criteria for believing that our partner observes in a similar way;

3. that we have (subjective) criteria for believing that our observations agree really and not merely apparently with his.

Only on such a basis have we good reason for believing that a phenomenon is intersubjectively observed and publicly observable.

If I am right in this analysis, then there can be no knowledge of intersubjectivity without previous ascertainment of intra-subjective knowledge. In fact intersubjective knowledge consists of a synthesis of intra-subjective knowledge. Or to put it most provocatively: The epistemology of intersubjectivity reveals that intersubjectivity presupposes critical subjectivity as its necessary, though not as its sufficient, foundation.

9. THE PHENOMENON OF REALITY AND REALITY*

> To the memory of Kurt Huber, my teacher at
> the University of Munich, martyr of the German
> Resistance to Nazism, and redeemer of the tra-
> dition of my alma mater, who started me on the
> problem of this study.

I. THE PROBLEM

One of the most common and most fundamental criticisms of
phenomenology has always been: What can a science of mere phenomena tell about reality itself? It may tell us what we *take* to be
real. But does this in any way guarantee that the supposedly real is
actually real? How can phenomenology decide the truth of what we
mean? Is not this the end and a rather quick end of every phenomenology?

These questions require an explicit answer. They concern the
fundamental relation between phenomenology and epistemology.
Implicitly at least, both idealistic and realistic phenomenology claim
that phenomenology is in a position to answer epistemological questions. Only neutralistic phenomenology would deny it.

In their primary tasks phenomenology and epistemology are certainly not identical. This must be emphasized against a phenome-
nologism which would dissolve all philosophy into phenomenology.
Nevertheless, there are very close connections between them. It is
these connections which I propose to discuss in this essay. The main
problem concerns the relation between the "phenomenon of reality,"
i.e., what appears to be real and what is actually real.[1]

---

* "The 'Reality-Phenomenon' and Reality," in *Philosophical Essays in
Memory of Edmund Husserl,* ed. by Marvin Farber (Cambridge: Harvard
University Press, 1940), pp. 84-105; and "Critical Phenomenological Realism,"
Philosophy and Phenomenological Research 1 (1941), pp. 154-76.

[1] The distinction between *Wirklichkeitsphänomen* and *Wirklichkeit* occurs,
for instance, in Husserl's *Cartesian Meditations* (Husserliana I, 71). Dorion
Cairns in his translation renders it as "actuality-phenomenon and actuality,"
adding that in the phenomenological attitude only the former is considered.

In fact, this may well be the crucial problem of epistemology. The central region of reality claimed to be accessible to our cognition consists of the immediately perceived objects, i.e., of the perceptual phenomena. The examination of their relation to reality must therefore be a major task of every epistemology. In asserting this I imply that it is the task of epistemology proper to examine the justification of the claim to knowledge made by our cognitive acts, i.e., by our perceiving, by our thinking (insofar as such thinking aims at knowledge proper), and by the corresponding products of thought such as propositions, conclusions and hypotheses.

Theoretically, the examination of this *quaestio iuris* would require the direct comparison between the phenomena as presented to us and the "real" reality apart from such presentation. Simple as this requirement may sound, for reasons of principle its fulfillment is impracticable for all subjects who are involved in the actual process of cognition. For the second term of such a comparison would never be given us by itself, free from any relation to us, but only as another phenomenon. Every epistemology claiming to be really critical will have to acknowledge this essential limitation. Epistemology can never pretend to pull itself by its own bootstraps from subjective involvement to the higher level of an ideal umpire.

This predicament suggests at once the question: Is not all cognition essentially and permanently confined to mere phenomena ("appearances"), as a moderate or skeptical phenomenalism asserts? Or more radically: Are there perhaps only phenomena, as radical phenomenalism of the positivistic brand asserts? In order to answer these questions the phenomena themselves will have to be subjected to a thorough analysis. There is at least the possibility that in their very structure they already refer to something beyond themselves. Analyses of this sort are the foremost task of a science of phenomena, i.e., of a phenomenology in a specific sense. It has to make a thorough inventory of everything presented in the very way it is presented, or, in other words, of the what and how of the phenomena.

Yet such an analysis can yield only information about what we *consider* to be real in addition to the immediate phenomena. It is here that our main problem emerges: How far can the phenomenon of reality tell anything about "real" reality? No definitive solution of this problem can be claimed for the following discussions, but only an attempt to bring some of the basic issues to the fore. Without such a refocusing there is little hope for breaking the stalemate between the major epistemological opponents and, in particular, for clarifying the issue between idealistic, realistic, and neutralistic phenomenology.

II. THE PHENOMENON OF REALITY

To begin with, three fundamental terms will have to be defined and interpreted, all the more because Husserl's exposition fails to give an explicit analysis of them. At first sight such definitions may look rather arbitrary. They are, however, based on a previous scrutiny of the phenomena, and are meant to render their intrinsic articulation.

1.   By *phenomenon* I understand everything presented to us *directly*, i.e., without mediating inferences, exactly in the way it is presented to us. This implies that I do not contrast phenomena and objects but only phenomena and non-phenomena, i.e., non-presented objects. Every object if presented becomes a phenomenon in this sense, acquiring thereby the additional character of phenomenality and losing it again if no longer presented. Accordingly, phenomena in this sense are not only, as it were, surface-phenomena, such as reflections, modes of appearance, perspective aspects, in short mere appearances; they also comprise what is given in and through these data, i.e., the appearing object itself in its role as being presented, in this sense the "depth-phenomenon."

2.   *Reality* means here the "standing-on-its-own" (in and of itself) of any object; as such it is independent of any observer and of his observation.[2] Everything real occupies a definite place of its own in the pattern of the real world. In contrast to this, *unreal* appearance has no place in reality independently of the observer. Something is real in this sense even if it is dependent on factors other than observers, e.g., in the way that color is dependent on extension for its possible existence, or acts are dependent on agents. In a similar way, something remains real if, in the causal line of its genesis or its continuation, it depends on third factors, ultimately on God; this applies even if such a real object has been created by acts of a real subject,

---

[2] Independence of the subject cannot be the essence of reality; this would make no sense in the case of the reality of the subject's real acts, which are obviously dependent on him; however, such independence is indeed a very fundamental and essential *consequence* of reality in all other cases.

as in the case of a work of art that is conditioned by a reality-producing artist. For being real it is enough that the real object stands "on its own feet," independent of the cognitive activities of the subject. Accordingly, the field of the real in the sense here defined is by no means restricted to physical or psychological objects. In this sense even "ideal" entities, values and ideals, duties and rights, and social entities may stand of and by themselves, i.e., be real. The question of the reality of phenomena of reality is raised here in its widest possible form.

3. The term *'phenomenon of reality'* stands not only for the phenomenon of an object's reality but also for the full phenomenal object which presents itself with the claim to be real; or better, reality-phenomena are phenomena which at the same time pose as real. In this they differ from "mere" phenomena, which make no such claim. Within these reality-phenomena epistemology will have to distinguish between authentic reality-phenomena which actually possess reality and merely seeming or inauthentic phenomena of reality which are merely supposedly real.

I have purposely refrained from defining the phenomenon as "what shows itself in itself" (*das sich an ihm selbst Zeigende*).[3] For the question is precisely whether what shows itself *is* actually the thing itself which it purports to be. If only those data shall be admitted as phenomena whose authenticity has already been previously established, the concept of phenomenon becomes useless for phenomenology. Before applying the term legitimately, we would then have to make sure that it is actually, and not only supposedly, the real thing which speaks out of the phenomenon.

A similar difficulty would arise if, making use of Husserl's momentous account of genuine perception as implying *leibhafte Selbstgegebenheit* (bodily self-givenness) of the perceived object, we should characterize the reality-phenomenon as the one in which an object is "bodily present." Again, this would mean that we could not speak about a reality-phenomenon legitimately before we have established that it is actually the real thing "in person" which presents itself, not a false pretender.

Phenomenalists might object to the concept of a phenomenon of reality as a contradiction in terms. Can a phenomenon ever contain

---

[3] Martin Heidegger, *Sein und Zeit,* § 7 A (Halle: Niemeyer, 1927, p. 28).

more than its own phenomenality? Are not phenomenality and reality incompatible from the outset? This objection is based on the widespread assumption that there is a hermetic separation between the world of phenomena and reality. It is high time to protest emphatically against this prejudice. Phenomena are by no means like a layer of films after the manner of Democritean *eidola* which are transferred from the object outside the sense-organs, thus blocking the passage back to reality itself. Reality and phenomenality do not exclude each other, either conceptually or structurally. What is real exists in and of itself and may, as far as its structure is concerned, at the same time be presented to us in its very reality. Again, what is presented to us as a phenomenon may, though it need not, be real at the same time. The phenomenal world is not a group of entities characterized and set apart by their special structure; rather it is held together merely extrinsically by the fact that the spotlight of observation catches them temporarily. In principle, therefore, as far as their structure is concerned, real things may remain exactly what they are, if they enter into relations with us and are presented to us. This event means only that they acquire the additional character of phenomenality.

However, all such considerations regarding the possibility of phenomena of reality become irrelevant in the light of the simple fact that there are phenomena, best represented by products of the imagination, which neither *have* nor *claim* any reality for themselves. They contrast with phenomena, such as that of the printed paper now confronting the reader, which enter with the claim of being taken to be real. To this extent all genuine perception implies perception of reality. But only in special cases does this reality-perception become explicit.

III. THE REALITY OF THE PHENOMENA OF REALITY

Are all phenomena of reality essentially real? Certainly there is no essential incompatibility about such a combination. But its actual occurrence and absolute necessity are restricted to the narrow field where objects are presented to us both completely and immediately, i.e., with full adequacy in one single grasp. Phenomena of this type cannot possess several "sides" from which they might present different more or less adequate aspects. In contradistinction to these, multilateral phenomena would essentially show themselves only partially at one given time and hence their successive aspects can always clash with one another.

All phenomena as such are presented to us with full adequacy, regardless of whether their transphenomenal referents are adequately given. They include such object-like phenomena as sound or color, our acts referring to them insofar as we are phenomenally conscious of them in the actual moment of their performance, and the conscious self performing or experiencing these acts, including his own existence. This threefold articulation expressed in Husserl's formula *ego cogito cogitata mea* may also be described as (1) our own existence as that of a believing being, (2) our acts of believing and (3) the thing believed insofar as it is believed. I shall call this field – in Husserl's terminology that of "pure subjectivity" or "absolute transcendental consciousness" – "subjectival." By the term "subjectival" (and its opposite, "non-subjectival") I wish to indicate that such entities are by no means subjective in the sense of having no real existence, of being merely misleading appearances, but that they are objective parts of the subject and his world. This subjectival sphere does not include all the psychological facts, but only a very limited part of them, namely only our present conscious view of our actual psyche and of other people's as well. We may be very much mistaken as to the real character of our psyche and our psychological experiences, and that not only through mistakes of memory.[4] There are even philosophers who are mistaken about the fact of their alleged (Cartesian) doubt. What they actually experience is not doubt but a mere talking about their doubt.

However, this subjectival reality constitutes only a very small fragment of our supposed total reality. Much more is believed to be real than this "subsistence minimum" of solipsism, from which the whole external world, the physical as well as other people's psychical world, would be excluded. Such "non-subjectival" phenomena of reality are not presented with the same adequacy as the subjectival field is.[5] In their case such an exhaustive presentation is even es-

---

[4] Cf. M. Scheler, "Die Idole der Selbsterkenntnis,' in *Vom Umsturz der Werte*. Translated by David R. Lachtermann in Max Scheler, *Selected Philosophical Essays* (Evanston: Northwestern University Press, 1973, pp. 3-97).

[5] In this connection a fatal ambiguity should be mentioned which attaches especially to the German phrase *sich (als wirklich) geben*, much used in phenomenological discussions. This phrase means not only "to present, offer oneself"

sentially impossible. For, whereas the subjectival phenomenon has only one side, as it were, and only one possible distance from the observer, the non-subjectival is essentially many-sided, may present itself from different points with different aspects and in changing position, even if it has no sides in a spatial sense but only aspects of varying distinctness. Moreover, non-subjectival phenomena imply certain "promises," as it were, concerning the aspects not yet present-ed, in fact even an infinite number of such "promises." If, for in-stance, a mountain-phenomenon claims reality, its reality is never completely given. Rather, one of its aspects refers to an infinity of other aspects promising to appear as real in the same way as it was foreshadowed in the first. This first aspect predelineates others, partly in full detail, such as the immediately adjacent zones of the front side (as far as given at all), partly only as to their general structure, such as the backside. In any case, a non-subjectival phenomenon of reality claims to be more than a mere piece of stage setting looking from the front as if real, to reveal itself from the back as a mere trickery like Potemkin's legendary villages (in which case, however, the painted sets were indeed real). The most striking example of such illusions is still the mirror-image or colored stereoscopic pic-tures. In all these cases the phenomenon of reality promises to hold up its reality-character in all possible directions. But this promise of omnilateral "resistance" turns out to be misleading in the case of the *mere* phenomena of reality when approached from some other side.

Thus a non-subjectival phenomenon of reality can prove its actual reality only by keeping its promises in the succession of its aspects. In the case of objects which are not immediately and adequately presented like the subjectival ones it is, however, essentially impossi-ble ever to go through all their aspects, even successively. Quite apart from the endlessness of their exterior and interior microscopic and ultramicroscopic aspects, even in the macroscopic field it is out of the question to cover all their aspects in succession. Hence there is always the theoretical possibility that, for instance, optical reflexes have been taken for objective properties so that the supposed real object suddenly explodes into an illusion in the way mirror-images do when taken as realities, for instance *in* an optical fun house.

(*sich darbieten*) but also "to pretend" (*sich ausgeben*). Phenomena primarily only pretend or promise to be real. But such a promise has still to be fulfilled or verified before we can say that reality is actually given.

Besides, there is still another more fundamental danger related to the fact that everything non-subjectival can appear essentially only in successive aspects, never simultaneously. These aspects may be ever so adequately and completely given. But who knows for certain what has become of the aspect which confronted us just a second ago and which, as we believe, has now turned away from us. At the present moment, when looking at the object from its back, as we believe, we have no guarantee that it still exists, that the Potemkin-village has not been taken down in the meantime and is just being reerected at the place where our glance will pass after another second. Extravagant as such an assumption may be, it cannot be discounted outright, once the epistemological problem has been raised; more-over, it is an assumption which is being made even by scientists in the case of the "secondary" qualities.

This consideration applies in an analogical way to non-subjectival phenomena other than the physical, and including "ideal entities" such as truth. They too pretend to remain "real," even when not constantly watched. Yet, failing the possibility of such checking, they are never completely presented.

Thus the actual reality of non-subjectival phenomena of reality never excludes the possibility of illusion and error. They all promise something beyond their actual content, and this transphenomenal promise may, in theory, always turn out to be deceptive, as they constitute only one-sided or many-sided appearances, the latter in the case of a skilfully arranged series of stereoscopic colored slides. All these considerations are based on insights into the structure of the non-subjectival phenomena and their essential relations to the subject.

Is there really no hope of obtaining an absolute guarantee for the non-subjectival phenomena of reality by another approach? Such hope is indeed implied in recent phenomenological philosophy. I shall now try to examine it.

IV. HUSSERL'S PHENOMENOLOGICAL REDUCTION IN ITS EPISTEMOLOGICAL SIGNIFICANCE

This is not the place for appraising Husserl's general contributions to epistemology. Only one particular and more problematic feature of his new method calls for interpretation and comment here.

"Phenomenological reduction" has become more and more the key to Husserl's phenomenological philosophy. No wonder this point has become the most controversial issue in phenomenology. Husserl also made it plain that the reduction is an operation dealing with the claim to reality of our ordinary beliefs. It is this aspect which makes it relevant to the present discussion.

Even according to Husserl himself it is far from easy to grasp the precise meaning of this operation, quite apart from the fact that his own accounts changed considerably over the years. Closer examination shows that the phenomenological reduction became for Husserl an increasingly complex operation. Of this complexity no final account appeared during his lifetime.[6] The following interpretation does not claim to agree with Husserl's later exposition of the subject. It is based on his most explicit account given in his *Ideas* of 1913.

Taking up Descartes' universal doubt, Husserl here starts from the possibility of questioning all non-subjectival phenomena of reality as to their reality. Reduction then performs the systematic suspension of our belief in the reality of these phenomena. Initially, in this operation this belief is by no means crossed out as invalid, but is only "bracketed." The reality of the phenomena is simply suspended.

On the basis of this reduction "transcendental" phenomenology analyzes the field of the phenomena thus transformed and examines them as to their essential structures and intrinsic connections. However, eventually the reduction is credited with much more: it prepares the ground for Husserl's peculiar phenomenological idealism (or better: irrealism).[7] Supposedly it turns out that the assumption of a reality parallel to the phenomenon of reality is not only superfluous but even absurd. To that extent, the reduction settles the epistemological problem along with the phenomenological one.

In view of such a result, the question seems obvious: Is reduction at all fit to decide the reality of a phenomenon of reality? I cannot but deny it. Reduction may be ever so important for sharply isolating

---

[6] For a fuller discussion of this increasing complexity see "Is the Reduction Necessary for Phenomenology? Husserl's and Pfänder's Replies" in *Journal of the British Society for Phenomenology* IV (1973), pp. 3-15, especially pp. 5-9 and V (1974), 257-261.

[7] Cf. E. Fink, *Die phänomenologische Philosophie Edmund Husserls in der gegenwärtigen Kritik, Kantstudien* XXXVIII (1933), pp. 321-383, reprinted in *Studien zur Phänomenologie* (Den Haag: Nijhoff, 1966, pp. 79-156, especially pp. 110 ff., 143 ff).

the sphere of those phenomena which are indubitably certain. Moreover, it may indirectly be helpful for discovering the full qualitative richness of the phenomena which is so easily overlooked owing to our excessive interest in the question of actual reality. But if it is correct that "bracketing" means simply suspending the question of reality, it can never be the means of deciding it. Breaking off the bridges across a stream can never be the way to determine what is on the other side, even if it should turn out that crossing over is really impossible or unnecessary because one might live as well without contact with the other shore. The possibility of such self-sufficiency would never give us the right to deny the existence of the world from which we have emancipated ourselves. As long as phenomenology keeps strictly within the boundaries determined by suspension, it can only be an epistemologically neutral phenomenology, neutral toward idealism as well as toward realism.

However, the decisive evidence for Husserl's idealism is more specific: After the reduction to the "residue of world-annihilation," i.e., the subsistence-minimum of solipsism, a phenomenological inventory reveals that the belief in a non-subjectival reality has its exclusive origin in the believing subject. Thus reduction, as implying at the same time a reflection upon the constitutive functions of our consciousness,[8] can reveal as the source of the world of objects certain "productive-creative" acts in the constituting "intentional" life of the subject. Non-subjectival reality supposedly turns out to be reducible to certain "hidden achievements of our intentionality" which constitute not only the "meanings" of reality but reality itself. To be sure, the meaning of the term "constitution" in this context is never fully clarified. At times it seems to stand for an "active" construction of the object itself by the subject, at others only for a "passive" self-constitution.

Thus far no detailed account of such an intentional constitution has been presented, neither during Husserl's lifetime nor in his posthumous writings. Certainly such an account would have to appeal to phenomena not immediately accessible ("hidden achievements"), and would require special uncovering procedures. This is clearly a risky step for a phenomenology used to description of the immediately given. Besides, the attempt to derive the phenomenon of reality

---

[8] On this point cf. Th. Celms, *Der phänomenologische Idealismus Husserls* (Riga: 1928, pp. 309 ff).

from constituting acts threatens to falsify the very phenomenon and to result in the kind of reductionism which phenomenology has always opposed. Finally, it seems paradoxical that the phenomenological reduction, conceived as a suspension of the question of reality, should be the means of solving it. This smacks of a sleight of hand.

However, in Husserl's *Ideas* another consideration seems to be decisive for denying independent reality to all non-subjectival phenomena of reality, namely an essential insight of a supposedly intuitive character to the effect that all being has its origin in a bestowing of the meaning of being (*Seinsstiftung*). Accordingly all phenomena of necessity would have to be *knowable* and, to be sure, knowable "not only for an ego invented as a pure logical possibility but for some actual one." [9] Yet this argument as it stands is hardly conclusive. Is a world of objects without an actual ego really so absurd, so intrinsically inconsistent? Must a world devoid of actual knowing subjects necessarily collapse, considering that such subjects are known only in connection with living organisms for which there is evidence only during a comparatively inconspicuous period of this planet and the stellar universe?

Husserl's phenomenological reduction, like Descartes' radical doubt, can never yield more than the region of the indubitably certain. But it is by no means evident that this is the whole of reality. The really crucial problem of epistemology lies beyond this point. Reduction, by cutting us off from reality, would make us utterly unfit for deciding it. It would be as "uncurable" as was, in Hume's words, Descartes' doubt.

V. DIFFERENCES AMONG THE PHENOMENA OF REALITY IN THEIR EPISTEMOLOGICAL SIGNIFICANCE

Are there no other means for establishing the reality of non-subjectival phenomena of reality and for distinguishing between genuine phenomena of reality and merely seeming ones? A thorough phenomenology of cognition and particularly of perception as envisaged by Alexander Pfänder's non-idealistic interpretation of phenomenology does not have to resign itself to this failure. Even phenomenally there are different kinds of phenomena of reality. These

[9] *Ideas*, § 48. pp. 90, 92; transl. pp. 136, 137.

differences permit the distinction in principle and usually even in fact between phenomena of reality that are trustworthy and others that are not.

To illustrate this point by a few familiar examples: The mere phenomena of reality which we face in a dream or when half-awake show a peculiar fluctuation and malleability as compared with the stability and inexorability of the phenomena of reality we have when fully awake.[10] Phenomena of reality occurring in states of excitement or prejudice appear tinged and colored, as it were, by emotion, as compared with those presented under conditions of cool observation. Whoever remains self-critical will be aware of these distortions and will postpone judgment in such a state of emotion until its removal. Likewise, in a critical frame of mind an abnormal condition of our sense organs can be recognized as influencing our phenomena of reality and consequently be discounted.

This is particularly important for the correct appraisal of such illusions in sense perception as described in Locke's notorious experiment with the three vessels containing water of different temperatures, where the lukewarm water in the middle one is felt as warm by the previously cooled hand and at the same time as cold by the previously warmed one. Critical perception will appraise such experiences in their full contexts and simultaneously consider the undercooling of the one hand and the overheating of the other of which we can be fully aware. Similarly a critical observer in touching a ball with his fingers crossed will be conscious of their dislocation and consequently not accept as veridical the impression of two balls. Likewise we realize immediately that the blurred phenomena of reality presented to us in the case of inadequate accommodation are less trustworthy than the clearly outlined phenomena obtained at proper focusing. But quite apart from such distortions on the side of the subject, phenomena of reality under imperfect illumination have not the same phenomenal weight as those perceived in full light. The blueness of distant mountains steeped in the haze of the atmosphere does not claim reality in the same sense as the blue object-color of a gentian. Similarly the bluish, reddish, or yellowish

---

[10] Criteria such as distinctness and vividness are less reliable: not only because even phenomena when we are fully awake may remain indistinct and blurred: dream-phenomena can, at least in part, display a tormenting over-distinctness and vividness, often leading to actual awakening.

shadings shown by snow in various illuminations as registered particularly by impressionistic painters will hardly be confused with the white object-color or raise any serious doubt about it. Even the so-called geometrical-optical illusions about size or shape of lines will not stand up under truly critical observation. Only at first sight will the semblance of inequality or of a bend in the lines prevail. Following these lines up carefully without paying attention to the misleading contexts will unmask this semblance or at least raise suspicion even before we use a ruler. Outside the experimental situation a critical observer would avoid quick judgment and only speak about "impressions."

Thus careful screening of the phenomena of reality can establish differences between them. Some will, if not immediately, at least in the successive examination of their different aspects, prove to be mere phenomena without reality, such as reflexes or irridescent colors which claim at first to be permanent colors in the object. In others, reality seems to be grasped immediately. One of the most important features here is the criterion of "self-evidence" which is still in need of much more phenomenological analysis.[11] Differences of the type here described occur in all kinds of phenomena of reality, even among value phenomena. Whoever scans reality only superficially will overlook these shades within the phenomena. A critical phenomenology of perception can identify and invalidate inadequate phenomena of reality and thus remove the most dangerous sources of illusion.

Important though these distinctions may be for reasons of principle, they cannot provide us with the same absolute certainty which subjectival phenomena of reality possess. Even screened non-subjectival phenomena of reality are never adequately and simultaneously presented. They will never allow us to get out of the subjectival field into the non-subjectival world in a way guaranteeing its reality beyond the possibility of illusion. Significant though the critical sifting of the phenomena of reality may be, much as it may point beyond mere phenomenality: measured by the standards of indubitability, we remain necessarily locked within the world of phenomena, however wide and elastic this "prison" may become. In the field of non-subjectival phenomena there is no absolute safety against an "evil genius," weird as such a possibility may be. The vantage point of a subject standing outside the non-subjectival phenomena and being restricted

[11] See above "Phenomenology of Direct Evidence (Self-evidence)."

to perspectival perception is essentially unfit for obtaining absolute certainty. Even phenomenology will have to put up with this result.

Does this mean that in the case of non-subjectival phenomena of reality all cognition of reality becomes impossible? Does this ultimate uncertainty entail the non-existence of everything non-subjectival? This was indeed the conclusion of radical "irrealism." Is it valid?

VI. DUBITABILITY AND DUBIOUSNESS

Thus everything non-subjectival, including its reality, remains dubitable in principle. Nothing even stands in the way of doubting the whole subjectival sphere, though such a doubt would have no reasonable chance of confirmation and would be essentially unjustified. However, in non-subjectival reality there always is the theoretical possibility that the doubt proves justified. But this does not imply that everything dubitable is unreal and only the indubitable real. Dubitability and unreality are neither identical nor necessarily connected.

For this reason epistemology cannot make headway on the non-subjectival phenomena of reality if dubitability is used as its criterion. Important as it may be for determining the field of absolute certainty, it cannot decide about reality in the intermediary zone between the absolute certainty of reality and the absolute certainty of unreality. Here doubt is significant only if it is reasonable, if it can offer "good reasons," in other words, if the phenomena of reality are *dubious*. Otherwise doubt is merely the expression of pathological scruples and therefore epistemologically irrelevant. The phenomenon of dubiousness, or deservingness of doubt, and not that of dubitability, is the one most significant in this zone.

The groundless denial of everything dubitable lays the burden of proof one-sidedly upon the shoulders of the affirmative party by asking it to prove the indubitability. However, no such one-sided burden of proof can be admitted in philosophy. Neither the affirming nor the denying party has a title to better treatment, if truth and not merely debating about it is our ultimate concern.[12] Unprejudiced

---

[12] It is therefore equally one-sided if Nikolai Hartmann, in *Zur Grundlegung der Ontologie*, pp. 156 f., shifts the *onus probandi* exclusively to the denying party. Where would that lead in the case of astrology or of superstitions in general?

epistemology will have to submit not only the arguments *pro* but also those *con* to a thorough "doubting" examination. If the *con* is not proved conclusively, it remains at best an abstract possibility. On the other hand, the critically scrutinized phenomenon of reality always contains important evidence *pro*. Wherever encountered it entitles us to disregard mere dubitability. To this extent we may stick to our everyday practice: all phenomena of reality claiming and upholding reality under thorough inspection may pass for real until their reality is made dubious by relevant counter-evidence.

But what is dubiousness? Under what circumstances does it occur? Or, in other words, what are valid reasons for doubting? This question in turn presupposes an analysis of the rather complex phenomenon of doubt, with regard to its structure, its kinds, and also its varieties. In the present context this may be omitted. Suffice it to say that dubiousness is closely connected with the phenomena of uncertainty or questionableness. The term 'dubious' accordingly points at the epistemological instability of certain phenomena and of the statements referring to them. To give a few instances of such instability: The phenomenon may be unclear or wavering, it may contain inconsistencies either in itself or in its presuppositions or consequences, or an assertion may rest on unverified assumptions, a conclusion on uncertain premises, etc. The systematic investigation of these cases is one of the major needs of epistemology.

VII. INSUFFICIENT REASONS FOR DOUBT: DESCARTES' ARGUMENTS

Here is an example of such an inadequate analysis: Descartes' epistemological doubt, radical as it pretended to be, questioned everything dubitable "not from mere lack of thought or fancy but for good and well-considered reasons." [13] I propose briefly to examine these reasons, bearing in mind that even Descartes did not consider them conclusive, once he had found sufficient grounds for believing in God's veracity as the ultimate guarantee for his criteria of clearness and distinctness.

---

[13] "Non per inconsiderantiam vel levitatem sed propter validas et meditatas rationes" (*Meditatio* I, *Oeuvres de Descartes,* ed. C. Adam et P. Tannery, VII, p. 21.)

Descartes' first argument against sense-perception was taken from the fact of sense-illusions.[14] He gave no detailed evidence, but simply referred to what since the days of the ancient Skeptics had been put forward against the trustworthiness of our senses. He did not consider the possibility that a critical attitude might enable us to distinguish these illusions from veridical perceptions. But even if illusions should be phenomenally indistinguishable from veridical perceptions, what has to be considered is:

1. Illusion, inasmuch as it implies the absence of actual reality, presupposes the possibility of grasping it by veridical perception. Besides, illusion can only be identified as such from the standpoint of subsequent veridical perception. The unmasking of an illusion is therefore rather a guarantee of, than a danger to, the possibility of veridical perception.[15]

2. Illusion in one case does not prove illusion in all cases, but at best the possibility of illusion in other cases. More can be established only by means of veridical perception free from illusion.

Descartes' second argument for the illusiveness of our perceptions was derived from the impossibility of giving a reliable criterion for distinguishing between the reality in waking life and the pseudo-reality in a dream: to put it bluntly, "Perhaps all life is nothing but a dream" (Calderón). Yet a thorough phenomenology of dream-experiences can reveal considerable differences between dream-consciousness and awake-consciousness. There is, for instance, quite apart from the degree of distinctness, the lack of critical attitude and acuity experienced in ordinary dream-life on the side of the subject, and the fluctuating instability and capriciousness of the world on the side of the objects perceived. But even without such distinguishing criteria, the unreality of dream-phenomena would make sense only with reference to a genuine reality refuting them as mere dreams.

If, finally, Descartes considered the abstract possibility of some ingenious trickery by an omnipotent deceiving demon, he left the realm of well-substantiated doubt based on the concrete doubtfulness of the actual phenomena of reality. Certainly his arguments are not exhaustive. But a phenomenological analysis of the traditional doc-

---

[14] "Prudentiae est nunquam illis plane confidere qui nos vel semel deceperunt." (*Ibid.*)

[15] Cf. H. Leyendecker, *Zur Phänomenologie der Täuschungen*, I. Teil (Halle: Niemeyer, 1913).

trine of illusions does not support the far-reaching conclusions so often drawn from them. There is no good reason for declaring phenomena of reality as dubious on principle, even if they are dubitable.

VIII. REALITY-CRITERIA

However, mere criticism of the arguments for the doubtfulness of non-subjectival phenomena of reality is by no means sufficient. A number of significant phenomena indicate affirmatively the reality of phenomena of reality: a fact which certainly does not exclude that these phenomenal criteria have been fabricated by Descartes' demon in order to fool us, but which because of this possibility must not be ignored. Without any claim to completeness, I nominate here the following:

1. Being *"already there"* (Already-there-ness)

Phenomena of reality present themselves to us with the character of having already been there before we arrived on the scene. This characteristic is perhaps most pronounced in the "aha"-like experience of meeting something familiar. In watching a phenomenon of reality constitute itself in our consciousness in slow motion, as it were, the indication to a reality of the phenomenon as standing on its own is almost irresistible, thus giving the phenomenon of reality added credibility.

2. Appearing and disappearing

Especially the verb to 'appear' in its ordinary sense implies that what appears comes into our ken from elsewhere, does not spring up or arise spontaneously at the periphery of our field. This may not be equally clear in the case of the verb to 'disappear' which can be understood not only in the sense of drifting out of sight, but of fading away. In any case a constitutive analysis of the process by which a phenomenon of reality comes into view can show clearly the difference between the way in which such a phenomenon gains and correspondingly loses in clarity of givenness as distinguished from the way in which a light or a flame rises up "from nothing" or fades off and collapses. Such phenomena clearly indicate that behind the change in givenness there is an ontic permanence not affected by such phenomenal modes of presentation. What "appears" in the marginal field of our consciousness stands on its own feet, what "disappears" is not being annihilated.

3. *Marginal Openness*

Our peripheral field of perception is never cut off sharply at its boundary. Phenomena at the periphery are given more and more blurredly. But this does not mean that what is so given no longer is phenomenally real. There is a clear phenomenological difference between a well-defined structure given dimly and a fuzzy structure given clearly. What we perceive at the periphery of the perceptual field are not merely fuzzy configurations, but usually well-defined structures given with decreasing clarity. Through this modification we can still see the phenomenon itself with its unaffected structure. And this structure appears as open in the direction of other structures beyond the perceptual field. This structural openness of what is given at the periphery of our field indicates that reality is not at an end where our field ends, that it is not boarded up at its periphery but goes on beyond. Openness indicates that the phenomena of reality stand on their own.

4. *Structural depth*

Finite objects, particularly of the three-dimensional opaque variety, always contain indications that behind their "front" and their exterior there are deeper and hidden structures not immediately accessible. Thus a sphere, in contrast to a flat disc, presents itself as going on beyond what is given to us from one angle. This becomes particularly clear at the shaded boundary of a spherical object such as the moon. This phenomenon of going on beyond the phenomenally presented side is an indication that there is more than merely a phenomenon of reality, i.e., that the partially given phenomenal object has a being of its own, "stands on its own feet."

5. *Non-dependency*

In meeting a phenomenal object, we may withhold and possibly withdraw from it all support of the type we lend to imagined objects, or even social or legal constructs. If nevertheless the phenomenal object maintains its independent status, this is certainly a good indication that it stands on its own feet and in this sense is more than a mere phenomenon of reality. Some of the phenomena will collapse, showing their dependence on the spectating subject. Others will maintain their being and in fact may behave in ways of their own, predictable or unpredictable. Such non-dependence is certainly a good indication of their reality, if not of their total independence.

6. *Probe-resistance*

In the wake of Friedrich Bouterwek, Pierre Maine de Biran and Wilhelm Dilthey, Max Scheler attached special significance to the fact that real objects put up a characteristic resistance to our will. Such resistance to an opposing or attacking will is certainly a strong indication of reality in some cases. An obvious exception is the real will itself. Also, this criterion cannot be applied to objects which are not within the reach of the will, such as non-material objects and even time and space. Alexander Pfänder used to refer to a specific mental act of shaking down (*rütteln*) under which real objects would hold up if tested for their ontic stability. Less figuratively this act may be called "reality probing (or testing)"; some phenomena under the impact of such a probe will yield, since their supposed reality is only make-believe. Others will escape unharmed. Such intactness is certainly a good indication that the phenomenon of reality is also actually real.

7. *Ontic coherence*

By this term I am referring to the fact that phenomena of reality never occur in isolation. They form parts of wider contexts. Now if such a context breaks up, if, e.g., the phenomena offered us on the stage do not fit in with the phenomena of the world outside the stage, their reality in the sense of everyday reality is endangered. Obviously the wider and more lasting this coherence among phenomena of reality is, the more in our encounters they fulfill our anticipations, the better are their credentials for standing on their own. This will heighten their chances of being real. But, as in the case of coherence as a test of truth, coherence alone is not sufficient as a criterion of truth immune to the trickery of an omnipotent evil genius.

IX. INTERIM BALANCE: THE CASE FOR GENERAL REALISM

Thus far all I have shown is that a realistic solution of the problem of the reality of our phenomena of reality is possible. But what can we know about the nature of the reality to which the reality criteria in the phenomena of reality point? Before attacking this final problem I would like to summarize briefly the main results of the preceding phenomenological investigations as follows:

1. There are phenomena of reality, i.e., phenomena which purport to be real.
2. The reality of subjectival phenomena of reality is absolutely certain.
3. The reality of non-subjectival phenomena of reality is always dubitable.
4. Only what is actually dubious, not what is merely dubitable, should be denied reality.
5. Non-subjectival phenomena of reality are not dubious as such but merely dubitable in principle.
6. There are phenomenal criteria in the phenomena of reality indicating their actual reality.

And yet the fact that there are indications for the reality of the phenomena of reality does not yet establish their concrete relation: Do they coincide? Or are they distinct, either partially or even completely? This is the problem which I now propose to discuss.

X. THE PROBLEM OF THE GENESIS OF SENSE-PERCEPTION IN ITS EPISTEMOLOGICAL SIGNIFICANCE

For a full understanding of the traditional problems in epistemology and for a proper appraisal of the difficulties which our cognition of reality encounters one aspect must not be overlooked, although at first sight it may seem to be extrinsic to the question. Unconsciously, at least, it has dominated the whole discussion of epistemological problems. Even a phenomenological approach cannot ignore it altogether.

Somewhere in the analysis of sense-knowledge the question has to be answered: How can we explain the actual genesis of sense-perception? Primarily, this may seem to be a task for psychology in collaboration with physiology and physics; for, with regard to the origin of sense-perception, a decisive share of physical and physiological factors cannot reasonably be denied. Thus, in the process of our normal visual perception, physical influences upon the retinae of our eyes, upon the optic nerves, and, ultimately, upon the "visual cortex" in our brain are indispensable. Ultimately, all these organs are themselves phenomena of reality and so are the causal links between them. Through an ophthalmoscope we can observe even directly two inverted, slightly diverging two-dimensional physical images of the perceived objects on our retinae. It should be emphasized at once, however, that these images are merely physical phenomena of reality, likenesses of objects to be perceived by an outside observer; they differ basically from the images which the owner of such a sense-apparatus experiences (whatever an image may mean in such a case). Without these physical images, or, at least, without one of them, real visual sense-perception would never arise. Physicophysiological processes, therefore, do not only play an accompanying part, but have causal significance for the origin of our sense-perception.

As a mere natural event, it seems extremely mysterious how our perceptual phenomena can arise from these physico-physiological processes and, in particular, from the physical images in our eyes. Before, we seemed immediately to perceive and to grasp objects outside our bodies, not only miniature images within, as they may be identified by ophthalmologists. How shall we bridge this gap between the physical and the phenomenal aspect of perception and explain the structure of our phenomena genetically? Is there a way back, as it were, from the retina via the cortex and the mental processes to the original object outside which supposedly started the whole chain of physical and physiological processes? Among other things, on this path back to the original source outside, the physical images on the retina would have to be inverted, merged, unfolded in three dimensions, and, above all, would somehow have to be projected into space before they could be translated into anything like our conscious phenomena of reality. And even this would be only a first step. In this matter we could hardly get along without extremely daring, not to say "metaphysical," hypotheses, the foundations of which would be rather scant, if not utterly gratuitous.

But even if there should be no prohibitive obstacles to our explaining this retransfer of our unconscious retinal images into the perceptual phenomena of reality which supposedly are their causes, such a situation would have rather serious implications: Can we, in this way, ever hope to get hold of reality itself and not only of its effects upon our bodies, its images or off-prints, no matter how closely modeled upon the original they may be? If we projected these images to the place where their originals stand, it would still be only the image but never the original which we would encounter. To be sure, this consideration would affect only sense-perception and not other kinds of perception, supposing there should be such a thing as non-sensuous perception, for instance with regard to time, to value-characters, or to ideal relations and states of affairs (*Sachverhalte*). Still the difficulty would be fatal for a basic area of our knowledge.

Thus the consistent application of the physico-physiological theory would not only require extremely bold and questionable hypotheses; it would even have to declare as impossible the actual perception of the real object that stands at the beginning of the whole chain of perceptional processes. Identity between phenomenon of reality and reality would be prohibited by the very nature of the process of sense-perception.

In fact, such a naturalistic account of sense-perception would be untenable, since it would be intrinsically inconsistent and self-defeating.[16] It makes sense only on the assumption that the physical objects, as the "stimuli" for our sense-perception, our sense organs, and the physiological process within, are ascertained realities. If we had merely images of them, the problem to be explained would lose its meaning. In this case, our initial data would consist of the *image* of the physical object, of the *image* of the physiological process, and of the *image* of our sense organs, and the only legitimate question would be: How can the first image cause the other images? But this would mean abandoning the original problem. This problem makes sense only as long as it is possible to know some real objects themselves. If this is denied, as the consistent application of such a theory of cognition would necessarily demand, it becomes self-contradictory; it destroys its own foundations. One might think of calling such a reversal of a *petitio principii* (i.e., an argument which implicitly takes for granted what has to be proved) a *fuga principii* (i.e., an argument which denies in the end what it presupposes at its start).

[16] Cf. also B. Russell, *Mysticism and Logic*, p. 135.

This may be the proper place for a more general observation. Epistemology as the critique of knowledge in general has been usually ruthlessly critical of everything except itself. Epistemologists too often fail to raise the question: How do we know what we assert about knowledge, its structure and its working? An epistemology of epistemology itself seems more than an empty reiteration of the same question on a higher level. Unfortunately, there is good reason to remind certain epistemologists, in their highly speculative accounts of how knowledge works, of this omission and of their first and paramount obligation to be critical of themselves.

The connection between physiological process and act of cognition is certainly extremely complex and difficult to understand.[17] It may be that we shall never be able to explain completely how events in our brain and in our sense-organs can lead us back to the perceived objects outside, which supposedly start the whole perceptual process, without any direct evidence of causal links such as can be found between the physical and the physiological processes leading from the object to the cortical process. It may be that we shall end up with an "ignoramus, ignorabimus" just as in the case when we attempt to explain the genesis of qualities out of quantities, or of new qualities from a layer of more primitive qualities in "emergent evolution." Sense-perception, seemingly the most primitive type of perception, appears also as the most enigmatic phenomenon as soon as we try to explain its genesis; assuredly it cannot be interpreted in a merely mechanistic way.

But even if we should be unable to account for the origin of sense-perception, this would by no means imply that its object, reality, is inaccessible. So far, the physical and physiological facts of sense-perception, based as they are on the assumption of the possibility of such knowledge, constitute no conclusive argument against this possibility.

XI. DUBIOUS PHENOMENA OF REALITY IN THEIR EPISTEMOLOGICAL SIGNIFICANCE

Up to this point it may seem legitimate simply to acquiesce in a direct critical examination of the phenomena of reality which would

[17] For the most recent account of this connection cf. W. Köhler, *The Place of Value in a World of Facts* (New York: Liveright 1938, pp. 132 ff).

let them pass as real if under such examination they can hold their own. Yet a considerable modification of this policy is unavoidable as far as sense-perception is concerned. To be sure, critical phenomenological examination of our immediate phenomena of reality in themselves will be able to eliminate the most common objections to the reliability of our sense-mediated perception. As pointed out above (p. 140-42) this applies particularly to the seeming contradictions between conflicting colors in the same object, to its varying perspective sizes and shapes, and even to the simultaneous impression of hot and cold temperatures in sufficiently disorganized sense-organs (whose derangement is usually noticed as such).

One might hope that the application of such critical precautions will be sufficient for rehabilitating all sense-perception and our phenomena of reality as given by it. Unfortunately even then some of the non-subjectival phenomena of reality, if thus examined, remain dubious in my specific sense. Illusions may still occur; more than that, they do occur and are bound to occur. One principal reason for such dubiousness consists in ultimate mutual inconsistencies between our various phenomena of reality.

However, this line of reasoning may at once be challenged: Is there any sense in which phenomena can be said to be inconsistent among each other? How can they possibly clash? Does not one phenomenon just follow the other without any question of compatibility or incompatibility arising? If this should be correct, my stand would be greatly simplified. There would be no longer any obstacle to maintaining that all phenomena of reality are necessarily veridical. Especially perspective realism takes this simplifying view. For it there are only series of phenomena, as exemplified, for instance, by the successive perspectives of a penny. There is nothing beyond this series, and none of the aspects has any preference over the others. Such an "assemblage of all my present objects of sense" is even called a perspective, obviously a rather artificial use of the term.[18] Thus,

___

[18] More technically, Bertrand Russell defined a perspective also as a "set of all those particulars which have a simple spatial relation to a given particular." (*The Analysis of Mind*, p. 98; *Mysticism and Logic*, p. 140). I am not quite sure how far this characterization would also apply to E. B. McGilvary's perspective realism, though in his article on "Perceptual and Memory Perspectives" in the *Journal of Philosophy* (1933, pp. 309 ff.) he explicitly embraces this interpretation.

applying the celebrated principle of "Occam's razor" (*entia praeter necessitatem non sunt multiplicanda*) we can make a clean sweep of the rest of our phenomena of reality – if only the phenomena were obliging enough to comply with our conveniences of simplification and move out of our way. Leaving aside the question whether a perspective in *this* sense has anything to do with what we ordinarily and phenomenologically mean by a perspective,[19] one might object that these series lack any unifying cores and afford no account of what "percepts" will enter what "perspectives." For instance, it would no longer make sense to speak of rails as parallel, since all their "perspectives" show them to be ultimately converging. Besides, such an account would dissolve the world into a rather unintelligible maze of series of aspects, without any source that would account for their structures and their variations.[20]

But more important is another point: It is by no means the case

---

[19] One of the main objections to this perspective realism seems to me its insufficient analysis of what is originally and genuinely designated by the term "perspective." In spite of Husserl's penetrating studies, the phenomenology of perspectives is not yet sufficiently developed to provide a reliable foundation. Some very pertinent analyses can be found in A.O. Lovejoy's *The Revolt Against Dualism,* pp. 120, 173 f. A few observations which have bearing upon our subject may be inserted here.

1. Apart from other less dangerous ambiguities, as lined up, for instance, in Webster's Dictionary, one should distinguish between perspective as the *standpoint* from which an object is viewed ("as seen from this perspective") and perspective as the particular *picture* obtained if an object is viewed from such a standpoint; e.g., a painting gives a particular "perspective" of an object.

2. With regard to the second and more momentous phenomenon, the most significant fact is that each perspective is a perspective *of* something beyond itself and all other perspectives of its series. A mere perspective without something *of which* it is a perspective makes no sense. In other words, a perspective is essentially transparent with regard to an objective entity beyond. With regard to this "perspectivized" object the perspective pictures (with one exception, namely, that of the frontal perspective) are essentially distortions of shape, of color, and of other properties of the object, insofar as their isolated inner structure is concerned. Yet, owing to their essential transparency, these distortions themselves reveal something of the real structure of the object when they are taken in their full context and in their systematic modifications, such as the perspective distortions of parallel rails or of cubes, as distinguished from those incomplete and therefore ambiguous perspective patterns as they occur in psychological experiments about reversible figures.

[20] Cf. also Lovejoy's *reductio ad absurdum* of the perspectivist dissipation of objects. If applied to the past it would imply that "the being of the past is entirely contained within the present and its characteristics determined by present organic conditions." *Op. cit.,* p. 125.

that our phenomena of reality are isolated from each other like frames on a movie strip. Rather, each phenomenon of reality is intimately interwoven with the preceding and the following phenomena of reality. This connection consists of countless references within each phenomenon of reality to other such phenomena. By such references these other phenomena are more or less distinctly foreshadowed or predelineated. Thus the phenomenon of reality of a non-transparent cube as seen from one angle foreshadows how its phenomena of reality will look from adjacent angles. The closer it is to our present aspect, the more precise is this predelineation of the aspects from other angles. As to the back of the non-transparent cube, we know only the outer contour and can predict only how it will look with regard to it.

Thus all phenomena of reality in visual perception include certain "promises" ("intentions" in one of the various senses used by Husserl) with regard to other phenomena of reality. These may be either fulfilled, as in the case of a house, or foiled, as in that of a rainbow's location, by the actual phenomena of reality to which the promises referred. In the former case the phenomena of reality mesh or cohere, in the second they fall apart. It is inconsistencies of this type that we have to consider for their significance.

First, there are some comparatively simple and familiar cases of immediate contradictions between phenomena of reality which cannot be eliminated by mere critical sifting. There is, for instance, a real clash between the phenomenon of the stick appearing straight when outside the water and the same stick appearing bent when dipped into the water at varying angles and proportions of its length. In each case the stick purports to maintain a definite shape and to supply us with the corresponding aspects from other angles and in different positions. But each of these "promises" is "broken" by what follows. Likewise, if we examine the case of the so-called contrast-phenomena, we shall find incurable inconsistencies. A grey center surrounded by a red field, if covered by tissue-paper, looks unmistakably greenish. No better knowledge about the color underneath will remove this phenomenon of reality.

But there are also less spectacular but more momentous cases. Even in critical perception we are generally convinced that we grasp the perceived object exactly in the condition it is in at the very moment of our perceiving it.[21] Now it may be considered an established scientific fact that the objects distant in space from the observer can never be perceived exactly as they are at the moment of our perceiving them. This is indeed one of the most popular arguments with all the schools of critical realism. Among phenomenologists, this point has been stressed particularly by Moritz Geiger. As evidence he introduces primarily the case of our perception of the stars.[22] We may discount such extreme cases as inconclusive.[23] But in principle the situation is the same in all cases of sense-perception. If the light between our eyes and our own hand held ten inches away from our eyes takes only one billionth of a second to reach our retina and subsequently our visual cortex, we cannot perceive our hand as it is at the moment of our actual perceivings, but only as it was shortly, if only infinitesimally shortly, before. Even more serious are the delays in the transmission of stimuli due to general conditions within the nervous system and their psychological equivalent and those which are due to the "individual equation" of the respective observer. In such cases our immediate perception, even if critically sifted, e.g., by G. E. Moore, seems to insist that we see our hand as it actually is at the very moment of our perceiving it. Here even a critical perception, inasmuch as it contains this claim and the promise of continuous confirmation from other angles, and the phe-

---

[21] It may be slightly different in the case of our auditory experiences, at least with regard to more distant noises. Reverberating sounds, such as an echo, rumbling thunder, or even distant noises, reveal to a critical observer not only distance in space but even in time, as far as the reported source of these phenomena is concerned. However, such experiences may be comparatively rare. As to the lack of precise localization in space in the case of sound-phenomena, cf. also Lovejoy, *op. cit.,* p. 19, n. 18.

[22] *Die Wirklichkeit der Wissenschaften und die Metaphysik* (Bonn: 1930, pp. 168 ff): "There is a difference in time between being and being perceived" (p. 170). Geiger's reference to our perception of the moon as a disc is less convincing, especially if we consider telescopic pictures; in these, we may recognize the moon immediately as an enormous cosmic body.

[23] To be sure, a detailed phenomenological analysis would have to consider that the peculiar glittering points presented to us when looking at a "star," a fixed star as well as a planet, even if seen through the biggest telescope, by no means purport to be cosmic bodies of the type of the moon. The interpretation of stars as cosmic bodies is probably of a comparatively late date determined by scientific theories and analogies. What we really perceive in such cases is a point-like glitter coming out of the depth of the night sky. Such a phenomenon tells us nothing about the distance in space of the light-source; at any rate it fails to tell us anything distinctive. See also Paul Weis, "The Perception of Stars," *Review of Metaphysics* VI, 1953, pp. 233-38.

nomenon of reality corresponding to it are discredited by the scientific evidence as essentially misleading. The incorrectness involved may be practically negligible. Yet, in principle, it has serious implications. It means that our perception, insofar as it depends on our senses, always lags slightly behind the coexistent reality. If our perception would attempt to catch the object as it was at the moment when it selected and reflected the conditioning light rays, it would have to make up for the time lost in their traveling propagation. In order to make the past present, the act of seeing would not only have to use no time; it would have to reverse time and undo facts. This is plainly an ontological impossibility. Therefore, our sense-perception can never give what is present, but only what has just passed. And, since the past no longer exists, we can never see the original object itself but only its "trace," which means its cast or likeness.

XII. THE IDEA OF A CRITICAL PHENOMENOLOGICAL REALISM

1. What invalidates phenomena of reality?

There is also a positive side to this negative conclusion. My last statement immediately suggests the question: What is it that in such a case discredits critical immediate perception? What kind of evidence is the basis of such an invalidation? Obviously, in our case, it takes its start from a general insight, namely, the scientific information that the propagation of light requires time, and that consequently a perception depending on this propagation must be a delayed one. What, in turn, is the basis for this knowledge of the need of time for the propagation of light?

Ultimately it is not only "rational" considerations but perceptions, as supplied by astronomical observations, which support such invalidations. In the specific case they are observations about the disappearances and reappearances of Jupiter's moons or the findings of Fizeau's experiments on the reflection of light rays. To be sure, the propagation of light at the rate of 186,000 miles a second is not directly perceived. What we actually see are only dots of light which appear either early or late compared with our calculated expectations. Now this prematureness or this delay can be measured perceptually. And since light is late in those cases in which its source is ascertained to lie at a greater distance from the observer, and is fast where its source lies closer to him, it seems obvious that it needs time for traversing distance. From the perceived delay in the time of arrival of the lightrays we may, then, legitimately infer the need of time in the propagation of light.

This implies that certain perceptions, such as those about time-differences in perception, in combination with certain insights about the essential relations between them and their causes, carry increased weight and consequently take precedence over the simple perception of the object that seemed to be presented simultaneously with our perceiving. It matters little whether the "naive" perception is more or less frequent. What counts is not the number of phenomena but rather their content and their intrinsic relations to each other. Eventually, those perceptual phenomena of reality that are supported by insight into intrinsic structural relations (*Wesenszusammenhänge*) invalidate others conflicting with them.

But we need not turn to physics for examples of such invalidation of phenomena of reality. They occur continually in our daily experience. Here we are again guided by orders of preference between the phenomena of reality which, with a remarkable finality, discredit some conflicting phenomena as misleading. Perhaps the most impressive illusions, trivial as they may have become, are still those experienced when looking motionless into a mirror, especially with regard to the interchange between right-hand and left-hand side. As long as we do not see the mirror as such, or, as in the case of our own image, recognize the deception at once, we can make the silliest mistakes (for instance, in galleries of mirrors or in so-called labyrinths). But as soon as we compare the conflicting phenomena of reality, try to approach or to touch or to walk around them, some of them are discredited directly as illusory. Their claim to reality collapses, they lose their reality-character which they had maintained successfully before.

2. What determines reality?

Thus the invalidation of certain contradictory phenomena of reality by the concrete order of preference among them makes possible the elimination of non-veridical phenomena of reality. But this elimination does not yet tell us how to determine positively what is actually real; for it is by no means certain whether any of the phenomena of reality are ultimately real. This problem requires special study.

a. Selective Synthesis of Phenomena of Reality

There is the possibility that, as a result of our examination of conflicting phenomena of reality, the surviving ones turn out to be real without any need of our going beyond. All that is necessary in such cases is the synthesis of the phenomena of reality, the elimination of the non-veridical ones, and, along with that, the decision in favor of the veridical ones. This procedure seems to yield a positive result in the case of direct contradictions between the phenomena of reality, e.g., in the case of the various aspects of the straight stick which seems to be bent when partly under water. Straightness, the aspect represented by the stick outside the water, does not only appear to deserve preference, but establishes itself as the one veridical aspect, in spite of the fact that the expectation of a straight continuation in the part dipped in water is frustrated. In these cases, nothing compels us to go beyond the range of the mere phenomena of reality. The synthesis which has to be performed is therefore merely a selective one. In this selection we by no means decide only in favor of the most frequent phenomena. One phenomenon, if thoroughly examined, tested, and understood can outweigh innumerable casual every-day observations.

The situation is the same in principle with other inescapable and indestructible illusions. In the case of the grey cardboard covered by tissue paper, we are never seriously in doubt whether it is the covered or the uncovered sample that shows the real color; nor are we in doubt whether it is the intangible object appearing behind the mirror or the touchable one in front of it that is real. In other words, even here we find a concrete order of preference, a hierarchy, as it were, among the contradictory phenomena of reality. One among them not only discredits and dislodges the others, but even establishes itself as the only veridical one. To be sure, it cannot be claimed that such a hierarchy among our contradictory phenomena of reality is an essential necessity. Still, as a matter of fact, I am not aware of any case where we remain in serious doubt as to which phenomenon takes precedence.

But what is the basis for this order of preference between our non-subjectival phenomena of reality? This question cannot be answered in general terms. What decides is the specific nature of the phenomena involved. Usually the preferable phenomena give more detailed and therefore more creditable information about their specific objects. The microscopic aspect, for instance, reveals more about the minute structure of a body than the macroscopic surface-appearance. Touch takes us closer to the material texture of a thing than vision. It would require very detailed analyses of the various types of phenomena to bring out these concrete orders of preference and to give an understandable account of them. The importance of these concrete orders of precedence can hardly be exaggerated. Because of them, conflicts between our phenomena of reality need not have the fatal consequences which, according to the "absolute idealists," disprove the reality of our phenomena in their entirety.

b. Constructive Synthesis of Phenomena of Reality

Such a selective, intra-phenomenal synthesis, however, is not always sufficient. This point can be illustrated best by cases as they occur in the realm of the physical sciences.

Critical and cautious though we may be, for our immediate perception certain materials such as liquids, crystals, or visible gases purport to be homogeneous and to fill space continuously. And these phenomenal appearances claim validity not only with regard to particular aspects; at first sight they make us expect that this apparent homogeneity will hold throughout all possible perspectives.[24] Even under the microscope most liquids, gases, glass, and crystals keep up this appearance.

There are, however, certain other phenomena which invalidate these expectations. Such an invalidation is implied, for instance, in the von Laue diffraction diagrams, i.e., characteristic patterns which appear when x-rays are sent through crystal-slides. This experiment yields not a homogeneous field but a grid-like pattern on a screen behind the crystal. There is no direct conflict between such a discontinuous grid-effect and the phenomenon of reality of the continuous crystal-slide. This does not arise until we try to determine the re-

---

[24] I believe that the denial of such homogeneity is due to a sophisticated overcaution inspired by our subsequent "better knowledge." It falsifies the verdict of the immediate phenomena. To me our phenomenon of a continuous medium such as water in its limpidity leaves originally no room for the atomic structure which, on the strength of subsequent scientific evidence, we have to hypothesize.

lations between the two and to understand the grid-effect in its connection with the slide. As soon as we engage in such an attempt, the question arises: How can a discontinuous diagram be intelligibly derived from something continuous in a way which would allow us, at least in principle, to trace its genesis and to comprehend it as necessary? It would be strange indeed if such an effect could arise from a continuous source. We must assume that from a homogeneous source (e.g., light, granting light is such a homogeneous source) an inhomogeneous product (the diagram) cannot originate unless the traversed medium (the crystal) is, in its ultimate structure, inhomogeneous, grid-like, particularly if the product (the diagram-effect) does not appear without the intercession of such a medium. In other words, a certain correspondence between cause and effect is required. We are here faced with those ultimate demands of intelligibility which are at the root of all scientific explanation even in the inductive sciences. It seems of paramount importance to spell out these postulates of essential understanding. True, even in this case there is no immediate conflict between the phenomenon of reality of the continuous slide-structure, which is presented and fully and adequately exhibited only with regard to their macrostructure, on the one hand, and the postulated grid-like microstructure on the other. The actual conflict occurs only between the macrostructure and the "promises" with regard to the microstructure which the macro-phenomenon seems to hold out, promises which afterwards fail to be fulfilled by direct phenomena in observation. It is only here that inferential considerations take precedence over the directly perceived phenomena of reality. There is even in this sphere an actual order of preference of intelligible, if hypothetical, construction over the inconsistent and unconfirmed promises of the phenomena of reality. Because of this order of preference we may infer, contrary to the definite but unconfirmed expectation based on the continuous phenomena of reality, that the traversed crystal must have an inhomogeneous perforated microstructure which, according to the laws of refraction, would account for the deflections of the light impulses and interference-phenomenon of the diagram-effect.

Thus, on the basis of certain phenomenal effects, we infer the misleadingness of certain portions of the phenomena of reality and, instead, introduce a new reality that is not contained in our phenomena of reality. We construct this reality according to those requirements which the intelligible explanation of the effect, for instance of the diagram-effect, demands, i.e., we make use of certain general, but nevertheless very concrete, insights as to how rays can change their straight course of propagation so as to intersect and to produce the grid-effects in question. Only some discontinuous obstacles could account for them. So we arrive at the idea of a discontinuous distribution of matter in the slide, making use of our mathematical and geometrical insights in determining the exact position and size of the micro-obstacles.

But where do we get the materials for such inferred entities? Often we are told that in the world of science we have to abandon all ideas of similarity with the macroscopic world of our phenomena. Actually, in scientific construction we do leave out most of its characteristics. But little as there may remain in this type of impoverished construction of a world which omits all the qualitative data of our original phenomena of reality, what is left can ultimately be traced back to phenomena of reality such as shape and extension (waves), resistance (mass), motion (energy, charge), etc. However transformed, the elements of our constructive syntheses stem from our phenomenal world. The physical world, which for the physicists and even for most sophisticated laymen forms the only real one, can in no way supply us with a world entirely different from the phenomenal world which we directly experience.[25] As far as the materials for any inferred reality are concerned, science can do nothing more than to play off one kind of phenomena against another. Only in their dismounting and rearrangement is it at comparative liberty. Here it may even leave out certain parts in the pattern, to be occupied by entities so far unknown (e.g., ultra- or infra-red color, postulated particles, etc.). Science, therefore, in certain cases transcends the range of our phenomena of reality. Still, ultimately it remains confined to the phenomenal material and to the possibilities determined by its nature.

A particularly important case of such constructive extrapolation concerns our phenomena of reality in general, inasmuch as they are mediated by our sense perception. We found that an understanding of these phenomena makes it impossible to hold that our actual phenomena are identical with reality itself. They are at best its "traces."

---

[25] Cf. Wolfgang Köhler, *op. cit.*, pp. 142 ff., in particular the following statement: "... there can not be a single trait in nature which has not at least one model somewhere in the phenomenal world."

Thus the pattern of original object and trace is used for an interpretation of our phenomena of reality according to which reality is constructed as something outside and before the trace.

3. Critical Phenomenological Realism

Single non-subjectival phenomena of reality, then, even if screened by critique of our perceptual data, are unable to offer any ultimate guarantee of reality. To believe the contrary would still be too naive [26] a realism, although it would already be a phenomenologically purified one. Isolated phenomena of reality rarely yield adequate certainty. In the case of non-subjectival phenomena of reality only their critical synthesis can result in an adequate guarantee of reality. And this synthesis, as we saw, is a selective one, when the order of preference between the phenomena of reality allows for an "immanent" decision. However, in cases where the demands of essential intelligibility make it necessary to go beyond these phenomena of reality, the synthesis will have to be a constructive one. Even in this case the certainty which we can achieve remains incomplete. But it is all we can reasonably expect, considering the nature of non-subjectival reality, our own predicament, and the nature of our cognition and understanding.

4. The Status of the Mere Phenomena of Reality

One final, if secondary, question has to be faced as a consequence of this solution: What is to become of the phenomena of reality which have been discredited as misleading? Surely they will not simply

[26] It is a task by itself to evaluate the 'naiveté" of so-called naive realism. "Naive common sense" as pictured condescendingly by many epistemologists is far from being as childish as they would have it; implicitly at least "the man in the street" shows more awareness of the structure of things than many epistemologists display. Realism could be designated as really naive only if it should adhere in an uncritical way and without closer examination to surface-phenomena or traditional interpretations; for example, declaring the sky to be a bell-shaped dome, or pretending that we see the sun move around the earth or see the stars as cosmic bodies, etc. It is to be admitted that on the surface the real "man in the street" is all too often an easy prey to the prejudices of his time, to preformed modes of thought, and to half-digested popularized science. Not this uncritical, narrow-minded mentality, but only the enlightened common sense of an independent, though unreflective and non-theorizing observer is truly representative of naive (which means literally original) realism.

vanish into nothing, even if they are now unmasked as mere phenomena. But what then is their new status?

Genuine phenomena remain uninfluenced by any subsequent theoretical interpretations or refutations, as distinguished from mere misinterpretations of phenomena, such as the misinterpretation of a scarecrow as a man; the latter "phenomenon" simply collapses and can no longer be reproduced, once it has been unmasked. By contrast genuine phenomena will continue their misleading "promises," as best exemplified in the case of an object in the mirror. Yet these promises will now be, as it were, cancelled, invalidated. But where is that mirror-object itself to remain? Certainly it is not where it pretends to be, i.e., at such and such a distance behind the glass. Nor is it only in our mind. It still remains somewhere "outside." But all that is left there is now a (real) picture representing the object in the same way as a painting represents its (unreal) object; it must be noted, however, that a painting never produces a full illusion of the painted object, as the mirror-picture or certain (mostly unartistic) trompe-l'oeil paintings may do. This seems to imply that the essential fact about such illusory phenomena of reality is a peculiar dislocation.[27]

Erroneously the phenomenon of reality is here located at a place where there is no real correlate, whereas in fact it is at some other place, in the specific case on the surface of the mirror at a certain angle of observation. Such a dislocation also takes place in the case of our phenomena of reality in ordinary sense-perception, where, as pointed out previously, the "traces" of the real objects are mistakenly identified with reality itself. Even so, they remain entities outside, except that they are not where they purport to be, but at some intermediary place, relative to a certain standpoint.

Of course, the situation is not everywhere the same. The dislocation may be of variable character and degree. It is least pronounced in the case of some illusory stage settings, where one side of the object may exist and is really at the place where it purports to be. But there are also more complicated situations. To give only one specific example: When hot air makes sections of a visual object behind it undulate, as it were, a careful observer will notice some very peculiar phenomena. In such a case I never have the impression that the

[27] On this point I largely agree with Samuel Alexander's account of the situation in Space, Time and Deity, vol. II, pp. 216 f.

object itself wavers. Rather, I notice at the same time, if only indirectly, a fluctuating medium between the object and myself. And as far as the undulating section of the object is concerned, it shows a peculiar ambiguity with regard to its location, namely, somewhere between myself and the real object as represented in its surrounding stable sections.

XIII. CRITICAL PHENOMENOLOGICAL REALISM AND GENERAL CRITICAL REALISM PROPER

A critical phenomenological realism as based on such principles does not coincide with a so-called critical realism which does not grant reality to any of the phenomena and, instead, tries to infer a real world different from the one presented to us in the phenomena. This would be the position of the most radical form of critical realism, which might be illustrated by Kant's contrast of the thing in itself and its appearances, as taken over and developed by Alois Riehl and other German critical realists.[28] Other representatives would be William Hamilton, Herbert Spencer and Oswald Külpe. In their inferences, the "critical" realists overlook that a world beyond all appearances would of necessity remain inaccessible to us, that we have no legitimate way of inferring anything non-phenomenal unless the entities inferred are already known to us from the phenomenal field, either themselves or at least in kind. Critical realism yields in fact nothing but undetermined x's as causes of our phenomena. Otherwise it transcends the "limits of possible experience." Even if there are indications in the phenomena of something beyond – and there are such references in considerable number – they can never entitle us to infer entities other than of a structure analogous to that of our phenomena.[29]

The case is slightly different with the Lockian kind of critical

[28] G. Dawes Hicks' "critical realism," though in many respects inspired by the Kantian approach, is definitely much closer to the position of a phenomenological realism as advocated here. *Thought and Real Existence* (London: Oxford University Press, 1936, especially pp. 27 ff). Cf. his *Critical Realism. Studies in the Philosophy of Mind and Nature* (London: Macmillan and Co., 1938, p. v.).

[29] The whole problem of analogous cognition would require special phenomenological examination. It may be mentioned here that it has an illuminating parallel in the theological discussion of our analogous cognition of God (*analogia entis*).

realism and its distinction between primary and secondary qualities. To be sure, even his theory is "representationalist," inasmuch as the mind remains locked up in the imprisoning ring of its own representative "ideas" and can break through only by causal inferences. At least, according to Locke, the primary qualities are not simply mysterious x's but the exact originals of our representing primary ideas. Although this makes the nature of the inferred world somewhat more concrete, it does not improve on the position in principle. The inference needed for breaking out of the "iron ring of ideas" still would have to transcend the limits of experience. Besides, the whole distinction between primary and secondary entities has long been discredited as based on insufficient evidence. Also, such a distinction leaves unexplained how the secondary qualities proceed from the primary ones. This whole distinction simply shifts the problem from physics to psychology, where there is no better solution for it either.

In contradistinction to such a "critical realism," the critical phenomenological realism advocated here for the phenomena of sense-perception does not claim to pass beyond all actual and potential phenomena and enter into a reality of an entirely different structure. It does not transcend the phenomena of reality, but either merely selects critically among those which directly or indirectly conflict, or rearranges them in a newly constructed pattern. It also strives for an integration of the phenomenal field by filling gaps left by a "naive" phenomenological realism that relies exclusively on *isolated* phenomena of reality once they are critically observed and appear sufficiently trustworthy in themselves. Such a "naive" realism seems to be unable to cope adequately with the constant conflicts among nonsubjectival phenomena of reality. Phenomena of reality can be considered sufficiently guaranteed only if they support each other in the progress of our perceptions and prove consistent with their necessary presuppositions and consequences. This postulate calls for a constant re-examination of all aspects and claims of an object, e.g., by touch, by walking around it, before we can decide about the reality of our phenomena of reality. In this light the old epistemological criteria developed by the middle or skeptical Academy, notably by Carneades, receive new significance. They include:

1. the so-called *pithanón*, i.e., the credible, a term which may here be interpreted as what holds its own under questioning;

2. the *aperíspaston*, i.e., what is not pulled back and forth, an

expression which here may be taken in the sense of what is consistent with other phenomena of reality;

3. the *perihodeúmenon*, the object walked around, a term which may signify here whatever has been probed under all possible aspects.

For the satisfaction of all these demands there are, however, essential limits. The fact that such a synthesis can be performed only successively excludes a complete and fully adequate perceptual experience of an object in space, especially in the case of highly changeable objects. With regard to the microstructure of physical objects, there are rather narrow limits to our cognition, ultimately those pointed out by the Heisenberg principle of indeterminacy. Finally, even a critical phenomenological realism never can eliminate the abstract possibility of the Cartesian demon. No epistemology can do more than demonstrate the unreasonableness of such an assumption and, in addition, collect the strong and almost compelling evidence for the reality of non-subjectival phenomena of reality.

A certain restraint, a renunciation of absolute certainty with regard to non-subjectival reality is therefore clearly indicated. But this gives us no right to demand "everything or nothing," and to turn our backs to non-subjectival reality beyond our phenomena of reality.

XIV. NEO-CRITICAL REALISM AND PHENOMENOLOGICAL CRITICAL REALISM

I do not want to conceal that this paper was written originally without any knowledge of the pertinent discussions in current Anglo-American philosophy, and particularly of the so-called New Realists and the American Critical Realists, for whom I shall use the abbreviation "Neo-critical Realists." Nevertheless, in view of the range and weight of their arguments, I would like to indicate briefly how critical phenomenological realism as here advocated compares with their positions. In doing so I shall not try to do full justice to the analyses in Arthur O. Lovejoy's Carus Lectures on *The Revolt Against Dualism*. I merely want to contrast the two positions, with a view to clarifying certain aspects of critical phenomenological realism.

There is one point in the program of the New Realists with which, as far as the principle is concerned, even critical phenomenological realism agrees, namely, the attempt to return as far as possible to the tenets of a genuine naive realism, while modifying them where they prove to be untenable.[30] On the other hand, New Realism gives too few unbiased phenomenological analyses of our actual data. Instead, here, as in Neocritical Realism, there is from the outset a preponderance of naturalistic, especially of biological and physiological, considerations. Besides, New Realism, as developed, for instance, by E. B. Holt, makes too light of the phenomena of illusion and error.[31]

Hence the "dualistic" Critical Realist retains the distinction between given percept and real object. Neo-critical Realism in its original intention is anxious to avoid the pitfalls of the older critical realists, both of the Kantian and of the Lockian variety ("representationalism"),[32] while at the same time making provisions for the problems which beset naive and New Realism as well. Still, even this position is not without flaws. I shall point out a few of these remaining problems with a view to showing how far such realism does or does not agree with the critical phenomenological realism advocated before.

One rather fundamental difference concerns the understanding of what the Neo-critical Realists call "the given" or "the datum." For them the given is almost from the outset opposed to the real object. It stands for that much of the world as we *really* grasp, as contradistinguished from what we *believe* to grasp. Their conception of the given is largely determined by theory and, actually, by their genetic theory [33] of what, according to our knowledge of physical and biological facts, the data depend upon, and what could possibly enter our body [34] and ultimately our mind (whatever the latter may mean in the rather metaphysical and somewhat materialistic theories of some of the Neo-critical Realists such as Durant Drake). There is the definite danger that naturalistic considerations of this type about the possibility of givenness influence and falsify the description of what is actually present in our consciousness. Thus the "given" of Neo-critical Realism is in fact a reinterpreted phenomenon, reconstructed

[30] *The New Realism, Cooperative Studies in Philosophy* (New York: 1912, p. 11).

[31] *Op. cit.,* p. 372.

[32] R. W. Sellars, "Knowledge and Its Categories," in *Essays in Critical Realism* (1920) p. 211.

[33] Cf. C. A. Strong on "The Nature of the Datum," in spite of his initial definition of the datum as "what we are immediately conscious of" (p. 223).

[34] *Ibid.,* p. 225.

in the light of our scientific knowledge of the causes of our sense-perception.[35]

As to the nature of this given datum, the Neo-critical Realists sometimes give accounts of a highly speculative character. With all of them the given is described as a "character-complex," an account which, phenomenologically, is questionable, to say the least. Those who, like C. A. Strong, A. K. Rogers, and Durant Drake, follow George Santayana, interpret it as the "essence" of the real object, as distinguished from its existence, and even assert that the given is essentially universal.[36] But the distinction between essence and existence in its traditional meaning can hardly clarify the relation between the given and the object itself. In principle, the essence is a part, sometimes called a metaphysical part, of the real object, but nothing like a link between the object and the subject. However, this interpretation appears to be by no means universal among Neo-critical Realists. Thus, with Lovejoy the given appears to be a *particular* with an existential status of its own; unfortunately, he also failed to give an adequate phenomenological account of the nature of the given.

Besides, the Neo-critical Realists left the cognitive relation between the given and the real object strangely undetermined. On the one hand, they were anxious to maintain that the given has to be distinguished from the object known. On the other hand, they were just as eager to deny that it is an inference which takes us from the given to the object.[37] Consequently, the object known, though not given, must be presented in some third way.[38] It seems doubtful that Neo-critical Realism has thus escaped between the Scylla of New Realism and the Charybdis of the old critical realism. Would such a non-inferential, but still mediated, knowledge be any improvement on the inferential one, inasmuch as it still transcends the field of what we actually perceive or experience? Would it be able to break through

[35] Only after the completion of this article I saw Professor John Wild's essay on "The Concept of the Given in Contemporary Philosophy" in No. 1 of *Philosophy and Phenomenological Research* (pp. 70 ff.) which is directed primarily against "empiricist" and positivistic misinterpretations of the given. In spite of a slight divergence in the use of the term "immediately given" I am in substantial agreement with his account.

[36] For example, *op. cit.*, p. 232.

[37] *Op. cit.*, p. 4 (Drake), p. 194 (Sellars), p. 241 (Strong).

[38] "We affirm it through the very pressure and suggestion of our experience," (p. 195).

the "iron ring of ideas" which imprisoned the older Critical Realism? What would be our justification for any claim of passing beyond the field of the given? As long as the given does not somehow contain or clearly foreshadow the real object, no tenable account of such transcendence seems possible.[39]

How does critical phenomenological realism compare with Neo-critical Realism with regard to these points?

First, as to the concept of the given: The given is here essentially the phenomenon free of any subsequent interpretation, just as it presents itself apart from any theoretical considerations of the possibility of such givenness, which are only apt to make us falsify the structure of the given. Besides, unlike Neo-critical Realism, it does not immediately consider the given as opposed to what really exists, but as what, after reflection, is left of our immediate phenomenon.

Nevertheless, it would be a mistake to assume that the phenomenological concept of the given needs no further clarification. This applies to the concept of immediate givenness (*unmittelbare Gegebenheit*) as well as to Husserl's "bodily presence" (*leibhafte Selbstgegebenheit*). To give only some general indications of the direction in which such clarifications would have to move the following three layers of phenomenal givenness would have to be distinguished:

1. In a very general and primitive sense, what is given means the *object given* as such, for instance, the book or the table as now seen in a certain perspective;

2. In a more restricted sense, what is given is that much of this object as is fully presented, i.e., especially its frontal aspect, through which the object itself is being presented; we might call it the "*giving*" *datum*.

3. However, the given may also mean what, as a result of a reflective act of perspective reduction which "turns off" all automatic perceptual interpretation, appears to be present in our perceptual field, for instance in visual perception, the color areas in their various shades, shapes and sizes, which, as a rule, are entirely different from those ascribed to the "given object." This is in fact what every perspectivistic painter has to do. This given datum seems to be what Husserl calls *hyle* or sense-datum. However, nobody would assert that only these residues of such a dis-

---

[39] Brand Blanshard, *The Nature of Thought* (Londen: Allen & Unwin, 1939, vol. I, p. 440).

mantling reduction are given. Rather, this layer of givenness constitutes an artificial set of data restricted to the *conveying stratum* of given percepts, which, generally, in its transparency is simply overlooked.

In the discussions of this essay the first meaning, i.e., the phenomenon as the given object, was the most important, although, in a detailed examination of our knowledge, the other meanings must not be neglected. I am not aware of such distinctions in the concept of the datum as developed by the Neo-critical Realists.[40]

However, the decisive difference lies in the fact that in critical phenomenological realism the given has no immediate reference to physical or biological facts, as it has with Neo-critical Realism. For this reason in phenomenology the given is a concept of much more immediate application. Moreover, it would be utterly misleading to conceive of phenomena as general essences. Essences can be obtained only by a specified kind of abstraction ("eidetic reduction," in Husserl's terms), but never by simple sense-perception.

It may be more difficult to distinguish between the Neo-critical position and that of critical phenomenological realism with regard to the relation between phenomena of reality and actual reality. There is definitely a dualistic element in my new account of this relation, inasmuch as the phenomenon of reality in sense-perception has been interpreted as the "trace" of the real object, to be distinguished from the real object that leaves behind the trace; they no longer coincide. On the other hand, the relation between the two is considerably closer than it would seem according to most Neo-critical Realists. To be specific: In the case of a conflict between our phenomena of reality, either, owing to specific conditions, i.e., owing to the intrinsic order of preference between the phenomena of reality, some of them take precedence, as a result of which the yielding ones undergo the *capitis diminutio* of forfeiting their claims to reality, while the prevailing ones keep the character of reality for good; or none of the phenomena of reality has a real claim to reality, which, in this case, has to be reserved for reconstructed entities behind them. In this second case, however, the causes of the phenomena of reality are clearly indicated and foreshadowed by their effects, i.e., in the case of sense-perception, by their traces as represented by the phenomena of re-

---

[40] Some indications may be found in Strong's distinction between the sensation as a meaning and the sensation as a fact (*op. cit.*, pp. 234 f.).

ality. By no means are these "transcendent" realities mere x's. Thus, even where we do transcend the field of the immediately given, we transcend it in a direction which is well foreshadowed. In no case are we to turn away from the guidance by the phenomenal structures.

I am not sure whether such a conception of the relation between phenomena of reality and reality is completely incompatible with all forms of Neo-critical Realism; for instance, in Lovejoy's interpretation of memory and forecast,[41] reality seems to have substantially the same structure as the given. There is no point in drawing unnecessary dividing lines. What really matters is whether it is possible to solve the puzzles of epistemology by phenomenological methods. Only thus shall we be able to come to terms with certain vexing epistemological problems which phenomenology seems to have evaded thus far, but will have to face, once the comparatively elementary tasks of description and analysis of the phenomena have been accomplished.

---

[41] *The Revolt Against Dualism,* pp. 305 ff.

PART TWO

AT THE THINGS (ESSAYS *IN* PHENOMENOLOGY)

10. TOWARD A PHENOMENOLOGY OF EXPERIENCE*

This paper does not aim at a comprehensive phenomenology of experience. Its main purpose is to show how the phenomenological approach can add to a fuller understanding of a phenomenon whose prestige stands almost in inverse proportion to its lucidity. "Experience" is easily the most eulogized title of contemporary philosophy. Hence it has become its most overextended and diluted concept. Any attempt to clarify the nature of the phenomenon in depth and to examine the rights of experience must therefore begin with a demarcation of its field.

I. THE PROBLEM OF DENOTATION

I shall attempt this demarcation of the denotational field of the term 'experience' by telling what I intend to exclude from it. At first sight such a procedure may appear highhanded and only of private interest. However, the lines I shall draw are based on previous study of "family resemblances" which make the incisions in the continuum of the phenomena a matter not only of convenience but of requiredness: they indicate the places where the articulation of the phenomena calls for such incisions.

I shall not try to take into account here with John Dewey "all the complex series of transactions which occur between the live creature and its environment." [1] Such a definition, at least if taken literally, would have to include mere physico-chemical exchanges of energy

* This article, published before in *American Philosophical Quarterly*, Vol. 1, No. 4, October 1964, is a development of a paper which was read in a symposium on "Experience" before the Metaphysical Society of America at Notre Dame University in March 1960.
[1] See, e.g., Gail Kennedy, "Dewey's Concept of Experience: Determinate, Indeterminate, and Problematic," *Journal of Philosophy*, vol. 56 (1959), p. 802.

between the organism and its surroundings, e.g., a plant absorbing carbon dioxide and discharging oxygen. I shall disregard also "experiences" such as accidents of good or bad luck as long as they remain unnoticed. Finally I shall ignore "experience" in the sense of the stock of more or less shaky generalizations, maxims, or "knack" which may make a person "experienced." No doubt there are connections between all these uses. But for the purposes of the present discussion I want to focus on what, if I am not mistaken, the classical debates about experience have always been about: the kind of individual occurrences in which a potential knower makes cognitive contact with an individualized object. However, I want to make it clear at once that this characterization is not meant as a definition of the essence of experience but merely as an attempt to stake out the field for structural investigation, which eventually may lead to a structural definition. I shall use as a paradigm of such an experience the reader's awareness of the page on which these sentences are printed with its black marks against a white ground, beginning with the visual experience, matched by the experience of absorbing its meaning and by whatever other experiences may follow upon this reading experience.

II. THE RECORD OF PHENOMENOLOGY

I shall start out with a brief account of the phenomenological exploration of experience thus far. Such an account seems to be particularly appropriate since phenomenology is often suspected of being hostile to experience.

Thus it is worth pointing out that Brentano, the major inspirer of Husserl's phenomenology, started his reform of philosophy with a new psychology "on empirical foundations (*auf empirischer Grundlage*)" taking experience actually in a sense which included a certain ideal intuition (*ideale Anschauung*). True, Husserl himself in setting forth the idea of his pure phenomenology coupled this with an attack on empiricism, an attack aimed at safeguarding the right of insights into general essences against the monopoly of experience of merely particular facts. It is all the more important to realize that in spite of this anti-empiricist facade Husserl subscribed to the positivist principle of unconditional adherence to the given without addition or diminution, so much so that he claimed: "we phenomenologists are the true positivists." [2] But the decisive evidence is his actual approach to experience in his phenomenology of consciousness. For here the study of the essential structure of experience is one of Husserl's major concerns, and this, among other things, for the weighty reason that perceptual experience is the only valid evidence for our knowledge of the "real" world. Husserl's studies on *Experience and Judgment*, as developed under his supervision by Ludwig Landgrebe and published posthumously,[3] contain in fact some of his most concrete pieces of phenomenologizing, precisely in the sections on experience. Specifically, they show pre-predicative experience of our life-world as the matrix of all our predicative and scientific knowledge.

The same interest in a widened and deepened conception of "phenomenological experience" is manifested in Max Scheler's writings, particularly in those dealing with our experience of value. More recently, among the French phenomenological existentialists, Maurice Merleau-Ponty devoted much of his attention to this subject. His approach could perhaps be characterized best by a formula like "Against Empiricism; for lived experience (*expérience vécue*)," i.e., for experience as the manner in which each existing perceiver lives his body and his world.

What I am going to present in the following sections does not pretend to be a faithful exposition of common phenomenological doctrine or of that of any individual phenomenologist. However, I have made a special effort to incorporate into my version what I consider the most valid parts of Husserl's pioneering analyses. These seem to me often unduly neglected even by phenomenologists. But I must warn that whatever strange novelties I shall seem to peddle may turn out to be heresies which the master could rightfully disown. However, he should receive the primary credit for whatever may appeal to the reader.

III. SOME PHENOMENOLOGICAL FINDINGS ABOUT EXPERIENCE

An attempt to present merely what is distinctive in the phenomenological conception of experience would presuppose a panoramic survey of all the classical and recent literature in the field. This, I

[2] *Ideen zu einer reinen Phänomenologie*, 20.
[3] *Erfahrung und Urteil* (Prague: Academia, 1939); translated as *Experience and Judgement* by James Churchill and Karl Ameriks (Evanston: Northwestern University Press, 1973).

am afraid, is beyond the scope of this paper. But, trying to make a virtue of an impossibility, I might actually do better by simply presenting what seem to phenomenologists some of the central characteristics of experience, leaving it to the reader to decide whether there is anything original and possibly helpful about them. However, I shall make a special attempt to stress features which I hope will be of particular interest and possible value to professed empiricists. I shall do so by formulating eight compact theses on which I shall comment, as I move along, concomitantly.

3.1. Experience is an "intentional" act in which an experiencer is directed toward an experienced object

No different from other intentional acts, such as imagination, thought, or practical "intentions," experience refers to objects other than itself *of which* it is experience. In this sense of a reference beyond itself, experience has essentially a minimum of meaning, and meaningless experience is a contradiction in terms. The articulation of the global phenomenon in which experience occurs into the intending experience and the intended object of experience involves that any phenomenological study of experience has to pay parallel and equal attention to what is experienced as it is experienced and to the ways in which our experiencing approaches it. Thus in describing the experience of this page we shall have to attend not only to the phenomenal characteristics, the perspective aspects and the modes of clarity with which it is given but equally to our ways of looking at it from various angles successively and in different attitudes, doing it, for instance, searchingly or doing it merely casually.

It should be realized that common parlance does not restrict the use of the word "experience" to acts of experiencing but that very often we also call the object or "content" of this act "an experience." Nevertheless, it is only by the grace of the experiencing act that the experienced object receives its title of being "an experience." Even in epistemological discussions of experience we often understand the word in a more global sense in which act and "content" are embraced by the term. It is all the more important not to overlook the articulation within this global phenomenon and not to lump them together. More important, we must be aware of the fact that our experiencing is set off against the object of our experience in a characteristic and unique manner. Neither is part of the other.

3.2. A full experience is a synthesis of several intentional acts

Our experiences do not simply follow each other in single file, as it were. They are object-focused. And they are not always directed toward separate objects. Often, and perhaps in most cases, they have identical foci. In other words, the intentions of several experiencing acts may converge upon one and the same object of experience. It is only when these acts coalesce in this manner that we can properly speak of having experience of an object. The experience of the present page implies a whole series of intentional acts, whose concentric meaning has been formed by a synthesis of all impressions the reader has had since he first "laid eyes on it," moved toward it, or turned it.

3.3. The experience of an object refers beyond itself

No experience is sharply circumscribed by precise contours. At its periphery each content melts into a background of dimly given data, which in turn refer beyond themselves toward other potential data; and each act of experiencing borders on other acts which may present more and different aspects of the same object. Each phase of an experience is thus surrounded by tracks or pathways to only partially given and even to aspects not given at all. Such references can then be fulfilled or frustrated in subsequent phases of experience. In the reading experience of this page, where our moving glance focuses on a limited area of the text, we find ourselves referred backward and forward over the page to what is thus far only marginally given and beyond to what is still completely beyond our glance. We are also referred to the reverse of the page, to preceding and subsequent pages, and to the whole book in which this text appears.

3.4. Experience has temporal structure

There is no such thing as a merely instantaneous experience. Rather, experience has a temporal pattern opening from the very start toward future phases and subsequently also toward past ones. These past phases "sink down" toward deeper levels of consciousness, where they are submerged by more recent arrivals, and become "sedimented," to use Husserl's suggestive metaphor. They are at first still within the range of immediate retention, but soon they are available only to the recuperating effort of recollection. Future phases stand before us only in the mode of approaching expectation. The experience of this text at the present moment is suffused by at least several minutes of the reader's first and second impressions, and illuminated by what he may still experience if he feels sufficiently encouraged and at leisure to read on.

3.5. *Experience extends to any type of individual objects*

Experience is not restricted to so-called sense-experience.[4] For the phenomenologist there are experiences of relations, meanings, values, requiredness, other minds, social and cultural phenomena. Any kind of cognitive contact with particular data is an occasion for genuine experience. We experience not only each other's epidermises (or rather, their perspective appearances) but also each other's encompassing bodies, personalities, and maybe even thoughts and feelings.

3.6. *Experience forms the pre-predicative stage of our cognitive life*

The predicative stage of judgments and propositions with its polarization into subject and predicate differs essentially from the unpolarized structure of our immediate experience. But predicative knowledge has its primary foundation in such direct experience. Perception is its primary form, but so are feelings and other first-hand ("primordial") acts. The way to judgmental knowledge is prepared by a sequence of articulating acts of which Husserl in *Experience and Judgment* has given some highly original accounts. From the plain seizing of the originally given via its retentive inspection and explication for its detailed structure we gradually approach the stage of "substratum" and "determination" which allows for expression in logical predication.

By way of illustrating something of these highly complex relationships I would like to call attention to the situation in which we find ourselves when, after having spent some time in a room, we want to describe it. Evidently this presupposes explicit refocusing and reorganizing of the original experience.

---

[4] "So-called" – for what entitles us to call it *sense*-experience? What do we know about our senses that accounts for the structure and the content of these experiences? And how do we know about these "senses"?

3.7. Experience constitutes the experienced

In introducing Husserl's term 'constitution' I have to point out immediately that it allows for a number of more or less extreme interpretations, and that it has given rise to considerable confusion and controversy among his followers. I shall here confine myself to a minimum sense of the term under which it means no more than that each object of experience establishes itself, or "settles" in our experience by "taking shape" before our eyes, as it were. Again the example of this text should help to make this concrete. Before encountering it we had a number of more or less vague anticipations based on such clues as our previous acquaintance with printed texts, which provided something like the steel frame of a building. But when we got sight of it first we had little more of a picture than that of a block of paper. As we opened it, this block rapidly took on more definite characteristics. Empty lots in the perceptual field were filled with pages, headlines, text, etc. At the present stage at least a few perspectives of this page have established themselves for the reader, sufficient to picture how the page would look from the bottom, etc. But even then many blanks remain to be filled by reading on before the picture of the entire article will stand complete before the reader's mind.

3.8. Experience is a combination of receptive and spontaneous processes

While there are certainly receptive phases in all experience, especially in its initial stages, it would be quite mistaken to see in experience nothing but a passive process. Experience is permeated by spontaneous activities which Husserl called achievements (*Leistungen*). Kant's transcendental analysis of experience opened up the field for their investigation. Husserl, in tracing the active achievements of *Erfahrung*, described specifically the exploratory inspection, the laying hold of and keeping hold on the object of experience, and its "explication." To him there is an entire hierarchy on constitutive acts conditioned by the first occurrence of empirical raw material. As a whole, experience is a network of receptive and spontaneous processes, of undergoing, in which the active phases are in the ascendancy the closer experience approaches the predicative stage of articulated knowledge.

To appreciate this I hardly need remind the reader of the way in which he first experienced this page and still continues doing so. After receiving his first impressions from it, he let his eyes range adventurously over its expanse before he began, more or less methodically, to look at it in an orderly fashion by reading.

IV. THE GIVEN AND THE FOUND IN EXPERIENCE

Closer attention to the active factors in experience suggests a reconsideration of the concept of "the given." Among the many things taken for granted in our thinking about experience is the belief that the object of experience is "given." At least some philosophers, mostly critics of phenomenology, realize that the term 'given' is highly ambiguous. Thus it may stand either for the sense data (whatever they may be), for the perspective appearances of an object, for the sides which they present, or for the global object with all its sides. But few if any students of experience seem to have inquired what the very idea of givenness implies. Obviously the term is a metaphor. How many of the features of the idea of "giving" or donating genuinely apply to the given as it occurs in experience?

Now the metaphor of giving or donating implies first of all that the initiative for the process lies with the giver, that the gift passes from him to the receiver or addressee. The latter's role in this process may seem at first to be primarily passive. Yet actually there can be no gift without some activity on the part of the recipient. Not only before the law a gift cannot be accomplished without being accepted; without acceptance the gift is a failure, drops to the ground, as it were. One may try to force a gift on a potential receiver; but it is obvious that something forced down his throat is no longer a gift. There can be no *giving* without free *receiving*. Otherwise the given is at best the offered. But what exactly is accepting? It presupposes a certain openness and readiness on the part of the receiver to take over and hold on to what has been handed to him. This is certainly more than a merely passive posture. The recipient has to actually "open his hands," "close them" around the gift, and to "keep them closed" until he can deposit it within his domain. Other gestures can be equally expressive of the act so symbolized.

How far do these features of the metaphor apply to the act of experience? In important regards they do. Whenever a new datum enters our ken, it is not the experiencer who has the initiative. He is certainly passive to the extent of undergoing the impact of the "first impression" and of continuing to be affected by the influx of subsequent information. At this stage, it is the experienced object which does all the talking. On the other hand it is certainly the case that nothing can be given to the experiencer without his openness, his readiness, and his willingness to receive. To the non-receptive subject, to the merely captive audience, nothing can be given, it can only be offered, and then it is mostly wasted. Now openness and readiness is to a considerable extent a matter of active control: we can open (or close) our mind and we can get set for an experience or alternately guard ourselves against an experience. Even after this phase, experiencing always requires the active operation in which we lay hold of or assimilate whatever enters our opened field of experience.

But is this kind of receptive experience, an experience of the wait-and-see type, the only type of experience to be considered? Actually the very word "experience" and its equivalents in other languages suggest something much more aggressive. For "ex-perience" in English refers to the extract or outcome of a special trial (the stem of the word is related to the Greek verb *peiráo*): hence the literal meaning of the word comes very close to "experiment." Similarly in German the word "*erfahren*" includes the root "*fahren*," i.e., to drive, to travel. Hence *erfahren* expresses originally the attainment of knowledge by an outgoing effort.

Now there is indeed a type of experience in which the primary initiative lies with the experiencer. Such experience is based on seeking, not merely waiting, and terminates in finding, not merely receiving. This "finding experience" deserves separate and detailed exploration, since this is clearly the type which is at the base of all research experience. To this extent the found is even epistemologically more important than the given.[5] In the present context I can give only a first sketch of this type of experience.

[5] It was a happy coincidence and confirmation for my thinking on this matter when Professor C. I. Lewis, in an unrelated letter of September 10, 1954, pointed out to me that "any directly discoverable item is found" and that "the given" in his writings was to be understood in the sense of "the sensuous found." I would not be prepared to replace the concept of the given completely by "the found." It seems to me rather that there are two types of the experienced, the given and the found, corresponding to two kinds of encounters with the world, the giving and finding experience. Yet the found in its distinctive nature has been comparatively neglected, although it would seem to be much more significant epistemologically.

Can there be such a thing as seeking without an object sought? Plato's *Meno* denies this, thus preparing the ground for his doctrine of innate ideas. I submit that there are at least two basic types of seeking. One is the merely exploratory, curiosity-directed exploring of new ground without looking for anything in particular. The other is definitely a search "for," directed by some more or less definite idea of what we are looking for. Such a search, but only such a search, can be successful and unsuccessful. There are of course all forms of transition. At times we may not even know what we are looking for until we find out by a discovery "This is what we had been looking for." In fact we cannot even be happily or unhappily surprised in our search if we have not at least "the remotest idea" of what we are after. But there is the limiting case of the merely exploratory search in simple surveying, free of expectations that can be fulfilled or disappointed. This, however, does not eliminate the possibility of the kind of surprises which result from a sudden change in the pattern of experiences to which we have become accustomed.

Now what is found as a result of a merely exploratory search constitutes itself on the basis of an approach which simply follows the lead of the phenomena. To be sure, finding something in the uncharted sea around us implies some criterion of what could be considered a find, as distinguished from our experience in those intervals of our exploration where we find "nothing." Somehow the found must present itself as sufficiently different, set off against the ground of the preceding experiences to give us the idea that here is something new. Then we can match our findings with each phase of the probe and chart the results.

The situation differs considerably when the search is undertaken under the guidance of a pattern of what we are seeking for. Not only shall we be looking for clues in the phenomena which will fit into this pattern, we shall also be exploring the field in a very different manner, following up leads in accordance with the pattern to which we want to match our findings. The found itself will present itself right away with a fringe of references in anticipation of what is to be found next and what may fulfill or disappoint our expectations. True, such a pattern of anticipation may very well prejudice our search. But the found is still master of itself, though it is not *our* master. We are no longer at its mercy but can put it on the witness stand, as it were.

V. TOWARD A PHENOMENOLOGY OF THE CONTEXT
OF EXPERIENCE

At this point I would like to make a first attempt to relate the phenomenological conception of experience to a concept which has become prominent in the discussion of non-phenomenological empiricism – that of the context of experience.

I must confess that thus far I have not yet come across a precise definition or description of this term in the contextualist literature. I gather therefore that its basic meaning has to be derived from ordinary usage. Here I understand a "context" to mean the correlate of a "text" which is surrounded by the "context." Or are we to understand that the text is not only the excluded core of a surrounding context but "part and pattern" of it? This would of course already be a widening of the literal meaning.

What, then, according to the contextualist empiricist, is the relation between an experience and its context? Is the context merely the outside frame for the "text" of experience? Or is it the whole, of which experience forms an integral part? If the former, then the context is at each given moment transempirical. But even if the latter is true, at least part of the context reaches beyond immediate experience.

Once these questions are cleared up, we can and must raise the further question: How do we know about the context? The question is particularly urgent for the transempirical concept of the context.

Now phenomenology, and particularly the phenomenology of constitution, should be in a position to tell us how the phenomenon of the context presents itself. Yet actually the term "context" does not often appear in phenomenological accounts of experience, and if so only incidentally.[6] But this does not mean that the thing meant is absent. The terms that occur most frequently are 'horizon,' 'field,' '*Umwelt*' (the best English equivalent is probably "circumambience"), or, in the most comprehensive sense, 'world.' Obviously these expressions would cover only the transempirical sense of the contextualist's context. How, then, is it constituted for the phenomenologist?

Suppose we focus first on the thematic core or "text" of a con-

---

[6] For a phenomenological discussion of context (or "thematic field") I can now refer the reader to Aron Gurwitsch, *The Field of Consciousness* (Pittsburgh, Duquesne University Press, 1964, especially pp. 318 ff.).

figuration anywhere in a room – say, the table in front of us. In perceiving it as such, we are already aware of the concentric belts of decreasing clarity that surround it. These continuous zones terminate in a marginal fringe which melts away into the open blankness of a *terra incognita*. Now, while keeping the focus of our primary attention on the perceptual core, let us try to watch and describe what connects it with the areas of diminishing attentional illumination. There is considerable variety in this regard in different perceptual fields. But there is probably something typical about the situation in the visual field. Here we may notice what may be called 'leads' or 'tracks' which run from the thematic field into the marginal zones and beyond. Outlines of objects and shadings may serve as illustrations. Now these tracks carry, as it were, references, or anticipatory "intentions" to the field beyond, foreshadowing not only what may be found in adjacent areas but also the perspectives in which they will be presented. They are decreasingly definite for the lateral aspects of an object we confront, and quite indefinite, though rarely absent, as regards its back.

What is thus vaguely presented or adumbrated as surrounding the focus of our experience constitutes the first and necessarily inadequate appearance of the field or context. Nevertheless, this is the original first-hand way in which we know about fields and contexts as such. Still, no isolated act of experience gives us adequate knowledge about our world. Only the further progress of our experience can orient us in this gradually constituted field. Its constitution takes place when we follow up the anticipatory references, making their vague content "thematic," or converting it into the "text" of our attention, while the previous core becomes marginal context and finally drops off into the background. From such a second step we may then proceed to check on other anticipations of our original intentions or on those which have newly formed during our second step. It is in this manner that the context, first presented only vaguely and peripherally, constitutes itself into a firmer framework on an equal level with the first thematic text. But only when in the process of a sustained, but by no means rigidly patterned, sequence of confirmations, infirmations, and revisions it has constituted itself with a reasonable amount of clarity and stability, can the context claim equal rights with the text. And never can it achieve priority over it. For even after the constitution of the context it is not only the context which determines the meaning of the text, it is also the text which supplies new meaning to the context. There is equality in interaction.

Nothing of what I have outlined here should be construed as an attempt to discredit or even to question the legitimacy of the concept of context, or the validity of contextualism. It is merely meant as an attempt to show that the concept of "context" is in need of further experiential analysis. A phenomenology of "text" and "context," which would thoroughly explore and describe their constitution in consciousness, may be one way of buttressing this promising development in latterday empiricism.

VI. ON THE METAPHYSICAL SIGNIFICANCE OF A PHENOMENOLOGY OF EXPERIENCE

In conclusion I would like to discuss, however briefly, the question: What is the bearing of such a phenomenological analysis of experience upon metaphysics? The relation between phenomenology and metaphysics in general is one of the most open and controversial issues among living phenomenologists. It should also be mentioned that Husserl, who in the beginning phases of his phenomenology vetoed all speculative metaphysics, eventually, in his *Cartesian Meditations*, presented his idealistic monadology under the title of metaphysics.

All I intend to do in the present context is to outline what kind of connections might be found between the preceding analysis of experience and a conception of metaphysics which I have to define dogmatically. Be it understood, then, that by a metaphysical statement I mean here any statement which claims to reveal the fundamental reality of the world as a whole beyond mere appearance.

Is there anything metaphysical about the preceding study of experience in this sense? Two aspects in particular need discussion before an answer to this general question can be given:

1. Is the preceding analysis free from metaphysical assumptions?
2. Does it add anything to the stock of metaphysical insights?

In answer to the first question I plead: not guilty. Phenomenology suspends all belief in a reality beyond consciousness. This applies also to beliefs such as those in the reality of possible external causes of our experiences, whose truth sensationalism naively presupposes.

Specifically, phenomenology does not commit itself at the start to any belief in organisms as described by such sciences as anatomy, neurology, or physiology, or in an environment as described by the physical sciences. Only when the results of these sciences have been phenomenologically scrutinized and buttressed can phenomenology incorporate them.

This does not mean that phenomenology is without any presuppositions. No methodical examination can begin from the proverbial scratch. At least it will have to use such tools as logic and language. But these non-metaphysical presuppositions are not meant to be beyond all examination. They are always subject to phenomenological testing and retesting and in this sense accepted only on approval. I do not believe that in this respect phenomenology is any better or worse off than any other critical philosophy.

So much about the metaphysical assumptions of a phenomenological analysis of experience. What about the ultimate metaphysical significance of its findings? Is phenomenology the necessary and sufficient presupposition of any future metaphysics built upon experience? It would be preposterous to make such a claim at this time.

Can it at least promise a metaphysics of experience, i.e., a final appraisal of the essential structure of experience and of its place in the real world? This expectation too would be premature. All that phenomenology can attempt is to clarify the essential structure of experience. To decide whether or not such experience occurs in actual life is not its business *qua* phenomenology. Nevertheless this much may be claimed: The act of experiencing is part and parcel of the indubitable sphere of Husserl's absolute consciousness. Hence phenomenology can supply us with metaphysical knowledge about this one part of the universe.

The situation is much more complicated with regard to what is experienced, i.e., the object of our experiencing. Here we must remember that at least in its initial stage phenomenology suspends all claims to reality for everything that transcends the phenomena of consciousness. Its original stance is therefore one of metaphysical neutrality. The question is whether in its further development it can pass beyond it.

The following answer may serve at least as a hypothesis: As far as the "what," the content of our experiencing, is concerned, experience in its synthetic progress is able to supply increasing completeness, consistency, and corroboration. But it can never be exhaustive. All our knowledge of the content of the experienced world can therefore be only relative and subject to correction. If one wants to call the ultimate knowledge so achieved metaphysical, such metaphysics can never be absolute; at best it can have probability value.

As far as the "that," the being of this experienced world, is concerned, phenomenology is in an even more precarious position. Husserl himself developed a peculiar transcendental idealism according to which the transcendent world owes its being to the constituting acts of the pure ego. Yet few other phenomenologists have followed him to this radical conclusion. Some have tried to formulate a phenomenological realism, whereas the French existentialist phenomenologists seem to be advocating an intermediate solution according to which existence and the world form a reciprocal system. Obviously in this matter phenomenology has not yet been able to reach a unanimous verdict. And frankly I do not see how it could reach it at all, as long as it sticks to its original mandate of exploring the phenomena *qua* phenomena, regardless of whether they are real or not. Any decision that goes beyond this is, strictly speaking, transphenomenological. To be sure, even such a decision need not be an arbitrary decision. It can be based on good reasons, including phenomenological reasons. But these can never be compelling reasons.

Personally I believe that a philosopher is entitled to make such metaphysical decisions. And I am not sufficiently concerned about the purity of the phenomenological faith to abstain from them in the name of the phenomenological suspension of belief. But I also wish there were more purists who would not dilute phenomenology for the sake of metaphysical prizes.

My all too sweeping conclusion, then, is that pure phenomenology as such is not a sufficient foundation for any future metaphysics of being as a whole. It can only supply a metaphysics of consciousness, including that of the experiencing consciousness, as one of its constituents. Besides, it may supply relevant, though not conclusive evidence for transconscious reality. Once phenomenology has done more of a solid job in screening this evidence, it may become the indispensable foundation for metaphysics. But today phenomenology had better concentrate on this foundation until it can support a superstructure that will not prove top-heavy.

11. A PHENOMENOLOGICAL ANALYSIS OF APPROVAL*

I. PURPOSE

The primary objective of the present study is to test a certain type of phenomenology inspired by Husserl's early work, but not to imitate it in detail.

Its secondary purpose is to demonstrate the powers of this method in the case of a phenomenon which occupies a strategic position in recent discussions of ethics: the phenomenon of approval. This phenomenon has been little analyzed in itself and has seemingly been considered unanalyzable. Such an analysis is lacking not only in emotive theories of ethics such as Edward Westermarck's, but also in Charles L. Stevenson's recent analytic philosophy of ethical language, in whose "models" approval figures prominently. By analyzing approval phenomenologically I would like to show that what may be unanalyzable to one type of so-called analysis may not be so to another.

Thirdly, I hope to make a critical contribution to ethics by determining the proper place of approval in the "economy" of ethical life and, more generally, of the theory of value. It may well turn out that this place has been vastly overestimated, and that approval should be demoted from its present place of honor.

Finally, I would like to use this study as an occasion for clarifying the relations between linguistic analysis and phenomenological analysis. Such a clarification is still very much in order.

Since I wrote a first version of this paper, George Pitcher has published an excellent article on this subject,[1] which was followed by

* From James M. Edie, ed., *Invitation to Phenomenology* (Chicago: Quadrangle Press, 1965, pp. 183-210).
[1] "On Approval," *Philosophical Review*, LXVII (1958), pp. 195-211.

some perceptive remarks by Robert A. Gahringer.[2] My substantial agreement with their conclusions almost made me abandon my plan to improve on my own paper. But on second thought this very agreement seemed to me worth recording, since Pitcher and Gahringer make no claim of having used phenomenological methods. If their approach can be labelled at all, it would seem to me to be in the tradition of linguistic analysis at its best. Nevertheless, our results differ in a number of points which may make it worthwhile to air our disagreements in public. I believe that there are several places in which an explicit phenomenological approach can demonstrate its additional fruitfulness.

II. FIRST DISTINCTIONS

Even a phenomenological analysis cannot dispense with ordinary language. Not only does it need it in order to describe its findings. The fine distinctions and at times even the seeming idiosyncrasies of current usage are revealing indications of important differences in the phenomena and deserve at least careful confrontation with these phenomena. Besides, it may well be doubted that phenomena other than those given in sensory perception could ever be discovered without the steppingstones of linguistic symbols. Actually these are simply the precipitations of previous direct experience.

Now in the case of the language of approval current English usage shows a significant difference between the plain transitive verb (to approve something) and the verb followed by the preposition "of" (to approve of).[3] It seems to me that these two usages are indicative of a real difference in the phenomena. In order to sense this difference one merely has to insert or drop the preposition "of" in contexts in which we have used the alternate wording. We then notice that having said that we approve the minutes of the last meeting, we cannot simply insert the preposition "of" without saying something quite different: To approve of the minutes as phrased by the secretary does not mean to approve them. On the other hand we speak without hesitation of approving of modern art, but we could not very well drop

---

[2] "A Note on Approving," *Journal of Philosophy*, LVIII (1961), pp. 45-50.
[3] As a matter of fact, only English seems to have this distinction. Other languages such as French and German use the verbs *approuver and billigen* only transitively.

the "of" from such a phrase without being corrected promptly by any idiom-conscious linguist. Gahringer even pictures a situation in which we may have to say that we approve a certain measure but without approving *of* it. Also, while we may very well disapprove *of* the minutes as drafted by an inexperienced secretary, we cannot very well say that we disapprove *them*, but only that we refuse to approve them.[4]

I submit this asymmetry in the English language throws significant light on the difference between two kinds of approval. Inspecting and comparing the referents of the two usages reveals that we are faced here by two significantly different phenomena. I shall call the referent of the transitive term "sanctioning approval," that of the prepositional phrase "acknowledging approval."

Sanctioning approval is an act which transforms the object of approval by conferring on it a certain type of validity, putting, as we say, a "stamp of approval" upon it. "So be it," "fiat," "placet," "aye" are all expressions of this kind of approval; "to okay it" is a particularly expressive American way of voicing this approval. The corresponding negative act of disapproval is the one by which we veto a course of action, reject it, refuse to put a stamp of approval on it. This may also be expressed by such phrases as "non placet," "nay," or by gestures such as turning thumbs down, or by some other form customary in parliamentarian language. In both cases the object of approval or disapproval emerges from the operation altered, vested with a new quality, a gestalt, which is essentially subject-related and subject-dependent. The approved "stands as read," is properly validated. It should be noted that only proposed courses of action or projects are suitable material for this type of approval.

Acknowledging approval or approval *of* something implies a very different relationship between approval and its object, compared with the one in sanctioning approval. It does not confer any new "stamp" on it. Instead it assumes that the approved is already "valid" in its own right and is in this sense independent of our approval. The only thing which such acknowledging approval may be said to add to the

---

[4] This has been pointed out to me by my colleague ,Carl Wellman, to whom I am indebted for many critical suggestions. See also J. L. Austin, *How to Do Things with Words* (New York: 1962, pp. 78 ff.), for the difference between "I approve" (performative), "I approve of" (mixed), and 'I feel approval" (report).

approved is the prestige which goes with the fact of having won over one more acknowledger and possible promoter.[5]

In the present context I shall be mainly interested, like most theorists of value, in the second type of approval. This is also the approval to which Stevenson's analysis of ethical language refers. Henceforth I shall refer to sanctioning approval only in passing, insofar as it can throw a light on some features of acknowledging approval.

III. THE INTRINSIC STRUCTURE OF ACKNOWLEDGING APPROVAL

Some preliminary remarks about the general nature of phenomenological analysis may be in order before I begin with the concrete analysis of acknowledging approval. For thus far there is no explicit theory of this analysis to which I could refer.[6] An outline of such a theory seems to be particularly desirable in view of the related and possibly rival claims of the new analytic philosophy. In the present context all I can do is to offer a few programmatic statements, which the ensuing demonstration will have to bring to life.

1. Phenomenological analysis focuses primarily on the phenomena, i.e., the referents of our discourse, ordinary or scientific, not on their linguistic expressions, which seems to be the first and ultimate concern of analytic philosophies.

2. Phenomenological analysis is not engaged, as analysis mostly is, in constructing alternatives for original statements which may be inferior in clarity and less economical number of constituent terms. Phenomenology aims primarily at a reflective study, as faithful as possible, of the phenomena in their directly presented articulation,

---

[5] It seems tempting to speculate on the original meaning of the preposition "of" in the case of acknowledging approval. Thus one might recall that the preposition "of" originally had the meaning of "away from." Hence one may wonder whether the phrase "to approve of" hints at the fact that the acknowledging approver keeps the object of approval at a certain distance, sizes it up from afar and responds to it from the outside. There is no such distance-keeping in sanctioning approval. However, I do not feel confident that such an interpretation can claim backing from linguistic science. Certainly the Oxford English Dictionary does not support it explicitly. And I do not want to draft language into the service of phenomenology without its consent.

[6] For some further hints see my *The Phenomenological Movement* (The Hague: 1960, pp. 669 ff.).

with their constituent parts, their connections, and their whole-making characteristics.

3. Phenomenological analysis pays special attention to the way in which these phenomena present themselves in our consciousness. This means not only that it attempts to describe statically the various aspects under which an object presents itself. It also includes an attempt to show in what systematic order such an object "constitutes itself," i.e., establishes itself in consciousness. As far as I can see, linguistic philosophy, even when it has become interested in the phenomena, not only in linguistic utterances, has not yet paid explicit attention to these modes of givenness of the phenomena.

4. There are at least two legitimate phenomenological approaches to the structure of a phenomenon:

a. One such approach, patterned in analogy to an anatomical dissection, will start from a concrete example and examine painstakingly area after area of the phenomenon in itself as well as its connections with adjacent phenomena. Examining the connection between the components of the phenomenon makes it possible to discover the character of the bonds between them and particularly how far these are of a merely "accidental" or of an essential character. To the extent that it is possible to establish these relationships, the pattern or structure of the entire phenomenon will become "intelligible." It is the grasp of this structural pattern which is involved in the much vaunted and much taunted essential insight (*Wesensschau*), which is certainly not a simple task and should be handled with great care.

b. Another approach to the phenomenon may begin with its general structure by way of determining first its generic type and then proceed to studying its modifications in the case under examination. In practice this approach takes the form of the familiar search for the genus and specific difference as expressed in definitions. Finding the proper genus for a phenomenon will involve us in a study of at least its basic structure. The search for its specific differences will direct our attention to its distinctive modifications.

In the present context the second or definitional approach promises quicker results. This is my reason for adopting it here. An additional reason is that thus far most discussions of approval seem to consist in attempts to classify it by assigning it its proper place in the family of psychological phenomena. This presupposes of course a valid or at least accepted framework of psychological classes. Thus Charles Stevenson bases his analysis of ethical language on the division of psychological phenomena into the two classes of beliefs and attitudes. I do not intend to question the rights and the adequacy of such a classification explicitly. But I believe that applying it critically to phenomena such as approval as presented through a phenomenological approach will also reveal the defects of this conceptual framework. In order to do justice to this phenomenon new and different patterns of psychological analysis will have to be introduced.

IV. APPROVAL IS NOT A BELIEF

It will be comparatively easy to show that acknowledging approval is not a belief, at least not in any of the conventional senses of the term 'belief,' where it stands for a dispositional state in which we hold a certain proposition to be true and the state of affairs to which it refers to be "the case" or "a fact." This description would certainly not apply to sanctioning approval. But it would be equally inadequate for acknowledging approval. It may be true that such approval presupposes or even includes certain beliefs about facts and even about their values. But approving means certainly more than mere theoretical believing. Even before trying to determine the positive character of this "more," I submit that in approving of birth control the approver commits himself personally to a much greater extent than when he merely believes that it is all right. This is no mere belief *that*. It is at least to some extent involvement *in*, a response to the propositional belief.

V. APPROVAL AS AN ATTITUDE AND APPROVAL AS AN ACT

At least half of the difficulty in deciding whether acknowledging approval can be classified as an attitude is due to the lack of a clear conception of the class "attitude." A phenomenological clarification of this concept is here out of the question. It would presuppose a conscientious survey of the field designated by the term "attitude" and by equivalent terms as a basis for determining its essential structure and its types.

Suppose for the sake of argument we decide, with Ralph Barton Perry, to call an attitude whatever expresses an interest; then there is hardly any valid reason for refusing acknowledging approval admission to such an *omnium gatherum*. The same would be true if we included with Stevenson "purposes, aspirations, wants, preferences, desires, and so on," a formulation which allows us to add an indefinite amount of similar phenomena. But does such a vast collection reflect the articulation of the phenomena, bringing out, for instance, the "family resemblances" to which Wittgenstein's analysis pays such remarkable attention? Or if we understand by "attitude," as Gordon W. Allport did, "a disposition or readiness for a response"? Then it is obvious that *sanctioning* approval is not an attitude. But the case is different with *acknowledging* approval. Normally when I approve of something I shall develop a disposition or readiness to respond, which may persist even when, at the moment, I am preoccupied with entirely different matters. Is this enough to assert that approval is *nothing but* a dispositional attitude?

Before deciding this, I consider it important to introduce a distinction which has been overlooked thus far. The best way to do this is to pay attention to the question of how acknowledging approval is formed or "constitutes itself" in our consciousness. No psychological and especially no causal investigation is intended, but simply a descriptive account. Now it seems to me that the static approval of, e.g., honesty, to which we have been referring thus far exclusively, has always gone through a formative stage. I shall not exclude the possibility that some such static approval crystallizes, as it were, almost unnoticeably, and certainly without our being able to remember exactly how this happened. But I submit that in the case of more outspoken and deliberate cases of approval the formative phase consisted of a specific and conscious *act of approving*, which may even be pinned down to a specifiable date. This is certainly the case with the kind of reflective approval which is involved in ethics. In this sense and to this extent I maintain that the primary phenomenon in the area of acknowledging approval is the formative act of approving, which in due course leads to a more static and lasting approval as its precipitate, as it were. As to this sedimented result of our act of approving, I feel little if any hesitation to call it an attitude. But it seems to me entirely inappropriate to talk about the formative primary act as an attitude. It is to this formative act of approval that I shall now transfer my attention.

VI. THE ACT OF APPROVAL

In calling the formative process which constitutes the attitude of approval an act, I seem to presuppose that this term has a precise meaning referring to a clearly marked phenomenon. I am well aware that such an assumption would be far from safe. Unfortunately I cannot fill the gap by improvising a theory of the general structure of acts for the present occasion. But I hope that I can by-pass this difficulty by assigning to the term the following minimum meaning: Acts are more or less episodic events or occurrences in the stream of experience which take place or are "enacted" in an "agent" or experiencing subject. Examples are acts of judgment, of inference, of will, of commendation or condemnation. The main groups of such acts are theoretical acts such as judgment or inference, emotive acts such as enjoyment or disgust, and acts of will such as accepting or rejecting. Into which one of these groups, if any, does the act of approval belong?

1. *Approval Is Not an Act of Judgment.*

Some of the eighteenth century British moralists, e.g., Richard Price and William McDougall, attempted to reduce the act of approving to a judgment about an object, notably to a judgment about its value. But I submit that to judge something as good is not the same as approving of it. Mere judging can be a perfectly detached affair. To approve means to abandon this detachment. To transform a judgment of goodness by an umpire into approval calls for an addition to this judgment, and to change the judger into an approver requires a change in his attitude which remains to be characterized. Obviously in separating approval from value judgment I do not want to exclude a close connection between them, about which more will have to be said later.

2. *Approval Is Not an Emotive Act.*

I shall probably be on much more contested ground in denying that approval is an emotive act. It might be relatively easy to show that sanctioning approval is not an emotion. But I hold this to be true also of acknowledging approval. This approval is certainly not an emotion in the sense of an emotional state such as gaiety or sadness, happiness or depression, anger or rage. In approving the approver is not "moved" in the way in which he is moved in such an emotional condition. For here he does not undergo something but does something. It is of course true that most acts of approving are accompanied by all kinds of emotions. But so are practically all other experiences. It also seems noteworthy that very often we approve of a matter while feeling anything but emotional satisfaction, doing it, for instance, reluctantly or regretfully.

3. *Approval Is Not an Act of Will.*

It may thus seem that approval belongs among the kind of acts which are commonly called acts of will. But even here I have to make reservations. It is true that sanctioning approval may be considered a voluntary activity in the sense in which legal acts such as resigning, giving notice, etc., are acts of will. But this is not the case with acknowledging approval. Such approval may of course *lead* to volitional actions. But acknowledging approval itself is a much earlier stage of our practical life, where acts of will in the proper sense do not yet enter.

It seems therefore that in order to accommodate acknowledging approval in the class of acts, a new and different division has to be found, or rather that a new type of act will have to be recognized. To discover this type, there is need for a fresh start.

VII. APPROVAL AS A REFERENTIAL ("INTENTIONAL") ACT

The clue which I shall use in this new and direct attack will be an insight which ever since Franz Brentano has been basic in all phenomenological research. According to it, most, if not all, psychological phenomena are acts in a more technical sense than the one in which we spoke of acts thus far. They are characterized by what has been called, none too felicitously, "intentionality." This means that the acts refer beyond themselves to what Husserl called "intentional objects." Thus every consciousness is consciousness of something. More specifically, every perception is a perceiving of something perceived, every thought a thinking of something thought of, every act of will a willing of something willed. Husserl stressed particularly the significance of the parallelism between act and content and the need of describing the structures on both sides in close correlation (without confusing them in the manner of "psychologism"). In further developing this method he also paid increasing attention to the way in which the intentional objects constitute themselves in our consciousness. Studying the constitution of an object in this sense means specifically watching the typical way in which it establishes itself before our "mental eyes," or "takes shape," as it were.

Applying this pattern as an undogmatic clue to the analysis of approval yields the at first sight not very exciting proposition that every approval consists in the approving of something approved.[7] Furthermore, approval is an intentional act in which the approved constitutes itself schematically in the following manner: (a) An object presents itself *for possible* approval. (b) Approval is actually *given*. (c) The approvable object is thereby transformed into an approved object. In examining this sequence I shall begin with a consideration of the object or theme of possible approval, which might also be called the *approbabile*, then turn to the act of approving, and finally consider the output of this operation, the approved or *approbatum*.

1. *The Approvable Object (approbabile)*. What kind of objects are possible candidates for approval? I shall omit a detailed collection and consideration of the concrete objects that can or cannot be approved by virtue of their peculiar content, all the more since Pitcher has studied this question painstakingly and successfully. Here I only want to determine the ontological character of the objects which are suitable candidates for acknowledging approval.

Does it make sense to approve of isolated entities, of objects, or even of mere qualities? At first blush this may seem quite plausible. For we speak not infrequently of approving of a person, a piece of equipment, a certain color, or institutions and laws. But closer examination reveals that there is a considerable difference between the comprehensive, undifferentiated way in which we like or love a thing and the way in which we approve of it. What we mean to say when we approve of it wholesale is that we approve of there being such a thing, and particularly of its being where it is, say of a certain piece of furniture being in a certain place, etc. In other words, even in the

---

[7] To be sure, there is a story about Bismarck who, when challenged to defend his repudiation of a certain proposal, is said to have replied: "I do not know the honorable gentleman's opinions but I disapprove of them." Even such a blanket disapproval, however incomplete it may be, implies that there must be some kind of a target for it.

case of such sweeping approvals the real object of approval is not an isolated thing as such but a state of affairs concerning it. In these cases we approve of all the states of affairs pertaining to this object so completely that it does not seem worthwhile to specify.

If this is correct, then the primary and major objects of approval are essentially not things but states of affairs, expressed in propositional phrases, whether these are stated in nominal form (philosophical journals), or in articulated sentences ("that there be philosophical journals"). It would lead too far to embark here on a full-fledged analysis of states of affairs, as ontology has to do. Suffice it to say that each state of affairs includes at least a substratum and an attribute.

Equally important is the realization that it is not simply the state of affairs as such of which we approve. What we are concerned about is always the question of its possible existence. To approve of the mere possibility of a utopia would be inane.

However, all these are merely minimum requirements of the approbabile. Further specifications will be added after we have considered the nature of the act of approving and its essential contribution.

2. *The Act of Approving.* By way of contrast let us first look briefly at sanctioning approval, which otherwise is no longer our concern. Sanctioning approval brings about a fundamental and intrinsic transformation in the structure of the object of approval: it changes it from a mere proposal of a course of action into a validated scheme or project. Sanctioning approval is thus a productive, in a sense even a creative, process.

This is certainly not true of acknowledging approval, which does not tamper with the intrinsic structure of what is approved. Nevertheless it does make a difference to its extrinsic appearance and role. In order to clarify the peculiar function and achievement of acknowledging approval, I have to refer to a certain type of act first described by Max Scheler and further explored by Dietrich von Hildebrand, the act of *Stellungnahme*, or as I shall translate it tentatively, the act of taking a stand or position. Scheler had pointed out that among the many types of referential acts ("intentional acts") which Brentano and Husserl had listed there were some that implied much more than the mere "having" of an object as its referent, as is the case, for instance, in mere perceiving or imagining. In phrases such as "to rejoice *at*," "to be pleased *with*," "to be happy *about*," "to be grieved *over*," the prepositions "at," "with," "about," etc. suggest more than mere reference, as in "awareness *of*." These acts imply a reaction, a characteristic response to the object referred. Thus joy is to be understood as an answer to its object. More specifically, Scheler thought that these acts are answers to its *value*; hence he called them "value responses" (*Wertantworten*). Such value responses were, however, not to be confused with acts of value *cognition*. Scheler thought that taking a stand is a separate and actually a secondary act performed in response to a value cognition, which it presupposes. This primary act of value cognition was described as one of intentional or referential feeling (*intentionales Fühlen*) in contradistinction to mere non-referential feeling (*Gefühl*) like pleasure. In this sense the acts of taking a stand, and specifically the acts of value response, were to Scheler dependent acts.

Whether or not Scheler's characterization of acts such as joy or grief as acts of taking a stand is quite adequate need not concern us here (I frankly would question it). In the present context not the example but the *type* so exemplified, the act of taking a stand, is what matters. And the prime need is to throw as much light as possible on this act, which has not yet been sufficiently explored. The standard classifications of acts, psychological or otherwise, do not seem to have room for it. For neither is the act of taking a stand an emotive act nor a simple act of will, although it is related to both of them. Perhaps its main characteristic is that it is a performing act; something is immediately brought to pass, as in making a decision or in adopting a project. Actually the metaphoric expression "taking a stand" is capable of a meaningful translation into more concrete characterizations:

1. It implies that, before taking a stand, we do not yet have a definite "position," but move about, drifting or shifting, from one possible location to another.

2. Taking a stand, we select one of these possible positions, move up to it, and install ourselves in it.

3. Most important: we now adopt this position for good, identify with it, and commit ourselves to it.

With this general picture of the acts of taking a stand in mind, let us now return to acknowledging approval or disapproval. Can it be considered as a proper instance? Scheler, and he alone, mentions it

(*Billigen und Missbilligen*) as one of many members of the class along with "being pleased and displeased" (*Gefallen und Missfallen*), respect and disrespect, striving for retaliation or spiritual sympathy.[8] But beyond mentioning these acts he does not analyze them any further. I now propose to do this explicitly in the case of approval.

I maintain that acknowledging approval is essentially an act of taking a stand. In fact, it is such an act in a much more genuine sense than less deliberate reactions such as joy, regret, etc., which are Scheler's primary examples. What happens when I give my approval to an object of possible approval is that I take up a position with regard to it, that I move up to it, and that I declare myself for it. In this sense the act of approval goes considerably beyond the mere "favoring" or "being for" something, as Pitcher and Gahringer have well observed. Favoring something or somebody (a "favorite") is a different, though related matter. If I favor a certain political party, this means only that I prefer it to another party, but it does not yet mean that I approve of it in the sense of a real commitment. In favoring I may stick to the position of a mere sympathizer or well-wisher, who maintains neutrality, however benevolent. In giving my approval I step down from the fence of neutrality. Hence, in the normal course of events, approval is and should be openly expressed, even if for special reasons it may have to remain concealed. By contrast, favoring may as well remain a completely internal affair.

Approval is, however, not the only such act of taking a stand. There are acts of sidetaking other than approval. There is, for instance, mere unreflective siding, joining, associating or dissociating, accepting or rejecting, welcoming or opposing, moving or seconding, and even affirming or denying. None of these is identical or even necessarily connected with approving. We may simply be joining "for the fun of it" or in the manner of camp followers or bandwagon climbers.

What, then, is the specific difference of approval as an act of taking a stand? Briefly: in genuine approval we take a stand *on* something, i.e., we do so in response to certain claims on the part of the cause at issue. A particularly good expression of such standtaking is the act of signing or subscribing to a statement, a petition, or a

---

[8] *Der Formalismus in der Ethik und die materiale Wertethik, Gesammelte Schriften* II, p. 128.

protest. Approving implies acknowledging a claim of the object of approval.

But it also means more by way of a commitment than mere side-taking. The approver gives something, however intangible, to what he approves. This gift may best be characterized by the word "support." It need not be physical, but can be merely "moral support" in the sense of giving whatever "aid and comfort" may be in the interest of the cause. Again, in the normal course of events such support should be openly expressed and communicated.

On the other hand approving does not imply that the approver surrenders head over heels to what he approves of and abandons all critical reserve. On the contrary, the approver, in contrast to the fanatic, maintains enough independence to give leverage, as it were, to his moral support. Approval is in this sense action at a distance.

Before leaving the analysis of the act of approval in itself, it may be well to recall that thus far I have discussed only the act of initiating approval. This act will normally lead to the formation of a permanent stance or attitude in the approver. The exclusive and premature attention to this secondary phenomenon has diverted attention from the primary or constituting act of taking an approving stand. The secondary attitude of approval may now be characterized as the *stance* the approver occupies or maintains in response to the claims upon his approval.

Finally, in the light of our findings about the act of approving I have now to suggest an important addition to what I said in the preceding section on the possible objects of approval. If it is essential to the act of approval to give support to the *approbabile*, then the question arises whether such support makes sense for *all* the states of affairs which would seem to be valuable, desirable, and worthy of our general appreciation.

Suppose we think of this universe, with Leibniz, as the best of all possible, or, with Schopenhauer, as the worst of all possible, worlds. Would it make sense in such a case to say that we approve or disapprove of the universe? Would not such a pronouncement seem downright ridiculous, even more ridiculous than Margaret Fuller's notorious acceptance of the universe, which brought down upon her Carlyle's cruel sarcasm (which was unjustifiably harsh coming from one who in *Sartor Resartus* himself had given the world his "eternal yea")? Similarly, would anyone in his sound mind and in more than a facetious mood say that he approves or disapproves of a sunset? And what of approving of such works as the Parthenon or the Sistina? Is there not something ridiculously arrogant, not to say smug and irreverent, about the act of approval if applied to such situations? If at all, they seem to call for entirely different responses than an approving nod. Approval has its proper place where it really "counts," where it "adds" something to the situation, where it "makes a difference." Otherwise the gesture of approval is, to say the least, incongruous for a human being cognizant of his place in the pattern of things. Philosophers who forget this and think that seeing goodness and sublimity in the universe means approving of it are apt to add fuel to the common ridicule of the philosopher as the arrogant appraiser and approver of everything (Candide's Pangloss).

In seeing the essential limitation of approval, Pitcher has gone so far as to say that only such matters can be approved as are under complete human control. I submit that this restriction is unnecessarily rigid and in fact leads to rather odd consequences or strained interpretations. Why shouldn't I approve of the elimination of crime, although it may very well be that it will never be completely under our control? It seems to me a perfectly sufficient basis for approval that the *approbabile* is *partially* under human control, and that it can be influenced by it. This, however, can become clear only if we realize that the reason for any limits to approval lies in the fact that approval makes sense only in cases where it "makes a difference" to the situation whether we approve or not. Wherever the object of approval is completely impervious to any expression of approval, it becomes as senseless as condemning earthquakes or "cursing the darkness." Thus we may say that the *approbabile* is restricted to such states of affairs as are within the sphere of influence of human beings without being under their complete control.

I even wonder whether an action which, in accordance with Pitcher's specification, is completely under our control is not quite unsuitable for approval. For the action which we control most is always our own. However, approving of one's own actions is hardly the proper thing to do. There are better and less complacent courses one could take toward these actions than to act like an outside supporter. It is only in the case of others than ourselves that approval or disapproval makes sense. Hence it would seem that approval applies precisely to those situations which are *not* under our most complete, i.e., our personal control.

3. *The Approved (approbatum)*. What, then, happens to the *approbabile* as the result of our approval? Or, to put it more phenomenologically, how does the object of approval constitute itself for us? A complete phenomenology of the *approbatum* would have to describe the various perspectives in which the approved appears, and to take account of the various modes of clarity or vagueness under which it appears. But this is not the context for detailed consideration of the features which approval shares with a good many other acts. My main concern is with the changes in the actual structure of the approved as the result of the act of acknowledging approval. The most obvious change is the transformation of the possible object of approval, the *approbabile*, into something actually approved, an *approbatum*. This does not mean that the approved acquires the stamp of validity which sanctioning approval confers. Acknowledgment adds to the acknowledged merely the tribute of a personal response, giving it the additional prestige of having made one more conquest among those who know about it. This may even bestow on it a peculiar type of power. It may manifest itself in various ways, especially in social recognition, where it would have considerable interest for the sociologist. But in the present discussion all that is necessary and important is to understand that and how approval functions in the constitution of the approved which affects the approved, although it does not change it in its internal structure.

Meinong, who coined the German term '*Objektiv*' as a counterpart to the term '*Objekt*' in order to designate the state of affairs as what is meant by a judgment, also invented the terms '*Desiderativ*' and '*Dignitativ*' for the counterparts of our desires and feelings. In similar fashion one might now think to use a term like "approbativum" for the object of our approval. While the parallel seems worth pointing out, I see little practical advantage and considerable disadvantage in cluttering up the field by the addition of another ponderous and unnecessary term.

I can sum up the result of my analysis of acknowledging approval in the following formula: Acknowledging approval is the act of taking a stand toward a state of affairs by which it receives moral support.

VIII. THE EXTRINSIC STRUCTURE OF APPROVAL:
ITS INCOMPLETENESS AND SECONDARY NATURE

Thus far I have attempted merely a description of the intrinsic structure of acknowledging approval and of its referents, the objects of approval. This, however, constitutes by no means a complete analysis of the phenomenon. For the act of approval has its place in the context of other acts from which it can be separated only artificially. It is to this context that I should now like to restore it.

The very act of siding with the *approbatum* raises the question as to the nature of the "sides" for or against which we decide. Is there something in the *approbatum* which bids us to take sides, thus making a claim upon us? A close inspection of the entire situation shows that this is indeed the case. Possibly the best way of showing this is by contrasting the act of acknowledging approval with one of mere taking sides unsupported by prior approval, as in watching a game. Here we may take sides perhaps just out of a whim or because we have a bias "in favor" of a team without really approving or disapproving of it. Genuine acknowledging approval is a very different matter. Here the object of approval is anything but an inert "victim" of our response. It presents itself as demanding approval and even as deserving of approval. In this sense approving is indeed in Scheler's sense an answering act responding to a situation, or, to use a Gestaltist term, a "requiredness," analogous to the way in which a question calls for an answer. Approval given without the intent of answering such a claim is not genuine approval but at best a taking of sides with our eyes closed. More specifically, to approve of something which we know to be bad or wrong is nothing but a *pretense* of approval. Ovid may be right with his *"Video meliora proboque/Deteriora sequor"*: Not doing what one sees to be better and of which one approves is all too common an occurrence. But a situation in which one sees that something is good or better and yet fails to approve of it (or even disapproves of it) would seem to be an essential impossibility. One might *talk* about seeing goodness and yet disapproving of it. But one cannot meaningfully *conceive* of it. Disapproval of the good would be no genuine disapproval but at best a spurious, forced *pretense* of it.

It seems worth pointing out that several languages, English among them, have taken account of these claims to approval by reserving special words for them. To be sure, in English the word "approvable" can be found only in the larger editions of Webster and in the Oxford English Dictionary, and this may not be sufficient to commend it to the good graces of the votaries of ordinary language. So it might deserve attention that, for instance in German, the word "*billigens-wert*" enjoys full and respected status in common usage and in the ordinary dictionaries, and so does "*approuvable*" in French.

If genuine approval thus consists in honoring the claims upon our approving which issue from the object of approval, the approved appears in a new role, namely as an *approbandum* in its own right, not only as an *approbabile* and an *approbatum*. More specifically: acknowledging approval in its very structure refers to approvableness or worthiness of approval as a peculiar character in the object to which approval means to respond. This insight has momentous consequences: it reveals that at the root of the entire phenomenon of approval is the *approbandum*, not the act of approval. A full phenomenological analysis of approval would actually have to begin here, instead of ending with it. Approval turns out to be a secondary and dependent phenomenon in the total picture of our evaluating life. Those who attempt to elucidate the theory of value and ethics by starting from the act of approval simply put the cart before the horse. I should, however, like to add that this insight itself is by no means new. It can be found in such unexpected places as J. S. Mill's *Logic*.[9] It also has been stated on occasion by such recent moral philosophers as W. D. Ross.[10]

However, the secondary role of approval in the economy of the

---

[9] "The fact affirmed in them [i.e., propositions of which the predicate is expressed by the words 'ought' or 'should be'], is that the conduct recommended excites in the speaker's mind the feeling of approbation. This, however, does not go to the bottom of the matter; for the speaker's approbation is no sufficient reason why other people should approve; nor ought it to be a conclusive reason even with himself. For the purposes of practice, everyone must be required to justify his approbation: and for this there is need of general premises, determining what are the proper objects of approbation, and what the proper order of precedence among those objects." *System of Logic*, Bk. VI, Ch. XII, § 6.

[10] "... it appears to me that it [i.e., the emotion of approval] is not just a feeling which arises in us, we know not why, when we contemplate a right action. It seems to presuppose some insight into the nature of the action, as, for instance, that it is an action likely to redound to the general good, or a fulfillment of promise. It seems to be an intellectual emotion, presupposing the thought that the action is right, and right as being of a certain recognized character." *The Foundations of Ethics* (Oxford: Clarendon Press, 1939, p. 23).

moral life does not mean that it is without interest, and that its phenomenology does not deserve and invite further exploration for its own sake. Such a phenomenology will, for instance, have to explore further the constitution of the *approbandum* in consciousness. Thus in a typical case the *approbandum* may present itself first as a mere candidate for approval whose claims are anything but evident. It may become a "nominee" before we can clearly "elect" it and answer to it wholeheartedly. Such procedures as "grading" offer excellent opportunity for watching the genesis of such claims and their characteristic pulls and counterpulls in their relevancy and irrelevancy.

Now it might seem that the claim of the *approbandum* is really nothing but its value, its goodness or excellence, in which case the phenomenology of the *approbandum* would fuse immediately with the general phenomenology of value, and approbation would be nothing but taking a stand in response to values. But this would be a premature conclusion. For one thing, if there is anything to the distinction between goodness and oughtness, between the right and the good, then the ought-to-be-approved and the good mean two different things, however closely connected. But there are even more definite reasons for believing that the two are not always connected or, even less, identical. To begin with, there are good things which do not call for acknowledging approval in the sense here specified. And perhaps there are even things which we have to approve of, however reluctantly, in spite of their partial badness. As to the former case, we have already seen that only such states of affairs call for approval which can benefit from our approval, regardless of the degree of their goodness and perfection. As to the latter, we have at times to give our approval to measures such as punishment, in which it is hard to see anything intrinsically good. Hence goodness and approvableness certainly do not coincide. Nevertheless it may be true that only what is less bad than its alternative, and consequently relatively better than it, can make claims on our approval.

IX. THE GROUNDS OF APPROVAL AND THEIR COGNITION

This situation suggests the following relation between the good and the approvable: Not absolute goodness but relative goodness constitutes the necessary, though not yet sufficient, ground for approvableness (we might call this goodness the "*probum*"). To make these grounds sufficient and make the *approbabile* worth approving, it must be at least capable of benefiting, however indirectly, from such approval.

If this diagnosis of the ontological relationship between the *probum* and the *approbandum* is correct, then the full knowledge of what is approvable presupposes an adequate knowledge of the values involved, the values of the state of affairs to be approved in the total situation, and the values that can be gained from the approval. Hence the problem of approval refers us back to the general problem of the cognition of value. It is of course beyond the scope of the present study to enter this field. I can only refer the phenomenologically interested to the trailblazing but by no means definitive studies of Max Scheler and to Alexander Pfänder's posthumous ethics.[11]

Instead, I want to raise one final question: Is it at all possible to separate the act of acknowledging approval from the cognitive acts on which it is based as its essential foundation?

Pitcher denies this for reasons that do not seem to me convincing.[12] Personally I cannot go so far. I consider it phenomenologically unavoidable to distinguish between approval itself and the cognitive acts supporting approval. But this does not preclude the possibility that they are parts of an encompassing whole. In fact, I maintain that genuine approval by its essential structure cannot occur apart from some kind of cognitive awareness of the reasons for approval. In this sense it may indeed be asserted that in itself approval is an incom-

---

[11] *Ethik in kurzer Darstellung*, ed. by Peter Schwankl. München: Wilhelm Fink Verlag, 1973.

[12] Specifically, he maintains that having at least one "basal reason for adoption" is the second constituent of approval, followed by a third to the effect that "anyone in the approver's position ought to be approving of it." Besides, Pitcher believes that this basal reason should be a general principle (e.g., "because I approve of reprimanding insolent servants"). As to this last point I confess that I am not yet convinced: Why should a "basal reason" have to take the form of a universal principle? Why is it impossible to approve of unique actions and works precisely because they are unique, for instance in art? Besides, it seems to me that even these basal reasons need not take the form of propositions. Why should not the perceived goodness of love be sufficient basis for approving of love without the explicit premise that "I approve of everything that is love"? But the basic question is whether basal reasons should really be included among the constituents of approval itself. This seems to me an unwarranted interpretation of the unquestionably close connection between approval and the supporting cognitive acts. Toward Pitcher's third constituent, the claim to universal validity of these reasons for anyone in the same position, I feel in principle much more sympathetic. Approval does indeed make a general appeal to be universally valid. But this is again no reason to include this appeal among the constituents of approval itself.

plete act, and that it forms an inseparable part of a larger complex of acts. Maybe this complex, consisting of the recognition of the reasons of approval and of approval itself, would deserve an embracing name. But none seems to offer itself thus far, and a synthetic label such as "reason-backed approval" would do little good. Also, such unity does not do away with the essential articulation within this complex, whose proper full expression would run somewhat like this: "I see that this is better, and I also can see that it ought to be approved, and therefore I will (perhaps reluctantly) approve of it." Approval then has its essential reasons. But these form as little a part and parcel of the approval itself as premises form part of the conclusion or legal reasons part of the court sentence.

X. TYPES OF APPROVAL

Having thus described the general structure of approval I want to pay some attention to its varieties. Here again I shall use ordinary language as my first guide. On this basis I distinguish the following dimensions of possible variation:

1. *Intensity.* We speak of "strong approval" and compare different approvals according to "strength." This usage seems to refer to the characteristic intensity of each approval, depending on the weight which we are willing to give to our act and indirectly to the *approbatum.* Phrases like "to approve greatly" point presumably to intensity. It should, however, be noticed that strength of approval is not simply a function of the value of the *approbandum* nor of its worthiness of being approved. The strength of our approval also depends on the degree of our personal involvement and interest, an interest which probably would make us more ready to take action on behalf of the *approbatum.*

2. *Conditionality of Approval.* When we speak of "wholehearted approval" as compared to "half-hearted approval," the reference is probably not so much to the intensity as to the unconditional or conditional character of our approval. Our approval may depend on certain conditions, not yet fulfilled, or we may have reservations, mental or outspoken, which qualify an approval that may otherwise be quite strong. There may also be weak but unqualified approval, for instance in connection with certain esthetic or utilitarian improvements.

3. *Emotional Tone.* When we speak of "warm" or "lukewarm" approval or similar "temperatures" of our approving, we may of course mean the same as intensity or conditionality. However, normally these adjectives would seem to express something else, i.e., primarily degrees of emotional satisfaction that go along with such approval, our being pleased or uneasy, our good or mingled feelings at the thought of the approved. For instance, in politics it makes sense to approve of certain awkward necessities strongly but with mixed feelings ("with one laughing and one weeping eye"), and thus clearly with little if any warmth. Whether or not there can be completely cold ("ice cold"), i.e., entirely unemotional approval, is something which I would not like to decide on merely a *priori* grounds. The judge or the artistic or gastronomical expert or tester would provide the chief test cases in this matter. Yet I do not see any reason in the nature of approval to deny this possibility, both in the case of sanctioning and of acknowledging approval. Incidentally, the fact of variations in the degree of emotional warmth, as well as the possibility of its total absence in the presence of the same intensity of approval, would be further evidence in support of the view that approval cannot be primarily an emotion.

Enthusiastic approval, in contrast to an approval that is "unenthusiastic" or "rather artificial," probably belongs in the same category as warmth of approval, particularly as expressed in applause, usually collective, that most telling language of approval.

4. *Quality.* Of potentially much greater importance are modifications in the quality of approval which may be signified by the adjectives of phrases such as "moral approval," "social approval," "esthetic approval," "scientifically approved," etc.

But we must not assume from the very start that such expressions stand for qualitative differences in the approving act itself. They may indicate merely differences in the sources or reasons for the same type of act. Or they may merely refer to different types of reactions to these acts.

XI. CONCLUSIONS

What is the significance of the preceding phenomenological analysis as applied to the problem of the nature of approval? At least three major points seem to me worth restating:

1. As far as the nature of approval itself is concerned, it turns out that the emotivists were right against the rationalists in holding that approval is not an act of reason or judgment. However, they were, wrong in asserting that approval is nothing but an emotion or emotive attitude. While it is true that most, and perhaps even all, approval is tinged by emotional tones and undertones, and that emotional responses follow the approving act, approval itself, in its actual and habitual form, constitutes a phenomenon *sui generis*, an act of siding with the approved in answer to its claims for approval.

2. Approval is anything but an unanalyzable phenomenon. By paying attention to its referential ("intentional") structure, we have observed a pattern of elements and relationships in approval itself and in its essential relations to other phenomena. Specifically the following features proved essential:

(a) the constituents of act and content, related by intentional reference;

(b) the act of taking up a stance in response to claims of the approved;

(c) the experiences which undergird approval, i.e., the acts which supply its essential foundation such as sensing the claims to approval and the values that form a necessary, though not sufficient, base for these claims.

3. Approval is by no means the one and only important experience in the sphere of value. To believe that "values are nothing but a matter of approval and that is the end of the story" would be to ignore the most important part of the total pattern. It may be the end in the sequence of value experiences, but it is only the beginning of the story as far as the exploration of the phenomena of value is concerned. For approval by its very nature refers back to such grounding experiences as the noticing of the claim to approval (approvableness) and of the value characteristics that make the object of approval worth approving. It is here that the real and most important task of a phenomenological analysis begins.

XII. THE EVIDENCE OF ETYMOLOGY

Before leaving the analysis proper of approval I cannot resist the temptation of indulging in lining up some evidence from etymology. It cannot be considered as conclusive by itself regarding the structure of the phenomena but as suggestive and corroborative about it.

It requires little etymological ingenuity to see that the verb to approve and the nouns approval and approbation are derivatives of the Latin *probare*, i.e., to prove. It is less generally realized that this word in its original meaning meant not so much a deductive demonstration as "to probe," to examine ("Prove all things; hold fast what is good"). Even the derivative "to approve" had originally the now obsolete meaning of "to give evidence," "show to be real." Later the root word carried not only the meaning of the Latin *probare*, i.e. to prove by demonstration, but also of approval ("video meliora probo- que . . ."). Thus the etymological history of the word suggests a close connection with empirically provable reasons, or, as Pascal might have put it, a *logique du coeur*.

What the prefix *ad-* in front of the original verb seems to express is adherence to, assenting to, giving support to such "proving," in other words, a personal response or reaction to the intellectual operation which tries to show the "probity," the propriety of the thing approved. It is in accordance with this original meaning that the word "approvable" seems to have carried, much more than now, the connotation of "being worthy of approval."

This literal meaning, linking up approval with rational proof, seems all the more remarkable, since the word "assent," which we nowadays reserve for cases of intellectual agreement, in its literal and etymological meaning refers to a sentiment, a mere feeling rather than to a proof. Thus it would appear that in English, as well as in Latin and the Romance languages, matters subject to approval were originally considered even more accessible to intellectual proof than matters reserved for "assent" or "dissent."

Similar testimony to the cognitive, if not intellectual, character of approval may be collected from the Germanic and Slavic languages. (Greek does not seem to have an exact equivalent.) Thus German *"billigen"* is related to *"billig,"* an adjective which stands for "what corresponds to the natural sense of rightness" (Hermann Paul, *Deutsches Wörterbuch* [Halle: Niemeyer, 1960]). The Russian word, *odobrénie*, contains the root *"dobre,"* i.e., the adjective for "good."

Just how much significance should one attach to such etymological observations? There is obviously the danger of overestimating the "wisdom of language" to the extent of crediting it with deeper insights than any one of its users ever had. Also we may easily fall victim to all sorts of literalistic oversubtleties on the one hand and equivocations on the other. Nevertheless, etymology reflects to some extent the history of common sense. For common sense too it a historical phenomenon. To go back to the original meanings of words and their components can thus acquaint us with the original views and perspectives of mankind. These may or may not have been closer to the truth. But they are certainly worth listening to at a time when we have lost the richness of connotations which words carried for earlier generations. Thus the fact that they felt that there is something provable in matters of value and oughtness is certainly worth weighing, even though by itself it would be no conclusive evidence for proving the case for ethical rationalism.

12. "WE": A LINGUISTIC AND PHENOMENOLOGICAL ANALYSIS[1]

> We felt that the right to say "we" required so much more than the simple "revolution" that was to resolve everything.
> Richard Zorza, *The Right to Say "We"*
> (New York: Praeger, 1970, p. 21)

> Monday
> Cloudy today, wind in the east, think we shall have rain ... *We?* Where did I get that word? ...
> I remember now–the new creature uses it.
> Mark Twain, *Extracts from Adam's Diary*
> (New York: Harper and Bros., 1904, p. 3)

This essay has three major objectives. The first is to me the most urgent one. I believe that it is time to challenge the social arrogance expressed in the universal tendency to say "we," "us," and "our" when one has no business talking for anyone but oneself. This tendency is part of the "arrogance of power" behind the patronizing usurpation of the right to speak for the "free" people of the world, when they have never been asked, or the arrogant claim to speak for the "old" or the "new" generation, for "we philosophers," and even for "we phenomenologists." It is time to check on the credentials for such impostures.

My second objective is more esoteric. I wish to show in a concrete instance that the seeming antagonism between analytic, and especially linguistic, philosophy and phenomenology is based on misunderstandings. Both have legitimate tasks. I would like to show how they can even cooperate and contribute to a cumulative answer to the specific issue I am raising.

[1] Published as "On the Right to Say 'We'," in George Psathas, ed., *Phenomenological Sociology* (Baltimore: John Wiley & Sons, Inc., 1973, pp. 129-156); read in part as Alfred Schutz Memorial Lecture at Boston University, April 13, 1972. The quotation from Mark Twain was contributed by my friend Charles Courtney.

My third objective is to initiate the exploration of a basic concept in the social sciences which, to the best of my knowledge, has not yet been tackled: the linguistic meaning of the personal pronoun "we" and the structure of the phenomenon that corresponds to it.

Obviously I shall be unable to reach all, if any, of these objectives. It is difficult enough to kill two birds with one stone. Three are bound to escape unhurt. This I won't mind. The important thing to me is to stir them up, or, to change the metaphor, to bell three cats.

Social philosophy, sociology, and even phenomenological sociology talk a great deal about "we," about "we-ness," "we-hood" and the "we-relation." But I am not aware of more than passing remarks about the language and the meanings of "we"-saying. For such purposes one would have to turn to the new philosophy of ordinary language. But even here I have not come across any general discussion of the pronoun "we" and its "grammar." [2] Pronouns are usually lumped together as "indexical signs," with no significant structural differences among them. This lack of differentiation is indicated by their symmetrical grammatical numbering. The chief example is the "I," with occasional references to the other persons of the singular. Only comparative linguistic offers observations such as the distinction between the inclusive and the exclusive "we."

Thus the linguistic analysis of we-talk in general is apparently unbroken ground. I enter it with some trepidation, but in the hope that what I can offer here will at least stimulate others to cultivate it in more definitive fashion than can I, for whom this example is largely a test case for possible cooperation between linguistic analysis and phenomenology. In making such a raid I have tried to utilize some of the new tools forged by its pioneering master, John L. Austin, in *How to Do Things with Words*.

---

[2] Since I gave the Schutz lecture Professor Joel Feinberg has drawn my attention to an essay by M. B. Foster, " 'We' in Modern Philosophy," in B. Mitchell, ed., *Faith and Logic* (London: Allen & Unwin, 1957, pp. 194-200). However, in this article Foster is concerned only with the way in which such analytic philosophers as G. E. Moore use the pronoun in their writings addressed to possible readers with whom they are not in direct contact. The neglect of attention to the first person plural pronoun is confirmed by Stanley Cavell, *Must We Mean What We Say?* (New York: Scribner's, 1969, p. 16). The most original but narrow treatment of the we-phenomenon by a "phenomenological ontologist" can be found in Jean-Paul Sartre, *L'Être et le néant*, Part III, Chapter 3, Section 3.

I propose to begin with a linguistic analysis of ordinary we-talk. I shall then undertake in two stages a phenomenological analysis of what corresponds to it in our experience, first determining the essential structure of the phenomenon meant and then of the ways and degree in which it is given subjectively. Finally, I intend to make some first recommendations on the right to say "we" in the light of these analyses.

A LINGUISTIC ANALYSIS OF WE-TALK

First Distinctions

In beginning with the we-talk of ordinary language I shall mention merely in passing such clearly secondary uses of the pronoun as the editorial "we" and the plurals of majesty and of modesty. Even if grammatically defensible, all of them seem to me morally questionable. The best case one could make for them is that in special cases they seem to deemphasize the self-important single ego or to express a generous identification with "fellow sinners." But mostly they are devices of evasion of personal responsibility and of false pretense. Some of them, such as the plural of majesty, have interesting historical roots originating in the period of double emperorship in the early Roman empire, leading later to an inflation of the single sovereign into a many-headed superman. As to the plural of modesty there is something cowardly, if not funny, in surrounding oneself with imaginary others, as if it were not much more pretentious to speak in the name of others as well as of one's seemingly self-effacing little I.

The situation is much more serious in the case of the editorial we, used all too often even in philosophical writing. I believe that only in very rare cases has an author any business speaking for his listeners or readers – only when he has good reasons to believe that they have already had a chance to share his own experience. Otherwise the editorial we is nothing but an underhanded attempt to overwhelm one's audience by persuasion, not giving it even a chance to test, accept, or reject one's opinions. I consider such seeming selflessness as sheer usurpation. Unless the editor speaks at least for a board or with special authorization, this is simply intellectual dishonesty and self-importance in disguise. Yet I know how hard it is to suppress it

– and that in spite of strenuous efforts I myself am likely to provide additional examples of this bad habit.[3]

I now turn to the use of the "we" in everyday discourse. Here I discern two basically different situations where use of the pronoun in its original sense occurs, depending on the presence or absence of those whom the speaker includes as his partners.

1. The *"we of copresence,"* as I shall call it, includes only people with whom the speaker stands in the kind of direct face-to-face relationship for which Alfred Schutz coined the term "consociates," as distinguished from mere "contemporaries." However, "copresents" need not be a small group of persons knowing one another personally. Even participants in a mass demonstration are copresent, although they know one another only "face to back." But they are at least in direct audiovisual contact with the speaker, to whom they can respond.[4]

2. The we in the absence of the we-partners I shall call the *absentee-we.* It occurs chiefly where the speaker talks to outsiders as a representative of contemporaries who are not only absent but whom he, at least usually, does not know in person; thus in the absence of any St. Louisians in the audience I can tell you Bostonians: "We in St. Louis are fond of your Boston Symphony broadcasts."

The We of Copresence

I shall focus first on the we of copresence. The word "we" like all personal pronouns is grammatically a substitute for a noun, such as a proper name or several names. As such it has at least indirectly objective reference and gives a certain amount of information about these referents, especially when it differentiates between the sexes. A pronoun differs from the represented nouns by not having a stable reference to one and only one referent. What name and object it refers to depends on the concrete occasion in which it is uttered and

---

[3] Even substituting the impersonal "one" for "we," as I am often doing, may be merely a partial remedy suggesting that I am speaking by way of generalization for everyone else–a generalization not to be taken lightly.

[4] The situation is different when the audience is addressed by transmission to another room, by radio, or by television, even though the listeners may have a chance to reach the speaker subsequently by telephonic questions. These are clearly transitional situations. Telephonic conversation, with or without visual screen, can establish copresence. And correspondents, though separated in time as well as in space, may use the we of copresence.

by whom. In this relativity to a variable point of reference pronouns are what is usually called "indexical signs" or "occasional expressions" (Husserl). However, personal pronouns do more than convey information about the nouns for which they stand. As uttered in a special situation they not only have "informative" meaning but perform certain functions that have not yet been sufficiently distinguished and described, particularly in the case of the "we" of copresence. I shall call these "formative" or, better, "transformative" meanings.

I shall begin with some informative meanings of the word "we":

1. "We" refers to more than one person, thus requiring multiple rays of meaning. It may mean these persons collectively, as in "we are together a part of humanity," or distributively, as in "we are all humans." "We" may refer to only two such beings, for which case a language like Samoan has a special form of the pronoun, the dual "we"; [5] but it may also include any number of referents; only, in the case of the we of copresence (consociates) it has to be a finite number.

2. "We" in this case refers to each and every member of this plurality in whatever is predicated of them. In this sense it makes a claim to "unanimity." Majority, however qualified, is not enough.

3. "We" points at a collection of referents standing in a polar relationship: the speaking "I" as the focal pole and the "we-partners" as counterpoles, as it were. And whereas the pronoun "I" is a self-referential sign referring back to the speaker himself, this is only partially true for "we," namely for its speaking I-pole. The situation may be different when all members respond to a challenge in unison by shouting "we," but even then the self-referential nature of the "we" is distributed over the contributory shouters.

4. The referents of "we" must be personal beings who the speaking "I" believes to be human beings. "We" is inapplicable to non-speaking beings, inanimate and animate, below the human level except in animal fables. Any attempt by an owner to include his domestic pets in a "we" can at best be a playful fiction.

5. "We" is basically equalitarian. Normally it can be applied only to personal beings of the same social standing or class. Especially in a nondemocratic or in a hierarchical organization such as an army a superior will hardly be included in we-talk in his presence by his

[5] "Ita-us" = for we two; see C. Bloomfield, *Language* (New York: Holt, 1961, p. 257).

inferiors, even if the superior may do this condescendingly with his subordinates.

6. We-talk makes sense only with regard to people capable of understanding the speaker acoustically and in a common language. It is senseless in the presence of a sleeping "audience" or one ignorant of the English language. In other words, "we" has a place only among mutually understanding partners.

7. "We" as used in English and many, if not most, other languages does not make it clear whether all those within reach are included, or some, in particular one or many persons to whom one is speaking, are excluded, either as individuals or as members of an "out-group." It is therefore not without interest that some languages distinguish between an inclusive and exclusive "we" – inclusive if addressing an in-group only, or exclusive if addressing an out-group, addressed of course as "you." [6]

I now turn to the formative or transforming functions of the we pronoun of copresence. When Austin claimed that one can do "things" with a phrase like "I promise," he referred only to utterances in the form of whole sentences. What I would like to show is that even single words such as pronouns have such power, much as this power has to be seen in the context of the total situation described by the surrounding sentences. [7]

The first of these transforming functions is that of social address. The we of copresence, whether inclusive or exclusive, is not merely informative, it also tries to do something to one's we-partners, to "tackle" them. It tries to make them (a) listen and (b) realize that they are appealed to as partners. But in what sense can such addressing be considered as a transformation of the situation? In itself the mere address does not lead to any change in the person addressed. However, such change does occur as soon as he pays attention to this appeal. His turning of face, his focusing on the speaker as his

---

[6] Bloomfield, *op. cit.,* p. 256 f. gives examples from the Algonquian language in which the inclusive and the exclusive "we" are distinguished by the prefixes "ke" and 'ne," respectively; the same is true of Samoan. The Spanish *"nosotros"* was originally exclusive like French *"nous autres"* but is now used also for inclusive purposes. See José Ortega y Gasset, *El Hombre y la gente,* Madrid. Revista de Occidente, 1957, pp. 139-140; English transl. *Man and People.* (New York: W. W. Norton, 1957, p. 111).

[7] That even single words have linguistic force is already suggested by W. Alston, *Philosophy of Language* (Englewood Cliffs, N.J.: Prentice-Hall, 1964, p. 36).

spokesman is what the address aims to bring about. Yet properly speaking addressing by itself is merely an attempt to make others "tune in," as it were. It merely exerts a certain social pressure or has "illocutionary force" (Austin). But only if such pressure is effective, and brings about a real change in the interpersonal field in the sense of Austin's "perlocutionary force," does it make sense to talk about an actual transformation of the social field. Strictly, we must distinguish therefore between the transforming intent and the transforming force or effect of words.

The primary example of this addressing function is the second person singular and plural pronoun "you" in English and its modifications in other languages such as the intimate "tu" in French and "du" in German, the more solemn or religious "thou" and the vocative case in Greek and Latin. Here the individual listener is tackled frontally, as it were. No wonder that so many languages try to soft-pedal this attack either by putting it in plural form, thus distributing the "shock," or by using the third person singular (Italian, Spanish) or plural (German) to divert the blow.

But the addressing function operates also, though in a less frontal manner, in the we of copresence with consociates, when the speaker expects the we-partners to be aware of the fact that he is speaking for them, that is, to listen and realize what he is saying to others. I do not mean to assert that always before saying "we" there has to be an explicit you-contact with these we-partners. It may be desirable to be on you-terms with a person before one includes him in one's we-talk, and some people might actually feel offended by it prior to having been formally introduced to the speaker.[8] In informal context the you-address may very well be implicit in the we-address. The main point is that the we of copresence, while uttered within the other's earshot, also addresses him. True, one does not address him "face-to-face." But there is also such a thing as an oblique addressing by implication, "face-by-face," as it were, appealing to him while at the same time inviting him to participate in some outwardbound action. "We protest" implies "You are my partner."

The addressing function of we-talk becomes even more explicit in

[8] In the following story from old-time northern Germany, a patriotic gentleman addresses an unknown elderly spinster: "Isn't it wonderful that we have another victory?" Spinster: "Sir, you have not yet been introduced to me."

the case of the exclusive "we." For here, in telling an outsider what "we others" think or feel, we still try to make him realize that he is being addressed.

But addressing and thus orienting one's consociates toward the speaker is not the only and the most characteristic "thing" done by we-talk. It is an attempt not only to attract his attention but to pull him over completely to the speaker's side, to claim him as an associate, or to "align" him. What is this function of alignment?

Perhaps the best way to exhibit this function is to compare it with those of other personal pronouns. At first sight one might think that there is a perfect parallel in their linguistic functions. But here one must not be misled by the categories of the grammarians as evidence of linguistic structure. This is not the place for analyzing all the functions of all the personal pronouns. Some of their peculiarities will serve as a foil for the analysis of the new we-function.

1. In saying "I," as in "I am talking," I am merely self-referentially pointing to myself; nothing else is "done" about and to the referent of my talking. Only by implication am I suggesting to my listener to transpose this "I" into the proper "you" or "he" if he wants to respond to me.

2. You-talk presents a very different picture, namely, the pure type of the addressing function as described previously.

3. The function of the third person singular is in this regard the very opposite of that of the second person. It not only leaves the referent untouched, normally it is used only "behind his back," and if used within his earshot, it has almost an insulting connotation, treating him as if absent. The third person pronoun has no social function in relation to its referent, since he is not even supposed to hear it. Its social function is restricted to describing to a second person someone not in present contact with either one of the speakers.

4. It needs little reflection to realize that the functions of the pronouns in the plural are more complex, since more than one person is referred to. The differences from the singular pronouns are perhaps easy to grasp in the case of the second and third person plural. For what is involved is simply the multiplication of the functions of the singular pronouns. In the case of the "you" in the plural, several persons are addressed at the same time. The only new feature is that they are addressed collectively, in this sense lumped together, with the understanding that they are in mutual social contact, not separate,

and are on the same social level, not superiors and inferiors such as God, man and animal, master and slave. In the case of the third person, "they," no such "lumping" is implied: "They" may be single or in a group. In fact, the "they" in English also has the function of the notorious "*man*" in German, the anonymous other or others, faceless and no longer individualized as to singular or plural.

In the case of the "we" of copresence the situation is very different. Here the speaker, in referring to himself and to others whom he wants to include, tries two things: (a) As to himself, he describes his own part and also commits himself to whatever the we-sentence predicates about him, at least in the case of an action; this implies doing it together with the we-partners. (b) As to the others, the speaker claims them *as partners* taking the same position as he himself does. This claim is, at least on the surface, mostly a factual one, asserting that the others already share his position. But it also implies the intent to make them acknowledge their alignment with him, the speaker. This involves a transformational function, especially in fluid situations. Here the use of the "we" may be an attempt of the speaker, more or less underhanded, to swing others over to his position and to make them join him. In both cases the use of the "we" uttered in the copresence of others involves an attempt to influence one's consociates and transform them into associates.

"We" as Used in the Absence of We-Partners: The Absentee We

The situation is basically changed when the "we" is used in the absence of those for whom one claims to speak. Not only is this "we" essentially an exclusive we, excluding all those addressed, there are also other important differences in both the informative and the transformative function with regard to the absent we-partners included.

The number of fellow-beings for whom the speaker claims to speak need not be known even to himself. Perhaps no one knows it. However, in this case, where the we-fellows are not delimited by presence within earshot, it is essential that "we" be specified as a certain class of persons such as "we sociologists" or "we phenomenologists." However, it does not seem necessary to restrict the range of absentee we's to contemporaries, although the right to speak for one's predecessors and successors is more than problematic. But as far as predecessors are concerned, a statement like "We Americans have always stood for self-determination" not only makes linguistic good sense but may, on the basis of the historical record, be even more justified than with regard to our contemporaries. However, a sentence like "We Americans will always stand for self-determination," which tries to commit even our unborn successors, is not only risky but unwarranted in principle, since we can have no evidence for their future actions. To that extent such a statement is sheer arrogance.

Even more important is the difference in the transforming functions of the absentee we. First, this is not the situation of a speaker addressing we-partners, since by definition the absentees are beyond the range of his direct address. Whatever addressing occurs is directed at the listeners in front of the speaker, and this address will take the form of the second person.

Moreover, the aligning function by which the speaker tried to enlist copresent we-partners is obviously impossible in any literal sense. Yet the speaker who talks in the name of his absent we-partners clearly means to commit them in some manner and degree. How is this possible? Clearly it presupposes some prior authorization or subsequent ratification. In this sense all we-talk in the absence of the committed is on credit, as it were. The decisive question is whether or not the speaker has some kind of a proxy for them. Without it, all we-talk in the absence of the we-partners is clearly false pretense. Hence the speakers' credentials have to be based on such explicit authorization as an election or a vote. This is perhaps not always possible and necessary. But unless he can produce good reasons as to why he need not bother about possible protests from his we-partners, he had better be on his guard – and so had his listeners.

(Note: An interesting case of the use of "we" occurs in philosophical writings as discussed in M. B. Foster's pioneer article mentioned in footnote 2. These writings address only potential readers, who are not copresent unless the papers were read to a live audience. Either they speak in the name of "we modern philosophers," who are likewise absent, or sometimes of "all of us," meaning the users of the King's English.

What is also interesting is that Foster points out that in using "we,"

the philosopher is not reporting a usage which he has observed in himself and among his associates. The utterance seems more like those which Professor Austin has taught us to call "performatory." In using the first person plural I am not merely describing a usage but I am subscribing to it, or expressing my own adhesion to it.[9]

However, Foster is concerned only with the "performance" of the commitment by the speaker to the use of a certain language. The aspect of claiming the we-partners for this use and one's right to claim them is never questioned or even mentioned. The fact that Foster is concerned merely with the absentee – we case also makes it of particular importance to him to determine what is the group or society of persons to which the "we" refers. It turns out to be "we men.")

Strengths and Weaknesses of Linguistic Analysis

Thus far I have attempted merely a sample of linguistic analysis. By studying the use of the pronoun "we" in various settings I have tried to determine its functions, attending to the phenomena meant by these uses only insofar as they are needed to understand these utterances. Beyond that I have made no attempt to analyze the structure of the phenomena referred to in themselves and for their own sakes.

Nevertheless, I submit that this analysis has yielded some important results even for phenomenology. Some of these may be merely negative in the sense that they can break up certain stereotypes that have interfered with the unprejudiced approach to the phenomena. Thus the linguistic study of the ordinary use of personal pronouns can help us to get rid of the type of thing-like entities that go with the substantivization of the live pronouns into "the I" (*das Ich*), or "the we," or we-hood, all terms that do not occur in our everyday speech.[10] Such linguistic monsters have invaded even the language of phenomenologists. There may be good reasons for introducing technical terms (even linguistic analysis has found it necessary to invent a meta-language); but it is more important to pay attention first to the concrete occasions in which the ordinary words occur, and what they refer to here.

[9] Foster, *op. cit.*, pp. 196-197.
[10] A particularly striking example of such hypostatization can be found in Fritz Künkel's *Das Wir, Die Grundbegriffe der Wir-psychologie* (Darmstadt: Wissenschaftliche Buchgesellschaft, 1972). His "we-experiences" (*Wirerlebnisse*) need not be denied by questioning his uncritical interpretation without prior linguistic and phenomenological analysis.

Also by immediately introducing such highpower terminology one may very well conceal the basic phenomena underneath a scientific superstructure. I maintain that this is exactly what has happened in social philosophy in the case of "the we." I hope that the previous examples have shown that the study of the concrete uses of the personal pronouns in actual situations reveals that "we" can mean very different phenomena. An embargo on all reifying substantivization could very well at the same time unclutter and enrich social phenomenology.

But this does not mean that linguistic analysis and even linguistic phenomenology can take the place of phenomenology. Even Austin knew and stated explicitly that linguistic analysis can supply only the "first word" [11] in the exploration of the phenomena. But he did not state who is to say the last word. He himself certainly never tried to go beyond the first word. Linguistic analysis can tell us what we actually do with words, for example, that certain utterances can make changes in the world, and, if I am right, then certain pronouns direct or even align people. But it fails to describe what exactly is taking place on the side of the phenomena, for instance, in the case of such performatory transformations. What is the structure of these changes? Linguistic analysis, after having distinguished different uses of these utterances, simply stops, as if, once the phenomena are properly distinguished, one knows all about them. That this is not the case is what I would like to show for the two main uses of "we" which I have distinguished.

Furthermore, it is not enough to establish the finer shades of meaning in present ordinary language. Language is no ultimate fact, it has developed historically. Hence it is important to understand why distinctions have developed, and, more specifically, what features in the phenomena are responsible for such differentiations. Such understanding requires insight into the phenomena themselves. To provide it is one of the objectives of phenomenological analysis proper. True, linguistic analysis supplies a grammar of ordinary language more differentiated and sophisticated than the grammar of the grammarians. In fact, for Wittgenstein the final goal of philosophy seems to have coincided with the discovery of a philosophical grammar (which

---

[11] "A Plea for Excuses" in *Philosophical Papers* (Oxford: Clarendon, 1961, p. 133).

at one time he oddly identified with "phenomenology").[12] Now grammar can tell the correct way of talking, for instance, in the case of the "we" and distinguish between "proper use" and solecisms. But no attempt is made to account for the rules of this grammar, leaving them as nothing but arbitrary brute facts of history.

Finally, in the case of performative expressions, all the reader is told is that certain utterances, for example promises, have the "force" to bring about such changes in the world as obligations. This sounds like word magic as practiced by sorcerers. At best such expressions can be understood metaphorically. What do the metaphors stand for? What is really going on when a word makes a difference in the world of facts? And how is such "word magic" possible? This calls, even clamors, for a description of the actual happenings in our experience – for a concrete phenomenology.

TOWARD A PHENOMENOLOGY OF THE WE-CONSCIOUSNESS

What I intend to do here is to give at least a first idea of how phenomenology can further enrich the study of the we-phenomena with a view to determining the right to say "we." I shall not waste time by a lengthy explanation of what is meant or rather what I mean by the still mystifying label "phenomenology." I hope this will become sufficiently apparent from "doing it," leaving it to further reflections what it is or was that I have been doing. But I still have to state what specific task I want to attack. From now on I shall focus no longer on what it is proper to *say* in a certain situation – which is the primary concern of linguistic philosophy – but on what it is that we *see* in it, describing the seen as fully and as faithfully as I can, and on exploring the ways in which it is given me, regardless of whether what I thus experience is ultimately real or merely a phenomenon. I shall try to demonstrate this kind of phenomenology [13] in two stages.

[12] Herbert Spiegelberg, "The Puzzle of *Wittgenstein's Phaenomenologie* 1929 - ?" *American Philosophical Quarterly,* V, 1968, pp. 244-256.

[13] This version is a slight simplification of the phenomenological approach advocated by Alexander Pfänder, which in turn is a development of certain key ideas in Husserl's pre-idealistic phenomenology. See my *The Phenomenological Movement* (The Hague: Martinus Nijhoff, 1965, pp. 180-185); and Alexander Pfänder, *Phenomenology of Willing and Motivation and Other Phenomenologica* (Evanston, Ill.: Northwestern University Press, 1967). Many of the substantive ideas in the subsequent section parallel those of Gerda Walther,

1. *Clarification of the Phenomenon as Meant* (*Phenomenological Ontology*). A phenomenological investigation as here conceived demands a clear understanding of one's beliefs about such phenomena as life, social relations, or values before looking for them in actual experience. This stage begins with the elimination of vague and distorting interpretations of the phenomena. But it has also to determine positively the typical or essential structure of the phenomena meant. In this sense it is a (non-metaphysical) ontology. This enterprise has been cultivated particularly by the early Göttingen-Munich branch of phenomenology.

2. *Exploration of the Phenomena as Given* (*Phenomenology of Appearances*). Clarity of meaning with regard to the phenomenon as meant is no guarantee that it is actually given. To establish this fact, one has to explore how far it is present in our experience. To many phenomena as meant nothing may correspond at all. Or they may be given only indirectly and partially, as they are presented in various perspectives. The study of these modes of givenness is clearly of crucial importance for the answer to the question of whether one can claim real knowledge about the phenomena meant. Adequate knowledge as conceived by Husserl implies that the phenomenon meant is given in such a way that all meanings are fulfilled and that no new perspectives can upset one's anticipations. Since, for instance, in the case of three-dimensional visual perceptions there can be infinite perspectives, adequate knowledge is impossible in principle. Even without such adequacy knowledge can still be direct and reach the thing itself or "in person" as it were; but knowledge of such objects lacks complete certainty. In any case, the knowledge claim has to be measured against *what* is actually given and *how* it is given. This is why the analysis of the phenomena as meant has to be followed by a critical investigation of the phenomena as given or of what appears.

Clarification of the We-Phenomenon as Meant

We-consciousness means consciousness of "we" or, better, of being we or us, and thus implies a distinction between the object of

---

who developed Pfänder's phenomenological psychology in "Zur Ontologie der sozialen Gemeinschaften," *Jahrbuch für Philosophie und phänomenologische Forschung,* VI, 1923, pp. 1-158. However, my conception of "union" and "unionizing acts" does not coincide with their conception of "*Einigung.*"

consciousness (Husserl's "intentional object") and the condition or state of being conscious (his "intentional act"). Although both would have to be examined in parallel manner, I shall in the present context concentrate on the object or content of the we-consciousness. What are its essential constituents? One particularly helpful way of determining them is by imaginative variation, adding or leaving off some, one at a time. I shall begin by leaving off such factors with a view to pointing out certain prestages of the full we-phenomenon.

I would like to focus on a specific case of we-consciousness, namely, the situation which my readers could experience in listening to a live lecture.

Prestages of the We-Phenomenon. Suppose, in listening to the lecture, each reader were to hear the lecture alone on his private television set. Suppose he also did not know whether anyone else was listening to it. Obviously in such a situation there could be no we-consciousness. Even if there should be parallel listeners on other sets, as long as they do not know of one another, the essential precondition for the formation of we-consciousness is missing.

Suppose now that he were in the same room as a member of an audience who knows that he has neighbors undergoing the same kind of auditory, if not intellectual and emotional, experience as he is. But assume also – and this is probably true for most – that they have not yet had a chance, and probably never will have, to make contact among each other, as it happens usually in the movies in contrast to theaters and concert halls. Now is mere awareness of parallel experiences enough to establish a social bond among them? I submit that this situation is conducive to developing we-consciousness, but that thus far the social relationship remains unchanged. Two witnesses to the same event, even if they know of one another, are not necessarily co-witnesses. In fact, the value of their testimonies will to no small extent depend on their not yet having taken up contact.

Suppose now you not only know about your fellow listener's experiences but also are in personal contact with him, either before these experiences or subsequently by talking with him. Is this a sufficient condition for developing a we-consciousness and the use of we-language? By itself such contact means only a "you" relation, in which each one sees his partner face-to-face at a certain (social) distance. At this stage, in discussing the shared experience, one might say: "You seem to have had the same experience I had" and even "you and I seem to see eye to eye on this issue." But there is an experiential difference once one substitutes for "you and I" and even for "I and thou" the single pronoun "we." There is more than verbal economy involved in a switch from one expression to the other. The two may be equivalent, and the former may be a stage on the way to the other. But phenomenologically they do not coincide. What is the difference?

Stages of the We-Union. At this stage on the scale of variations I shall introduce a substantially new factor. Thus far the partners in the social relation I have described have maintained their separate stations in getting to know and making contact with each other. But these positions themselves can be subjected to variation. They may be increased and decreased. Finally, instead of confronting one another across a social distance the partners in you-contact may perform a peculiar shift: they "turn their faces" and "move together," as it were. By "turning faces" I do not mean that they abandon their face-to-face relationship. But now they no longer confront one another, but face outward from a new common station. By "moving together" I mean an attempt to move from one's prior separate station to one single position, no longer separated by a social distance. Obviously all such characterizations are metaphorical and require translation into more direct phenomenological description. But such a description would require the framework of a phenomenological social psychology as outlined for instance by Alexander Pfänder. It is enough in the present context if they can be suggestive of phenomena still to be explored in greater depth.

But what is even more important here is to focus on what goes on after this shift: the link-up of the joiners in a new union. Here each abandons his separateness (though not his individuality) and enters an embracing whole, whose parts dovetail. In this whole each claims the other as belonging to him and is claimed by the other in return. In this sense and to this extent they might be said to identify and become "solidaric" through a kind of "soldering" which imbeds them into a "solid" unit, as the etymology of the word "solidaric" suggests. This change could and should be described even more concretely by attending to the experiences in each partner, such as their feeling no longer separate and alone, but of being "together," "united," "at one," or "merged." But all these expressions must ultimately be understood as invitations to enter and live through vicarious experiences all too easily ignored and made trivial.

What I have characterized thus far is clearly an ideal case. Few if any situations where one uses "we" in ordinary discourse attain this kind of solidarity. Yet I maintain that they all contain some degree of it. Nevertheless, it is important to distinguish between the following different types of we-unions:

1. We-unions may be *strong* or *weak* according to how much their partners have "invested" in them. The casual and unemphatic way in which we use the "we" in ordinary conversation certainly does not express the kind of solidarity that would resist questioning or pressure.

2. The union may be *permanent* or merely *temporary* and even limited to a single occasion, to be disbanded immediately after it has passed. Only a few we-unions are meant to establish lasting associations.

3. The union may be *superficial* or *deep*. Especially in their emotions partners may remain completely uninvolved. These dimensions of strength, duration, and depth can and must be explored by a phenomenological sociology.

Thus the we-union implies more than an external link-up, comparable to the riveting of beams into a steel frame, or to the jamming of passengers into a public conveyance, where actually physical closeness makes social closeness next to impossible. Union is not merely a matter of removing distance, physical or social, but the establishment of a new positive relationship within the union. It means that its partners not only "touch," but "embrace" one another in a nonliteral sense. By these terms I mean to suggest that each partner tries to include the other and his experience within his own parallel experience ("I experience you as experiencing happiness"), to participate or share in it. This need not mean that he experiences the other's experience exactly like his own. But whenever they hear or sing the same song together as "we," and not only as he, she, or they, or as "you and I," each partner in his experience is conscious of the other's experiencing, coexperiences it, and identifies with it. Thus the other partner's experience is part of the prime partner's own. Of course it does not form a real but merely an "intentional" part of it, is mentally included in it. Such coexperiencing may mean anything from mere awareness to full empathy. It is at best vicarious. Nevertheless, it is an integral element of the primary experiences. In this sense each partner enters the experience of the other. Their experiences interpenetrate. Obviously here even more than in the case of the personal union the interpenetration may vary in extent and intensity.

Among additional features essential to a fully developed and strong we-union are the following:

1. The union, being based on the reciprocity of the independent contributions of several partners, needs reinforcements to keep it viable. One of these is the belief, implicit or explicit, that one's own contribution is reciprocated, and that the union is not merely one-sided, as it happens only too often in friendship and love. One could speak here of trust in the reciprocity of the we-acts contributed by each partner.

2. But even this trust may not be enough. For if I cannot trust your reciprocating trust in me (and vice versa, you cannot do so), my primary trust will be misplaced. In other words, without a secondary trust in the other's primary trust in me and vice versa, the first trust and the union lose strength.

3. At this point there is clearly room for an infinite regress. Although theoretically possible, such iteration has diminishing phenomenological and practical returns. Only in rare cases may it be important to spell out and check on these higher-order trusts in reciprocity; usually they lack significance.

Other complementary features of a strong we-union are connected with the fact that we-acts and the coexperiences based on them essentially stand in a wider context. Thus the experiences of each we-partner are part of the setting of his personal world as their *background horizon*. The we-acts performed by a socialite mean something quite different from those of a person in a less socially crowded world. Now in coexperiencing his fellow partner's world each partner will see it only in more or less adequate perspective. Yet a full understanding of the other's world will include at least some perspective of it. In order to understand actions including the we-acts of a Chinese I have to have a picture of the world he lives in (as he needs one of mine).

Again, this is not the end of the story. For the other's social world as I see it in perspective includes his picture of my world as he sees mine, that is, very probably a caricature of it. This perspective of the other's perspective is what R. D. Laing calls a "metaperspective." Such metaperspectives of the other's perspective can of course again be reflected in endless iteration. My perspective of the caricature of the psychotic's picture of the "normal" world will be mirrored and probably again distorted in a possible psychotic view of the normal perspective on him. In principle there is no end to such iterations of perspectives. But their importance drops with each iteration. What is practically important for better understanding is to work on a correction of the distorting metaperspectives toward a gradual assimilation of the primary perspectives as the basis for a possible better we-union.

The main result of the preceding analysis of the ontological meaning of the we-phenomenon may be summed up in the following statements:

1. The phenomenon meant by the we-pronoun is a union of several persons into a whole in which they experience themselves as solidaric partners.

2. These partners embrace and interpenetrate each other's experiences vicariously in their coexperiences.

3. They trust in each other's reciprocal acts.

4. These acts are imbedded in one another's worlds.

In the preceding direct approach to the phenomena I have thus far avoided most of the terms applied to the we-phenomena in the past. Thus I have not used the term "we-relationship" (Schutz' most frequent term) not because I deny that there are characteristic relations between the partners of a we-union, but because what seems even more important to me is the encompassing union based on such relations of which the we-partners form integral members.

Defective We-Unions. Normally one might pay attention only to situations where all members of the we-group use we-language with each other and, perhaps more frequently, in talking to outsiders. But this should not make one overlook the case when there is no perfect reciprocity. In a nation torn by class struggle or an international organization torn by power groups some of these may cease to use we-talk in relation to the other members of whom they think only as "they" or "you." Such a we-group is certainly incomplete, if not "sick." If this sickness is incurable, the we-union has become an illusion or a fiction. Meanwhile it is important to realize that the we-phenomenon is not only dependent on one partner's perspective but interdependent on that of several, though not always of all of them. Such defects can occur both in the copresence and in the absence of the we-partners. In their copresence they are perhaps more likely to come to the surface, especially in a free, democratic atmosphere that does not suppress dissent. In the absence of the we-partners their reciprocating acts are not only likely to become marginal and potential, but finally to vanish, leaving the we-speaker unsupported in midair, as it were.

Exploration of the We-Phenomenon as Given

The preceding attempt to describe the structure of the we-phenomenon as really meant in one's everyday beliefs provides no assurance that such meaning is fulfilled in actual experiences and hence epistemologically justified. This can be established only by that branch of phenomenology which examines how and how far this phenomenon appears in intuitive experience (*Anschauung*). I shall therefore try to examine next some of the appearances of the we-phenomenon.

The Perspectives of the We-Phenomenon. Like all other social phenomena the we-phenomenon is given not only to one but to several subjects distributively. There is no phenomenological evidence for the existence of a we-subject to which the we-phenomenon could appear all at once. Consequently the we-phenomenon, as distinguished, for instance, from the you-phenomenon, can be given fully only in the composite experiences of the several partners making up the we-union. Here one has to distinguish between the viewing partner or I-pole and the viewed partners or counterpoles joined with him. Both are given only in the perspectives of each I-pole. What does this asymmetry mean for the givenness of the symmetrical we-union?

Obviously such perspectives are lopsided as compared with the balanced perspective one may have of an outside object of which one is not a part. One partner of the we-union, the viewing I, can be given only obliquely in acts of reflection, whereas the other partners are given straightforwardly and frontally, as it were. This situation is comparable only to that of the givenness of one's own body to vision from within the body, where one's head and the eyes cannot be seen directly. Thus it seems appropriate to consider the givenness of these two aspects of the composite we-union separately.

Beginning with the appearance of the other we-partners as the counterpoles of the we-union, one has to face up to the general problem of knowledge of other persons and their experiences. Settling this vexing problem is clearly beyond the scope and control of this essay. All that can and need be done is to proceed on the assumption that (a) such knowledge is possible, and (b) other bodies and other "minds" and their acts are given more or less directly. True, such knowledge is always inadequate: one can never exhaust all aspects of other minds in all conceivable perspectives, and one is therefore always in for surprises to one's anticipating beliefs concerning new perspectives, at least in principle. Some of these inadequacies in the perception of persons, for example, those affecting one's perception of other people's bodies with regard to their backs or their insides, may be irrelevant for our knowledge of their minds and mental acts. But even so there remains enough ambiguity, for instance in their bodily expressions, to make other-mind knowledge ambiguous and precarious. This general situation is modified by the specific factors entering the we-perception. Thus the other's abandoning of his separateness by joining a solidaric union may be given quite vividly through speech and gesture.

But, quite apart from ambiguous cases, one is never safe from deceitful pretense. As far as the second feature of we-unions is concerned, the interpenetration of the partners through vicarious co-experience, one is clearly on even more treacherous ground. True, one is not without clues for such an extension of direct experience beyond the immediately given. Furthermore, the others may bear us out in the case of more responsive partners. But they may also be merely trying to please us and lull us into overconfidence. This is particularly true of the trust in the union which one would like to find in others. There are perfectly valid tokens of their trust, but even so we cannot assess their trust directly. This is of course multiply true of the iteration of their trust (e.g., their trust in our trust of their trust) which can never be adequately given in principle but at best non-intuitively in the "etc."-consciousness of infinite series.

All this applies even more fully to our knowledge of their encompassing social world as horizon for the unionizing acts. At best we can construct and imagine parts of this world and depend for the rest on volunteered information communicated at our request. Thus the other half (in a dual union) and an even larger proportion (in a plural union) is given directly only in part, and never adequately beyond the possibility of error or deception.

What then about the self-knowledge of the I-pole of the we-union and his own unionizing experiences? One may hope to achieve all the self-evidence of the Cartesian *ego-cogito* for this facet of the we-union. But here too one has to be on one's guard against Cartesian oversimplifications. Self-knowledge, especially adequate self-knowledge in reflection, is anything but self-evident, once one becomes aware of the possibilities of self-deception, for which psychopathology and psychoanalysis have supplied unsettling evidence. Moreover, the general epistemology of self-knowledge poses serious problems, especially for the phenomenology of the temporal appearances of the self. Thus full thematic self-perception is possible only in retrospect, that is, in the retentive phase of memory, whereas instant self-knowledge is possible at best in the form of unthematic awareness, which does not allow for clear and distinct presentation. Although such circumstances do not invalidate the claims of self-knowledge, they certainly weaken claims to its absolute certainty. For some aspects they may be stronger than the claims to knowledge of one's partners in the we-union, for example, in the case of knowledge of one's own existence and of belief in it. But precisely in the area of one's unionizing acts one may be mistaken about one's ability to perform an effective union rather than a mere semblance of it, and to experience vicariously one's partner's experiences. Also, my trust in the others, and even more my trust in their trust in my primary trust, may be a mere semblance of real trust. Furthermore, my picturing of their social world may be a mere projection of what I would like them to see, not allowing for alternative interpretations. Thus there are special pitfalls in our reflective and nonreflective knowledge of our own we-perspective, but hardly differences in principle.

On the strength of this phenomenological examination of the two kinds of perspectives on the partners of the we-union there is reason to question the adequacy of direct we-knowledge. Even if one should claim a privileged status for the *ego-cogito* as the best possible case for reliable adequate knowledge, there is no convincing basis for an equal or even superior epistemological claim for a *"nos cogitamus,"* as it has been asserted. The claim for any certainty in this area can be assessed only on the basis of the previous findings about the two perspectives, the straightforward one on the other's part in the we-union and the reflective one on one's own.

Implications for Other Phenomenological Theories. At first sight it may seem that the results of the preceding analyses of the we-phenomenon conflict with most of the phenomenological literature on the subject. Thus Scheler boldly claimed that "we" had priority over the I and you, and to some extent Schutz seems to have backed him up on this claim. Certainly to Schutz the we-relation was a basic fact of the social lifeworld, which even Husserl's transcendental or "egological" phenomenology of intersubjectivity cannot account for. And to Binswanger and many advocates of "dialogical" philosophy the priority of the "we" seems to be nearly axiomatic.

What I have been doing thus far does not contradict such claims, especially if taken in a historical or evolutionary sense. It may very well be the case that we-consciousness preceded the development of an explicit individualized I- and you-consciousness. But the evidence presented for such vast claims seems to me anything but sufficient and certainly not phenomenological in a critical sense. What I wanted to show is that in one's personal experience the "we" has no privileged status. Linguistically, the pronoun "we" has a very limited place and function. Phenomenologically, what is really meant by "we" and given in experience is a certain union of individual persons supported by conscious special acts that require the support of I's and you's as partners, and these are given only in rather indirect and inadequate perspectives. In this sense the we-phenomenon is secondary compared with the I- and you-phenomena and "founded" upon them.

All this is a matter of a "static" phenomenology, describing how the we-phenomenon appears in consciousness. It does not yet raise the question posed in Husserl's transcendental phenomenology as to how this phenomenon is constituted in consciousness "genetically." Once one raises this question there seems to me no escape from claiming some kind of priority to the individual consciousness in which the we-phenomenon takes shape, if only in the form of "passive constitution." This does not require the adoption of Husserl's transcendental idealism. The previous studies seem to me to have produced important evidence for the view that the we-phenomenon owes its genesis and support to the we-acts of its members. In this light any sweeping claims for the priority of the we over the I appear to be unwarranted and certainly need phenomenological underpinning by showing how the we-phenomenon is given as something independent of the supporting acts of the we-partners. It is one thing to show that the I in its structure is essentially oriented toward the we, which is often attempted with considerable evidence. It is a very different matter to claim that the we is a more basic entity than the I.

Contributions of Phenomenology to Linguistic Analysis of the We-Phenomenon. Austin conceived of linguistic analysis as a means to "sharpen our perception of the phenomena" and to "direct our attention to the multiplicity and the richness of our experiences." In fact, an analysis of the meaning of linguistic expression cannot fail to describe to some extent the phenomena meant. To what extent? Linguistic analysis as such goes only far enough to distinguish meanings, not to analyze the phenomena for their own sake. As far as the we-phenomena not yet tackled by linguistic analysis proper are concerned, all that would be needed is to distinguish we-talk from you-and-I-talk by pointing out the different ways of grouping these phenomena. But such analysis need not explore the structure of the we-union and its varieties. This should be the primary contribution of phenomenological analysis in its concentration on the phenomena for their own sake.

Furthermore, most linguistic analysis seems to be satisfied with the discovery of the rules of grammar for the proper use of words such as pronouns, without trying to understand their reasons, if any. I submit that a direct study of the phenomena may supply such understanding, at least to some extent. Thus the rule that we-talk can apply only to personal beings can be understood when it is seen that only persons can perform the kind of we-acts that are essential to a we-union. Similarly the rule that the we of copresence, in contrast to the absentee we, must address the we-partners with the intent of aligning them with the speaker, becomes intelligible in the light of the fact that their cooperation is needed for the constitution and maintenance of the we-union, something that is not the case in the absentee union.

Implications of the Phenomenological Analysis of the We-Phenomenon for Social Science. Social science, like all science, aspires to "objectivity," at least in the sense of knowledge that does not depend on the so-called subjective factors in the observer's personality, such as likes, moods, or biases. It requires knowledge that can be checked by other observers on the basis of evidence publicly displayed. This does not prevent science from dealing with facts that take place within a subject and even with this subject's views, provided they can be established in a way that can be shared by several observers.

It is agreed, at least among followers of the Max Weber tradition, that the subject matter of social science is subjective in this second sense. But this is only part of the situation. If the present analysis is correct, then social facts are given only in the subjective perspectives of the social partners. The immediate implication of this situation is that the social scientist has to study in each case all the perspectives of all the participants and to correlate them in parallel columns, as it were. In a sense this is what opinion research is doing. But this perspectival research must also include the study of metaperspectives – the partners' perspectives of one another's perspectives – a task attacked explicitly by R. D. Laing and his collaborators.

It may seem possible to overcome this complication by such idealizations as Schutz' principle of the "reciprocity of perspectives" to the effect that standpoints are interchangeable and that differences in perspectives are "congruent" or irrelevant to the purpose at hand.[14] To Schutz these are assumptions "taken for granted," and they may be workable in most cases and pragmatically justified. But for a critical science and especially for a phenomenological approach it is a grave question whether these assumptions identified by Schutz are justified. Critical science and especially a critical philosophy like phenomenology can never take anything for granted. Besides, in the area of social tensions and conflicts it is a fact that the perspectives fail to be reciprocal and congruent. In all such cases there is then clearly no escape from such multiperspectival research.

This situation may suggest that the only objectivity social science can hope for is to put these subjective perspectives side by side and report about them. If this were universally true, something which has been asserted about certain regions of the world, namely that they contain no facts but only opinions, then indeed all that objective science could do is collect opinions and possibly examine them for consistencies and inconsistencies. But fortunately this need not always be the last word. The super-perspective of the scientist, to be sure itself a metaperspective, allows him to some extent to relativize the relativity of the original perspectives, to de-center them and to construct a new perspective in which the lopsidedness of the original

[14] Alfred Schutz, *Collected Papers,* Vol. I (The Hague: Martinus Nijhoff, 1962, pp. 1-13).

observers' perspectives have been neutralized. In this process the scientist's direct perspectives based at times also upon documents or other objective evidence can help. But this does not nullify the basic fact that the objectivity of social science is based on the raw material of subjective perspectives, reciprocal and nonreciprocal, which have to be explored conscientiously. This fact should also serve as a reminder that social science is usually at first remove from the facts. Such indirectness calls for epistemological modesty and humility. On this basis it can proceed with a critical selection from the direct perspectives of the firsthand witnesses, especially when they contradict one another.

SOME CONDITIONS FOR THE RIGHT TO SAY "WE"

I did not promise that this paper would result in a definite answer to the question of the right to say "we." This was my reason for its first title "*On* the Right" not "*The* Right," which could be understood as a promise to tell "all about it." To me the most important thing was to raise the question and to find ways of approaching an answer, but not of serving it up ready-made. Yet I owe at least a preliminary answer.

But first it is in order to clarify finally what kind of right I am questioning. Obviously I do not mean the *legal* right to use a particular personal pronoun in any way one wants, including lying. One might consider here the conception of a *logical* right, or *epistemological* right, depending on whether there are valid reasons for asserting that some people stand in a we-relationship rather than that they think about each other merely as "you and I." Also one may conceive of a *linguistic* right, under the rules of good grammar, including philosophical grammar, to say "we." Thus linguistically there is nothing wrong with using the pronoun "we" to include one's defenseless dead predecessors or unborn successors. All the more questionable is whether one has a *moral* right to do so. It is indeed this moral right to say "we" in the name of others which I would like to test. For there is indeed such a thing as an ethics of language and speech, little though it has been discussed thus far. The ethics of pronouns might well be one of its major fields. There are, for instance, also questions of ethics involved in addressing others by use of the second person singular, especially in languages which distinguish between the intimate address of friendship and the less intimate general form of the pronoun, as does French and German. But the moral right to say "we," which not only addresses but tries to align the other with the speaker, is a much more serious issue. Whenever I claim to speak in your name as well as in my own without your consent and especially over your protest, I have violated your moral right to the respect I owe you as a person.

However, such a blunt statement would have to be backed up not only by a clarification of the concept of moral right but also by a general theory of its foundations and its limits. If only for the sake of the argument I have to take it for granted that this concept makes sense and that there are definite good reasons justifying the claim to such rights. Nevertheless, I would like to point out what seems to me some of the most relevant considerations for an attempt to answer the question about the right to say "we."

The Case Against the Right

A remarkable book about "the adventures of a young Englishman at Harvard and in the Youth Movement" by Richard Zorza, from which I took part of my title and the first motto of this article, contains in the only chapter which resumes the title (*The Right to Say "We"*) and in the one paragraph speaking about it explicitly, the following continuation of my motto:

> No, that something [required for the right to say "we"] had to be the response of the whole youth movement, that whole new consciousness that we had seen developing, that we had responded to, that we had felt growing in ourselves as it grew in others. . . .[15]

There is obviously something odd about such a statement made in the name of "we," which at the same time denies the right to say "we" until certain conditions can be fulfilled in the future. But more important is the question whether these conditions can ever be met. For in asking for the response of the entire youth movement the author practically calls for the unanimous support of all those to whom he appeals. How far is such a demand realizable, not only in the particular case but in general?

As the linguistic analysis of we-talk earlier in this essay tried to

---

[15] Richard Zorza, *The Right to Say "We"* (New York: Praeger, 1970, p. 21).

show, "we" indeed makes a claim to unanimity among all the we-partners. Majority, simple or qualified, won't do and one dissenter can wreck the pretense of speaking in the name of a group. Now in the case of the we of copresence such unanimity can be established, at least in principle and certainly in small face-to-face groups. But in the case of the absentee we with its indefinite class membership, the establishment of unanimity by securing everyone's consent seems to be more than impracticable. At least in this case the right to say "we" for others seems to be indefensible in principle.

But there may be an even more general objection to the right to say "we" even in the case of copresents. If it should be true that no one can speak for another person without his consent, then he should always be given a chance to give or withhold it. Now, there is practically no possibility of ever consulting every copresent we-partner beforehand. In fact, the very idea of asking them in each case, "May I speak for you too and say 'we' in your name?" would seem to be almost absurdly unrealistic. Seen in this light all we-talk is necessarily usurpation. At worst using it means speaking under false pretense, if not lying. At best it is a belated attempt to persuade others to acquiesce with this pretense.

Even more important, the preceding investigations have shown that the we-phenomenon can never be given adequately to any we-partner, neither with regard to his own share of unionizing acts nor to those of the others. At best we can have incomplete evidence for the presence of these acts. Under these circumstances the right to say we is certainly essentially precarious and never absolute.

In Defense of a Limited Right

But this does not mean that this right is nonexistent. Although I would like to be much more sparing and scrupulous in the use of we-language (I have certainly tried hard to do so in this paper), I am not advocating its total abolition.

To begin with, is it really necessary to give the we-talk this strong and forbidding sense? Could it be the case that in saying "we" I do not yet assert that you are behind me unconditionally? The very fact that I say so in your presence puts my claim to the test and gives you a chance to protest, thus giving me the lie. The "we" is then merely an invitation to accept my "we" formulation and an attempt to simplify matters for you by way of a rejectable offer. Your very presence at my speaking constitutes your protection against my usurpation. Thus it seems at least possible to describe the aligning function of the "we" as an attempt to enlist others as free associates on approval, by tacit assent, or on disapproval, by open dissent and protest. The main need for justifying we-talk is then good, if not conclusive, evidence that one's partner reciprocates one's we-consciousness. In the case of dual union this is comparatively easy. But the larger the group, the more problematic such evidence becomes and thus the weaker is one's right to say "we."

This does not contradict the sad truth that the "we" is only too frequently misused as a persuasive device for capitalizing on the other's reluctance to protest and speak up. It may serve to shame him into accepting the speaker's judgment, perhaps even by flattery, as being credited with his views. I submit that this is the real threat of the usual we-talk, particularly when used in authoritarian situations, in teaching or in politics. "We" is one of the most insidious weapons in the arsenal of demagogues and dictators posing as democrats.

Nevertheless, I am prepared to defend a limited right to say "we" even without previous consultation of the prospective we-partners. To start with a rather obvious example: I would feel perfectly safe in making in a lecture the statement, "We have now spent 50 minutes together in this room," without fear of being contradicted except by some latecomers. What this signifies is that in cases where the we-statement refers merely to external circumstances and behavior, the evidence for sharing them is practically foolproof and the willingness of other we-partners to be included in a we-statement can be assumed, notwithstanding the possibility that in cases of disorientation or absent-mindedness they may not be aware of such external facts or they may see them very differently.

But the situation is clearly very different in the case of "mental acts" such as seeing, believing, feeling, or wanting, which are certainly not as plainly and fully given to the we-speaker as are external circumstances. Suppose I had said, "We have now seen and know that all we-statements are precarious." How dare I say this about you as I may about myself? Such a we-statement would be not only an unwarranted claim to knowledge about you but an interference with your intellectual independence, your right to give or withhold assent. For my own part I confess that I always feel put upon, if not antagonistic, when a speaker or writer, under the guise of chummy fraternizing, includes me in his we-talk without giving me a chance to dissociate myself from him. Does he want to flatter me or to shame me into acquiescence with what is actually patronizing condescension?

The situation differs considerably in the case of the absentee we, where only one of the "we" is present in talking to an audience. Here any immediate assent or protest or subsequent approval is essentially out of the question. Hence one may well wonder whether it is at all defensible to speak for absent we-partners. But the absence is so obvious that no one can be misled. To this extent the use of the absentee we should be harmless. Nevertheless, the temptation to take advantage of the absence of possible protesters occurs too frequently. Thus there is a need for specifying the conditions when the use of this "we" is legitimate.

The major question would seem to be what reasons the we-speaker has for assuming that the absent we-partners would support him in saying "we" if present. For now he speaks not only in their joint names, but as their separated representative. The clearest title is that of an actual proxy. Here the we-speaker, if he himself is ready to join with those he represents, may be considered authorized not only to cast the absentees' vote but, by adding his own, to speak in the name of a new "we." In other cases, such as elections, the we-speaker may have legitimate ground for thinking that at least the majority of his voters would authorize inclusion in the "we," and the outvoted minority consent to it, if they have really freely adopted the rules of the majority game. Yet here too the absent we-partners must have at least some chance of dissenting and dissociating from their spokesman if he no longer keeps in touch with them. To say "we, the people" and even more so "we, the United Nations" is a bold claim indeed, which can all too easily turn out to be a rhetorical fiction invalidated by the fact that none of the we-partners even knew that he was included by his representatives. (More honest, if less impressive, is the formulation "We, the Assembly of the United Nations" used in the "Universal Declaration of Human Rights.") In short, in the case of the absentee we one's right depends on the existence of live credentials testifying to the support of the absentees. Ultimately even the absentee we points back to the conditions for the legitimate use of the we of copresence. But even with antecedent proxies and subsequent ratifications of his we-talk the absentee we-speaker must be aware that he is not in actual touch with those for whom he speaks and whose very number he usually does not know. Under such circumstances the right to say "we" is at best precarious.

It should also be realized that there is no clear-cut division between the two we's. It may well happen that part of the audience of a speech is within earshot, whereas others are only within the earshot of a one-way public address system and thus are not strictly co-present. Hence the justification of the right to speak for those only within one-way reach will differ from those within two-way reach.

These considerations do not add up to a neat formula specifying the terms for the right to say "we." But they suggest at least a maxim: Limit we-talk to occasions where you honestly believe that your we-partners want you to speak for them. Without good evidence for such an honest belief one had better speak only for oneself. This is a matter of social humility for humans who cannot know one another's hearts. It is a matter of respect for their dignity. It is also a matter of intellectual honesty and moral courage.

13. THE RELEVANCE OF PHENOMENOLOGICAL PHILOSOPHY FOR PSYCHOLOGY *

I. THE ISSUE AND ITS BACKGROUND

I would like to begin with a brief exposition of the background for my choice of topic.

As far as psychology is concerned, one might well maintain that phenomenology has arrived in the American world, much more than it has in American philosophy, where it is still largely considered an exotic plant. Thus, in a recent symposium on behaviorism and phenomenology sponsored by the American Psychological Association at Rice University,[1] phenomenology was given equal ranking with behaviorism, apparently as one of the two major alternatives in psychology today. Among the participants, all native Americans, were such leading psychologists as Sigmund Koch and B. F. Skinner. And not only Robert B. MacLeod, long a spokesman for a phenomenology of "disciplined naïveté," pleaded the case for phenomenology. Carl Rogers, the founder of client-centered therapy, invoked phenomenology as the most important new ingredient of his "science of the person."

On the other hand, neither of the philosophers invited, Norman Malcolm and Michael Scriven, had any known ties with philosophical phenomenology. Even MacLeod, the most unequivocal proponent of phenomenology, stated "emphatically" that in his view, "what we call psychological phenomenology is not to be confused with Husserl's philosophy." (p. 51.) [2] Thus the phenomenology considered at the symposium was one without any live ties with phe-

* From *Phenomenology and Existentialism,* ed. E. N. Lee and M. Mandelbaum (Baltimore: Johns Hopkins, 1967).

[1] T. W. Wann, ed., *Behaviorism and Phenomenology* (Chicago: 1963).

[2] In a similar vein Alfred Kuenzli, in prefacing his anthology of articles on *The Phenomenological Problem* (New York: 1959), referred to Husserl as "not especially pertinent to the concerns of contemporary psychologists" (p. IX).

nomenological philosophy. Does this mean that phenomenological psychology has declared its final independence? If so, is this total emancipation a good thing for psychology as well as for philosophy? Was their indisputable connection in the past merely a historical accident without lasting significance? It is these questions which I would like to discuss by proposing the topic of the relevance of phenomenological philosophy for psychology.

One way of doing this would be to show the historical connections between the two in a way which would make it plain that they have essential links, even though they are now often forgotten. While this can be done and seems to me eminently worth doing, my own experience has shown me that this can grow into a forbidding enterprise. Such an attempt would have to consider more than just the lifework of Husserl, central though his position in the phenomenological movement was and remains, even after his radicalism took him increasingly more to left of center. For, as I would like to re-emphasize here, phenomenological philosophy is not synonymous with Husserl's work. A comprehensive appraisal of the contributions of phenomenological philosophy to psychology would have to include the work of Alexander Pfänder, Moritz Geiger, and Max Scheler, Heidegger's hermeneutic phenomenology, and the existential phenomenologies of Gabriel Marcel, Sartre, and Merleau-Ponty.[3] All I can do here is to present some of the evidence in the case of Edmund Husserl, too often looked upon as the antipsychologist par excellence.

Another and ultimately more valid way of handling the task would be to consider, without regard to the historical connections, the essential relationships between phenomenological philosophy and psychology. I shall try this to the extent of discussing some respects in which psychology presupposes phenomenology in a more than psychological sense. But I chiefly want to demonstrate it concretely by introducing an exemplary case where philosophical phenomenology and psychological phenomenology converge without being sufficiently aware of it, and where they may actually be interdependent. For I would like to make this clear: I am not thinking of

[3] I prepared such an account with the aid of the National Institute of Mental Health in *Phenomenology in Psychology and Psychiatry.* (Evanston: Northwestern University Press, 1972). A volume of translations from the writings of Alexander Pfänder, dealing mostly with his phenomenological psychology, entitled *Phenomenology of Willing and Motivation,* appeared in 1967 at Northwestern University Press.

a one-way street from philosophy to psychology but of a two-way exchange. It is philosophical phenomenology as well as psychology which stands to benefit from such a relationship.

But before I proceed with the task, I had better state in what sense I am distinguishing between phenomenological philosophy and phenomenological psychology. In so doing I do not want to suppress the fact that in the early days of phenomenology, i.e., around 1900, Husserl himself defined phenomenology as a descriptive psychology, much to his later regret. In trying to undo the damage, with only partial success, he stressed the point that phenomenology was not concerned with empirical facts, as is genuine descriptive psychology, but with the essences and essential relations of the psychic phenomena, regardless of whether any instances of such essences exist. But there are other differences. Phenomenology, conceived by Husserl as the science of the essential structure of consciousness, comprised not only the acts of consciousness, which he later called the noetic acts, corresponding to what a phenomenological psychologist like Carl Stumpf had called psychic functions: consciousness points essentially to referents beyond itself, to "intentional objects," to which Husserl later also attached the name of "noematic objects." These, too, belong to the rightful domain of phenomenology – for instance, by way of a phenomenology of the body or of works of art, which deal with their essential structures and their ways of appearing. These intentional or noematic objects lie clearly beyond the field of a psychology that is concerned merely with what are strictly psychic phenomena.

On this occasion I shall not raise the question of whether phenomenology, conceived as the descriptive science of the phenomena of consciousness, is itself essentially philosophical or rather a study that precedes all philosophy and science. All I want to consider is the relation between the phenomenology undertaken by such non-psychologist philosophers as Edmund Husserl in contradistinction to the one launched by such non-philosopher psychologists as Donald Snygg, the first representative of what I would like to call an American phenomenology from the grassroots. My question is then: Is what Husserl did under the name of phenomenology relevant for psychologists, particularly those who now do the sort of thing which these grassroots phenomenologists advocate?

I also feel a need to state what I understand here by the term "relevance," a term whose vagueness stands in direct proportion to its popularity. Unfortunately I am not familiar with any explicit discussion of this crucial term and shall have to draw some distinctions especially for this occasion.[4]

1. The strongest case of relevance is the one where something is both the necessary and sufficient condition of something else; this, according to Bertrand Russell, is the relevance of logic to mathematics.

2. The relevance is slightly reduced when the condition is necessary, but not sufficient; the relevance of mathematics to physics is of this nature.

3. A further weakening of relevance occurs when the condition is no longer necessary, though sufficient; thus for a science literary formulation in a particular modern language may be sufficient for its completion, but not necessary.

4. Finally, something may be relevant to something else even when it is neither its necessary nor sufficient condition. Nevertheless, its presence may make an important difference in the total situation, changing its entire configuration. It may be neither necessary nor sufficient for predicting a person's behavior to know about his phenomenal perspective and feelings. But it certainly adds substantially to a full understanding of his conduct, and is in this sense relevant.

Now in speaking about the relevance of phenomenological philosophy to psychology I do not mean to decide immediately what type of relevance is at stake. Clearly no one would claim that philosophy is the necessary and sufficient condition for a scientific psychology, nor even that it could ever be its sufficient condition. However, it may be that it is its necessary though insufficient foundation. This stronger thesis would be definitely in line with Husserl's views. But even a weaker thesis, according to which philosophy would merely "make a difference" without being indispensable, would be enough to establish its relevance for psychology.

Before discussing the systematic question, I would like to supply a minimum of historical illustration for the actual relationship between phenomenological philosophy and psychology.

---

[4] For confirmation and substantiation of my impression see Wayne A. R. Leys, "Irrelevance as a Philosophical Problem of Our Time," *Memorias del XIII Congreso Internacional de Filosofia,* IV (1963), pp. 173-185.

II. ON HUSSERL'S CONTRIBUTIONS TO PSYCHOLOGY

The belief is still widespread that Husserl was a sworn enemy of psychology. The fire behind this smoke is that at one crucial stage of his career Husserl had mounted his celebrated attack on psychologism. But this attack has to be seen and understood in its proper context: Husserl's attempt to keep psychology from overextending itself by an imperialism that would put it in complete control of the intellectual globe. At the same time he was concerned to help psychology in the pursuit of its legitimate tasks.

A full understanding of this seeming ambivalence in Husserl's attitude toward psychology would demand a close study of his spiral-like development. It would have to consider the philosophical inspiration of the mathematician "E. G." Husserl by the new descriptive psychology of Franz Brentano and the hope, expressed particularly in the "psychological and logical studies" of Husserl's *Philosophy of Arithmetic* (1891), never completed, of discovering the missing foundation of mathematics in such a psychology. It would have to take account of his seeming aboutface in the first volume of his *Logical Investigations* (1900), with its classic critique of psychologism, and his further shift in the second volume to a new correlative method that accorded both the psychic act and the transpsychic content equal rights. For this latter approach Husserl adopted the name of "phenomenology," defined as the study of the essential nature of consciousness in its intentional structure. But soon the scales tipped back toward the subjective pole of the relationship: under the title of "transcendental phenomenology" Husserl now undertook with growing insistence to locate the origin of all phenomena in a constituting subjectivity, a subjectivity that he always wanted to keep strictly separate from the merely factual subjectivity of empirical psychology, as he interpreted it, but which still implied the primacy of the subjective pole of the relation over its "objective" correlates.

However, this is not the place for plotting the curve of Husserl's progress or even of the variations in his proximity to empirical psychology – of which, actually, he did not keep abreast. Rather, the important thing in the present context is to give as clear a picture as possible of Husserl's basic attitude toward psychology. Especially his opposition to psychologism, first merely in logic and then along the entire front of philosophy, must not be interpreted as hostility to psychology as such. His concern was primarily the freeing of philosophy from the abortive attempts of psychologists after the manner of J. S. Mill to convert logic into a branch of psychology and to make the factual laws of thinking the foundation of the logical laws and their claims to validity. Moreover, in order to understand Husserl's antipsychologism it is necessary to realize that what he understood by psychology was the kind of psychophysics and psychophysiology which considered the psyche merely as part of a biological organism, to be explored by the experimental methods of the Wundtian laboratories.[5]

Phenomenology, as Husserl finally conceived of it, was anything but opposed to psychology as a science. The two are essentially interrelated.[6] A true phenomenological psychology, once developed, would "stand in close, even closest relation to philosophy." [7] Even with regard to the psychology of his time with its "immense experimental work and its abundance of empirical facts and in part very interesting regularities," Husserl expressed genuine admiration, particularly when it was in the hands of such experimentalists as Carl Stumpf and Theodor Lipps, who had seen the importance of descriptive clarifications before rushing off to the laboratories.[8] But Husserl's final verdict was damning and blunt enough: He denied the typical psychology of the time the right to call itself a rigorous science.[9] For this so-called science, in its eagerness to collect factual and experimental material, had failed to make sure of its basic concepts, and operated instead with the crude and uncritical terms of everyday language. Incidental discussions of terminological questions were insufficient to provide better foundations. Only a full-fledged phenomenology that had investigated the essential structures of the phenomena in their variety could make sense of the experimental findings. Empirical psychology, then, presupposes phenomenological psychology, a psychology that works out the funda-

---

[5] See the pertinent section in *The Phenomenological Movement*, pp. 149-52.
[6] "Phenomenology and psychology are closely related, inasmuch as both are concerned with consciousness, though in a different manner and in a different attitude." (*Logos*, I, 1911, p. 302). *Philosophie als strenge Wissenschaft*, ed. Wilhelm Szilasi (Frankfurt-am-Main: 1965). Also in *Phenomenology and the Crisis of Philosophy*, trans. Quentin Lauer (New York: 1965).
[7] *Ibid.*, p. 321.
[8] *Ibid.*, p. 304.
[9] *Ibid.*, p. 320.

mental distinctions of the psychological phenomena on the basis of essential insights (*Wesenseinsichten*).

What did Husserl himself contribute to the laying of such a phenomenological foundation for psychology? [10]

He did not write a systematic work on phenomenological psychology. What was published under this title were his notes for lectures that he delivered in 1925 and again in 1928.[11] There is no basis for the belief that he ever meant to publish them as an independent book. Nevertheless, the text now before us provides, at least in its second half (pp. 130ff.), the best picture of what kind of topics a phenomenological psychology in Husserl's sense would have to include and how he wanted it to treat them. Typical items are: the stratification of the psychic phenomena (Section 21), their unity (Section 24), perception (Sections 28-39), temporality (Section 40), the ego (Sections 41f.), and the subject as monad (Section 43). This is clearly not a complete system of phenomenological psychology.

However, we can also refer to extended chapters and sections in other works published or authorized by Husserl himself that take up the kind of psychological topics envisaged in "Philosophy as a Rigorous Science." Thus the analyses of perception in *Ideen*, those of the inner consciousness of time in the lectures edited by Martin Heidegger, and those of experience in *Erfahrung und Urteil*, as elaborated by Ludwig Landgrebe, contain a wealth of basic descriptions and distinctions which are of considerable significance for psychology.

But, especially in the present context, it would make little sense to insert here a complete catalog of Husserl's treatment of various psychological topics. The only meaningful thing would be to show concretely how he dealt with an exemplary phenomenon. The most obvious candidate would be his account of the intentional structure of consciousness. This would involve showing how each conscious act, e.g., our consciousness of the building in which we happen to be located, is essentially a consciousness *of*, namely, of the (intentional) object to which consciousness refers. In addition to this basic pattern, introduced by Franz Brentano's descriptive psychology, Husserl

[10] For a very helpful attempt to bring together Husserl's main psychological findings systematically see Hermann Drüe, *Edmund Husserls System der phänomenologischen Psychologie*. But it hardly justifies the use of the term 'system' in the usual sense, a term which Husserl himself usually rejected.

[11] *Phänomenologische Psychologie*, ed. Walter Biemel (*Husserliana*, IX) (The Hague: 1962).

pointed out that in intentional consciousness the immediate data of our awareness, such as our sense impressions of colors or textures, are ascribed to objects and in this sense objectified. Even more important, the referents of the many acts in which this building is experienced are ascribed to one identical object into which the different appearances or perspectives are integrated or synthesized.

But to give a full and meaningful picture of these investigations into the structure of consciousness would clearly exceed the frame of this essay. Instead I shall add something about the more general question of the role of phenomenological psychology in the total setting of Husserl's philosophy.

Quite apart from his early purpose in utilizing Brentano's psychology as a foundation for the philosophy of arithmetic, Husserl thought of psychology as an important, if not as the only, avenue to the new fundamental science of phenomenology, and particularly to its fully developed form: pure or transcendental phenomenology. This phenomenology was to be the study of the essential structures of consciousness purified from all "transcendent" existential beliefs. The purification was to be achieved by means of the celebrated phenomenological reduction, which was to "bracket," or, better, suspend all such beliefs and find the ultimate foundation for all philosophy and science in immanent subjectivity. One of the difficulties for this new radical conception of phenomenology was this: While in his *Ideen* (Section 31) Husserl had pointed out the theoretical feasibility of such a reduction on the basis of a free decision, he had not shown to his own and others' satisfaction why such a drastic step was necessary. Most of his later efforts consisted in mustering arguments for the rational necessity of this step. And one of his major reasons was the "crisis in psychology," a crisis which, as he saw it, could be overcome only by giving psychology a new foundation in transcendental phenomenology.

Husserl developed this line of reasoning in several places:

1. In his lectures on "Phenomenological Psychology" of 1925 and 1928, he tried to show how psychology is transformed, once it is based on phenomenological philosophy.

2. In his ill-fated [12] article on "Phenomenology" for the *Encyclo-*

---

[12] "Ill-fated": After having gone through four German versions, now published in *Husserliana*, IX, the German version of this article was not only seriously truncated but badly reformulated by a translator hampered by

paedia Britannica, Husserl began with a section on pure psychology, i.e., a psychology free from physical and physiological ingredients, along the lines of Brentano's descriptive psychology (or psychognosia), that focused on "intentionality" and was based both on a limited phenomenological reduction to "inner experience" and on an "eidetic" reduction to essences. In a second section Husserl tried to show how such a phenomenological psychology could serve as the foundation for transcendental phenomenology. For as Husserl saw it, there is a fundamental ambiguity in the way in which the world appears in our consciousness: in what sense is it real? This ambiguity calls for radical elucidation. Even phenomenological psychology shares the naïveté of all science in its simple belief in the reality of the natural world. But at least in focusing on the phenomena of "inner" experience such a psychology is already on the road to the subjective matrix. Carried through to the end it would lead to the complete transcendental reduction of all existential beliefs, as characteristic of transcendental phenomenology.

3.   Finally, in the *Crisis of the European Sciences and Transcendental Phenomenology* of 1935ff., Husserl returned to psychology as an approach to phenomenology – now, however, second to the new and more publicized approach, that via the study of the life world. He saw the reasons for the crisis in psychology in the incompatibility between an objectivistic approach in the style of Galilean science and the merely subjective approach from inner experience. Transcendental phenomenology would provide a new foundation for both in the constituting function of transcendental consciousness.

But the ultimate proof for the historical relevance of Husserl's phenomenological psychology could be supplied only by showing its traces in the work of the psychologists of his time. For a comprehensive study of these relations I can now refer the reader to a larger historical introduction.[13]

---

limitations of space. See the new unabridged translation by Richard Palmer in *Journal of the British Society for Phenomenology* II, 2 (1971), pp. 77-91 and my introductory remarks, pp. 74-76.

[13] *Phenomenology in Psychology and Psychiatry. A Historical Introduction.*

III. THE POTENTIAL RELEVANCE OF HUSSERL'S
PHENOMENOLOGY FOR PSYCHOLOGY

However, it is not from the historical effects that the full relevance of Husserl's phenomenology for psychology can be demonstrated. Anyhow, these influences have issued almost exclusively from the incipient phenomenology of his early *Logical Investigations*. The full-fledged pure or transcendental phenomenology of the *Ideas* and of his subsequent work has remained relatively ineffective. The most important question is therefore whether this phenomenology is essentially capable of and destined to make significant contributions in the future.

In the present context, I can offer merely the following general considerations.

1. A full empirical psychology worthy of its name must include a pure psychology of the phenomena of consciousness. This consciousness is essentially intentional. But in order to give an adequate account of intentionality we need the kind of phenomenological investigation which the traditional psychophysical psychology fails to provide. In other words, a psychology that does not abandon consciousness after the manner of strict behaviorism requires a description of the intentional structures as given in immediate experience, regardless of whether they are matched by physical counterparts.

2. Empirical psychology presupposes a framework of fundamental concepts or essential structures. Perhaps a more direct way of demonstrating this prerequisite would be to point out that the usual texts in empirical psychology simply presuppose a set of concepts such as function, act, content, perception, conation, etc. Rarely, if ever, are they accompanied by explicit definitions. In fact, these concepts often seem to be not much more than stipulations vaguely based on ordinary usage. Phenomenology is to put foundations under these seemingly arbitrary stipulations. It is to derive psychological definitions from what is called, perhaps a little pretentiously, essential insights (*Wesensschau*), or a little more concretely, from grasping the essential types that can be intuited on the basis of a systematic variation of the observed phenomena. Seeing and describing such essential structures might put an end to the appearance, if not the reality, of definitional anarchy.

3. Phenomenology can provide a genetic understanding of the way in which the contents of our consciousness take shape in our experience. Such constitution occurs either passively – when contents crystallize, as it were, without our doing, as in ordinary experience – or actively when we construct such contents, as in acts of judgment or in the imagination. Constitutive phenomenology, by paying special attention to these processes and describing them, leads to a much better understanding of the historic development of consciousness and its correlates than does a merely static description in the style of Husserl's earlier phenomenology.

Husserl claims that these steps – description of pure subjective experience, identification of essential types, and constitutive phenomenology – are indispensable to making psychology an exact science. If he is right phenomenology would of course be relevant in the strong sense. It would certainly be a serious challenge to all existing psychology that is still innocent of phenomenology. Personally I doubt that the plight of present-day psychology is that precarious. Thus in the field of description of subjective consciousness a lot of conscientious work has been done not only by psychology of perception and descriptive psychopathology but also by our psychological novelists. As for the reflection on the basic concepts of psychology, the reexamination of basic definitions is by no means absent from the theory and philosophy of psychology.[14] Even the field of constitution is not uncultivated; thus the recent development in Continental psychology of what goes by the name of *Aktualgenese* in the second Leipzig School of Fritz Sander is a careful attempt to study the genetic constitutions of *Gestalts*. Moreover, some of Piaget's genetic psychology attempts at least something parallel to, if not identical with, constitutive phenomenology.

My conclusion is that at least implicitly some of the tasks outlined by Husserl are being tackled, however inadequately, in current research in psychology. Their explicit treatment might indeed be of considerable help to the cause of a truly scientific psychology. But

---

[14] I am thinking here particularly of the recent development of a philosophy-based "philosophical psychology" (see, e.g., Donald Gustavson, ed., *Essays in Philosophical Psychology* [New York: 1964]). But apart from the question of the effect of these painstaking studies on the psychologists, the emphasis of analytic philosophizing on ordinary English rather than on the structure of the phenomena raises the question of whether it can avoid dependency on the accidents of historical language and reach essential types.

it would be strange if these tasks, urgent as they are, had not been discovered and attacked in ongoing research. Thus what I submit is that, while an explicit phenomenology can be relevant to psychology in its actual work, it is not indispensable as long as psychology implicitly attends to its phenomenological foundations. But this does not mean that a more explicit attack could not be of considerable value. Of this potential aid I would like to give an example.

IV. PHENOMENOLOGY AND FIELD THEORY: A CHANCE FOR CO-OPERATION

Let me now turn away from merely theoretical considerations of what may be called "metaphenomenology." Instead I would like to show in a specific instance how philosophical phenomenology could become relevant in an area of recent growth in psychology in a manner that would at the same time stimulate philosophical growth. I have in mind the conception of the phenomenal field as developed in recent psychology and as paralleled by Husserl's much dramatized, and perhaps at times overdramatized, conception of the life world.

Psychological field theory as such owes its major development to the work of Kurt Lewin. Long before Husserl's conception of the life world had become generally known, Lewin formulated his conception of a life space as the frame of reference for a person's actions and movements.[15] He even devised an elaborate system for plotting these movements by utilizing the patterns of mathematical topology.

What must not be overlooked in taking account of and paying tribute to these pioneering studies is that Lewin is exclusively concerned with problems of action. His life space is consequently defined in terms of "the totality of facts which determine the behavior of an individual at a certain moment" (p. 12). Also, the life space or "hodological space" is organized according to the chances of personal access, which is often blocked by obstructive barriers. Questions of merely theoretical perception or emotional relationship are not considered as such. Moreover, while Lewin stressed the difference between the physical field and the psychological field, he defined life space facts dynamically as *real* in the sense of having real effects on behavior, even though these effects need not be physical. What is

[15] *Principles of Topological Psychology* (New York: 1935).

even more striking is the absence of any references to phenomenology, striking particularly in view of Lewin's German background and at a time when Wolfgang Köhler, to whom the *Principles* were dedicated, along with other gestaltists put increasing emphasis on phenomenology. As a matter of fact, in 1917 Lewin himself had published a brilliant descriptive study of the phenomenal transformations of the landscape in stationary war, which he himself called a piece of "phenomenology." [16] I suspect that his later avoidance of the term is indicative of his wish to steer clear of all such philosophical entanglements, not only with Husserl's phenomenology but also with the "New Positivism" and its physicalism (*op. cit.*, p. 19). His chief concern was clearly to stay close to phenomenally observable behavior.

The "phenomenal field" as the basic concept in phenomenological psychology makes its explicit appearance in the first American text in the field by Donald Snygg in co-operation with Arthur W. Combs.[17] It is defined as "the entire universe, including himself, as it is experienced by the individual at the instant of action" (p. 15). As such it is contrasted with the "objective physical field." More specifically, the field is identified with "the universe of naïve experience in which the individual lives, the everyday situation of self and surroundings which each person takes to be reality." Snygg and Combs describe the phenomenal field as more or less fluid, as "organized and meaningful," for instance on the basis of the figure-ground relation. The phenomenal self forms a special sector within the total phenomenal field as its "most permanent part" (p. 76). It "includes all those aspects of the phenomenal field which the individual experiences as part or characteristic of himself" (p. 78).

This concept of the phenomenal world has been taken over by Carl Rogers, who also uses such terms as "world of experience" or "experiential world." [18] With the individual as its center, "it includes all that is experienced by the organism, whether or not these experiences are consciously perceived." The introduction of the term

---

[16] "Über die Kriegslandschaft," *Zeitschrift für angewandte Psychologie*, XII (1917), pp. 440-47, reported in Heider, Fritz, *On Perception and Event Structures, and the Psychological Environment* (Psychological Issues, 1, 3, 1959, pp. 112 ff.).

[17] *Individual Behavior: A New Frame of Reference for Psychology* (New York: 1949).

[18] *Client-centered Therapy* (Boston: 1951, p. 483).

"organism" may seem to imply a rejection of consciousness. However, at a later stage,[19] when Rogers emphasizes the noun "experience" for the phenomenal field, he makes it plain that "it does not include such events as neuron discharges or changes in blood sugar, because they are not directly available to awareness." Thus the term "organism" has clearly to be understood in a purely psychological sense.

Finally, I would like to mention a potentially even more sophisticated conception of the phenomenal world developed by Saul Rosenzweig in his theory of personality, also called "idiodynamics," an orientation that "adopts the dynamics of the individual as the fundamental ground of systematization in psychology." [20] A fundamental feature of this idiodynamics is the dominance of the "idioverse" (lately also called "idiocosm"), "the name given to the individual's universe of events." These events constitute "the population of the idioverse," which is to be explored by several methods, phenomenology among them. What seems to me significant about this conception is that here the idea of the phenomenal field is enlarged to that of the one encompassing world of the individual. True, thus far there has been no further development of the idea, and no concrete idiocosms of specific individuals have been described. But it should not be difficult to supply them as each idiodynamic biography is bound to do.

Similar conceptions can be found among sociologists and anthropologists. What is so often called "culture" in all its ambiguities seems mostly an attempt to describe that part of man's social field which is not only shared by men but is man-made.[21]

The rise of such concepts in different schools of psychology and social science is symptomatic of the need for a systematic study of the phenomenal world. Such a study would require a clear conception of the structural organization of this world, of its dimensions, and of the proper categories for describing it. How far has the new

[19] "Therapy, Personality and Inter-personal Relationships," *Psychology: A Study of a Science,* ed. Sigmund Koch, III (New York: 1959, p. 197).

[20] See especialy "The Place of the Individual and of Idiodynamics in Psychology: A Dialogue," *Journal of Individual Psychology,* XVI (1958), pp. 3-21.

[21] To my knowledge the only person who has noticed and stressed the parallel between cultural anthropology and phenomenology is Grace de Laguna in her article on "The Lebenswelt and the Cultural World," *Journal of Philosophy* LX (1960), pp. 777-791.

grassroots phenomenology been able to supply it? If it has, I confess that I have not yet come across any such attempt. Lewin's model of life spaces for action is a promising beginning. But apparently little has been done on the basis of this foundation in more recent phenomenological psychologies for the phenomenal field in its entirety.

How far is philosophical phenomenology able to fill this need? At this point I would like to introduce Husserl's conception of the life world, which, while foreshadowed already in texts from the twenties, made its full-fledged appearance only in the posthumously published sections of his incomplete work on the *Crisis of the European Sciences and Transcendental Phenomenology.*

In order to do justice to this conception, one must be aware of the context in which it occurs. This context is the attempt to show the need for transcendental phenomenology. Husserl wanted to demonstrate this need by a variety of approaches, all leading to the realization that the foundations for enterprises such as psychology or science in general can be supplied only by tracing their foundations in the subjective sphere, which Husserl called transcendental subjectivity. In the *Crisis* Husserl took a new approach to this goal by starting out from the everyday life world of the ordinary person, which is so different from the objectivized world of science. However, one must not expect of Husserl any sustained study of the life world for its own sake. All he needed for his purposes was the identification of those features in it that lead back to the fundamental layer in subjectivity in which they are constituted. Yet Husserl was increasingly aware of the fact that in order to show these origins he had to explore the life world to a much greater extent than he had done in his earlier work, where he had included the life world within the "natural world" explored by objective science.

Nevertheless, what can be found in the pertinent sections of the *Crisis* proved highly suggestive to those who consider the independent exploration of the life world one of the most important contributions made by Husserl's phenomenology. It contains at least the rudiments of a structural theory of the life world. One of its basic features is that it has a center in the experiencing subject (in contrast to the uncentered objective world of science), designated by the singular personal pronoun in the case of the private world of the individual and by the plural in the case of social group worlds. The life world is polarized around these centers and displays such spatial charac-

teristics as closeness or farness, being above or below, left or right –
all characteristics that as such have no place in the scientific world
with its objective coordinates. It also shows such emotional characters as "home" (*Heimat*) and "foreign" (*Fremde)*, familiar and
strange, old and novel. Husserl points to the cultural anthropology
of Lucien Lévy-Bruhl as supplying striking illustrations of what a
life world can include. But otherwise the published part of the Husserl papers does not show concrete examples of the conception. Yet
it would require little imaginative variation and extension of this
pattern to supply it.

How much toward a systematic phenomenology or, as Husserl also
calls it, an "ontology" of the life world has then been achieved thus
far? What we have is certainly nothing like a "rigorous science" in
Husserl's sense. Beyond the outlines of the basic structure of the
life world and some of the categories, spatial and emotive, which
would be distinctive to it, no general framework with basic propositions, definitions, and laws is in sight. What constitutes a "world"
in this sense? Is there only one life world per person? Or can a
person live "in several different worlds," as we often say? How far
are these life worlds articulated, subdivided, etc.? This is not a mere
matter of pigeonholing. Eventually any comprehensive account of
a person's life world needs a framework that would allow us to plot
its characteristic profile.

What has such a phenomenology of the life world to offer to the
psychologist in his need for a fuller understanding of the phenomenal
world? Clearly not a ready-made model or framework. But even in
its rudimentary form Husserl's phenomenology of the life world may
contain some new tools, some new dimensions, some suggestions
toward what a full-fledged phenomenological psychology of the phenomenal world requires.

I shall go even a little further than Husserl did by suggesting some
structural dimensions for the charting of life worlds. For instance,
life worlds are articulated according to zones and regions. By "zones"
I understand the concentric shells around the focal center of each
life world arranged according to its closeness to or significance for
the focal subject; by "regions" I mean the areas within the life world
organized according to the content of these zones, i.e., the material
fields of his interests. Obviously, zones and regions will intersect.

The articulation of the life world according to zones is foreshadowed in Aron Gurwitsch's important work on *The Field of Consciousness*, with its distinction between the thematic object, the thematic field, and the marginal field. True, his distinctions apply primarily to single perceptions. Yet they can easily be transposed to the perceived life world in its entirety. We can then distinguish between a central area, relatively well lit up, a penumbral belt around it, and a surrounding zone fading off from full shade into twilight and final darkness. Such zones may be based on degrees of acquaintance, according to familiarity or novelty of content, obviously a transitory division, since novelty will change to familiarity. But zoning may also be based on emotional closeness, which may be much more persistent; criteria for such emotional closeness may be preferences, real or imaginary, the latter in case we reflect on what contents we would rather like to have or to do without.

The articulation of the life world according to *regions* would have to be based on an inventory of the variety of objects and concerns with which we are in living contact. Here any attempt to be complete would be doomed to defeat. Typical regions would be one's own body, spatial environment, family, friends, and economic, political, cultural, and religious concerns. By way of an example, I shall merely try to indicate relevant features of the lived spatial environment. For the average adult middle-class Westerner this will usually be centered in his private room, surrounded by his house or apartment, oriented toward the street, placed within the town or city in which he happens to be permanently or temporarily settled. This immediate life environment usually stands in very loose connection and sometimes, in cases of disorientation, in no connection at all with geographical space, which is chiefly imagined space (though flying may do something for a better fusion of the two). Even this geographic space appears in all sorts of profiles, represented, for instance on maps of the United States as mirrored in the typical perspectives of the inhabitants of some of our "hub" cities.

Each person also lives in a special time world in which different parts of present, past, and future appear in different perspectives, are very differently articulated, are empty or full, have very different meanings. The importance of these time profiles has been shown especially by phenomenological psychopathology.

Man's social world is a most important area in his life world. What persons are included in it, by name or anonymously? How "close" or how "distant" do we feel to each of them? How do we rank them? How far are we aware of others' inner life worlds?

Then, what place do cultural products occupy in a man's life world? What does sport or art mean to him?

How does he see the entire cosmos in relation to himself? How much of his life is permeated by a sense of religious meaning?

The most detailed study of the structural dimensions of the life-world thus far (1973) is that by Alfred Schutz and Thomas Luckmann, especially in its second chapter on the "Stratification of the Life-world." [22]

In the present context there would be little point in developing a blueprint for a systematic study of life worlds. It is enough if this sketch can convey a sense of the vastness of the task and the need and chance to develop schemes and the proper categories for the description of life worlds, schemes that are indispensable for a fuller understanding of other individuals, sexes, generations, races, and ages. It is simply not enough to project ourselves into their places. We also need the directives for the proper exploration of the worlds for which these "places" are the centers.

Beyond such clarifications of the basic conceptions, philosophical phenomenology can apply the patterns of intentional analysis to a study of the phenomenal world. Not only specific intentional objects but the encompassing field and world are given in characteristic acts and differentiated modes of appearance. Hence a study of the content of the phenomenal world invites the parallel study of the various acts, as well as of the modes, perspectives, degrees of intuitive concreteness or emptiness, clarity and vagueness, etc., in which they are given.

Finally, the genesis of a life world, its transformations, and, in short, its history present new tasks for any kind of phenomenology. There is, of course, the merely factual or empirical task of tracing the growth and transformations of the phenomenal world in each individual life, its widening and narrowing, its revolutions and realignments. But in addition to preparing the ground by outlining such possibilities, phenomenology may again show essential and typical structures and laws pertaining to such "genesis." Thus one might well

---

[22] Alfred Schutz and Thomas Luckmann, *The Structures of the Lifeworld.* Translated by Richard M. Zaner and Tristram Engelhardt. (Evanston: Northwestern University Press, 1973).

hypothesize that any enlargement of the life world affects the relative importance of the central areas, or that modifications of the phenomenal world presuppose the loosening of the rigidity of one's native world, in short, an open attitude.

V. CONCLUDING REMARKS

I do not claim that phenomenological philosophy contains all the answers to the questions, asked and unasked, of empirical psychology. Such extravagant claims can only backfire – and it is no secret that they have backfired in the past. What I do want to suggest is that certain developments in both fields have converged far enough to make the comparing of notes and the exchange of questions and answers meaningful. American phenomenological psychology from the grassroots and imported phenomenological philosophy are not as far apart as is often believed. The precedent of William James, itself an influence on Husserl's phenomenology, is sufficient proof of that. Undeniably there are obstacles to communication. There is the disdain of aprioristically minded phenomenologists for empirical psychology. And there is the all too understandable aversion of the empirical scientist against the esoteric jargon of "the" phenomenologists. Both parties stand to gain from increased dialogue. Neither one has the right to pose as the authoritative teacher. Both have their unresolved problems – and their skeletons in their respective closets. And both have common foundations: the phenomena in their unexhausted and inexhaustible richness and wonder, and their common objective, the attempt to understand them as far as is humanly possible.

14. THE IDEA OF A PHENOMENOLOGICAL ANTHROPOLOGY AND ALEXANDER PFÄNDER'S PSYCHOLOGY OF MAN*

The immediate objective of the present essay is to serve as an introduction to the first English translation of selected texts from the writings of Alexander Pfänder, one of the early German phenomenologists, usually known merely for his psychological phenomenology and for his even more influential *Logik.* I want to show that his phenomenology may have particular significance today for all those who have an interest in the development of a philosophical anthropology and especially in the significance of phenomenology for this development.

But I hope that beyond that limited purpose this essay can also stimulate a more methodical and critical approach to an area where today philosophy may have special opportunities and responsibilities.

Recently there has been a lot of talk not only about philosophical anthropology but also about phenomenological or existential anthropology, and even about a phenomenology of man. But too often the appeal of such terms stands in inverse proportion to the clarity of their meanings and their concrete fulfillments. The idea that anthropology is vitally important and that phenomenology may have something important to contribute to it seems plausible enough. But precisely what it is that it can contribute, and how and why it should be able to do so seem to be questions rarely, if ever, raised explicitly.

What I want to do therefore is first to reflect on the relation of anthropology to phenomenology. I want to show what phenomenological anthropology can mean, once the phenomenological approach is clearly understood. I also want to show that thus far the real task has hardly been touched. Finally I want to produce some evidence for the assertion that perhaps the best fulfillment of this

* From *Review of Existential Psychology and Psychiatry* V (1965), pp. 122-136.

task can be found in enterprises which are still innocent of the label "phenomenological anthropology" such as Alexander Pfänder's phenomenological psychology of man.

I. ANTHROPOLOGY AND PHILOSOPHICAL ANTHROPOLOGY

The rise, or actually the revival, of philosophical anthropology in general, as the background for a phenomenological anthropology, deserves at least passing mention, especially in the Anglo-American setting, where anthropology is on the whole still identified with the empirical science of anthropology, a vast area of studies fascinating even for philosophers. The fact that lately this anthropology has become more interested in philosophical questions on its own is one of the encouraging signs of interdisciplinary bridge building.

Nevertheless, the idea of a *philosophical* anthropology may still grate on the more analytical, critical, and empirical nerves of Anglo-American methodologists. Let it be admitted, then, that this idea has its main origin in the more troubled and murkier waters of continental thought. Perhaps the most symptomatic and most impressive call to such an enterprise was implied in Max Scheler's statement of 1926:

In the approximately ten thousand years of history we are the first age in which man has become completely and unrestrictedly "problematic," in which he no longer knows what he is, but knows at the same time that he does not know it.[1]

Scheler himself died too soon to complete the philosophical anthropology he had announced. Its reconstruction from his posthumous papers remains to this day an unsolved task. All that is available now is his lecture of 1927 on "The Place of Man in the Cosmos," [2] with its strange dualism of blind cosmic urge and powerless spirit converging in man. Scheler might also have been the philosopher to develop a genuinely phenomenological anthropology. However, it must be realized that at this stage in his development phenomenology as such no longer played an important part in his thinking.

The challenge was reinforced by the new totalitarian doctrines,

---

[1] "Mensch und Geschichte", *Philosophische Weltanschauung* (Bonn: F. Cohen, 1929, p. 15).

[2] *Die Stellung des Menschen im Kosmos* (Darmstadt: Leuchter, 1928); English translation by Hans Meyerhof (Boston: Beacon Press, 1961).

especially by the Nazi myth of man the racial being, but also by the growing appeal of the Marxist view of man. Yet only a systematic and critical examination could answer such basic questions as those of man's essential structure, his distinctive features, his place in the universe, his dignity, and his destination. A mere empirical study of the varying patterns of culture, or even of cultural universals, could not yield the answers. Such questions require a philosophical approach.

II. THE IDEA OF A PHENOMENOLOGICAL ANTHROPOLOGY

Phenomenology, at Scheler's time the most influential movement in Germany, was the most likely taker of this challenge. In what sense and to what extent could it be expected to meet it?

In order to answer this question it might be best to consider first the peculiar powers and possible limitations of phenomenology. For I do not want to aid and abet the idea that phenomenology is the philosophical jack-of-all-trades.

Disregarding the varieties of today's interpretations of the phenomenological approach I shall here simply postulate three minimum requirements for any approach which has a claim to call itself phenomenological:

(1) A phenomenological approach must start from a direct exploration of the experienced phenomena as they present themselves in our consciousness, paying special attention to the way in which they present themselves, without committing itself to belief or disbelief in their reality.

(2) It must attempt to grasp the essential structures of these experienced phenomena and their essential interrelations.

(3) It should also explore the constitution of these phenomena in our consciousness, i.e., the way in which these phenomena take shape in our experience as it develops.

Now what would it mean to apply such an approach to anthropology? Certainly something very different from what the author of *The Phenomenon of Man*, Pierre Teilhard de Chardin, has given us in his exciting vision of man's evolution from point Alpha to point Omega, a vision which he himself sometimes called "phenomenological." One need not disparage it in denying it the title "phenomenology" in the sense of the phenomenological method as characterized above. Instead, a phenomenology of man based on this method would have to present first a picture of man *as he experiences himself immediately*, i.e., independent of all information which he may derive from science and scientific inference, as Teilhard de Chardin did so impressively. This would mean specifically:

(1) A descriptive study of man's consciousness of himself as man. Such a study would have to be articulated in line with the analysis of intentional consciousness after the manner of Husserl, i.e., it would have to distinguish what in his terms would be called the *intending ego*, its *intending acts*, and its *intended objects*, or if one prefers Cartesian terminology, the cogitating ego, its cogitations, and its cogitata. In the case of anthropology this would involve:

a. a study of the human self, with its characteristically human modifications, i.e., as an ego incarnated in a body, limited in its range of senses and in bodily strength, developing, maturing, aging, and eventually dying.

b. a study of human experiencing, i.e., of all the functions of this self, from sensing and perceiving to thinking, feeling, and willing in their infinite variety *as modified by the human situation*, e.g., by the limited range of stimuli to which its organs can respond, by the limitation of its memory and its imagination, etc.

c. the study of the human world with its human objects as experienced in a human life. For this human world too essentially belongs to man, if not as a part of him, at least as his essential habitat and as his essential counterpart. A particularly important area of this world, and in fact man's only access to it, is his own body as experienced by him. This phenomenal body must of course be distinguished from his anatomical body, as studied by the biological sciences and by physical anthropology. Only that part of this body which is given in his direct experience is part of the phenomenal body. Also, the human world includes man's creative expressions, his language, his various cultural enterprises, and his history as he experiences them.

A peculiar case is that of the human unconscious. One might first think that the unconscious is outside the sphere of a phenomenology which focuses on conscious experience. But insofar as even the subconscious can be made conscious through such more or less direct methods as psychoanalysis, it is at least a potential field for phenomenological exploration. There are hopeful beginnings in this direction.

Thus the primary range of phenomenological anthropology qua descriptive enterprise would be man and his world insofar as he directly experiences himself directly, but not beyond.

(2) Simply recording these phenomenal data is, however, not all that a phenomenological anthropology can do, particularly if it is restricted to personal accounts of each one's own experience of himself qua human being. To make such descriptions phenomenological, there would have to be at least an attempt to grasp the essential nature of these phenomena as sought by an eidetic phenomenology which attempts to separate what is essential to man from what is merely contingent to his essence.

(3) Another task of phenomenology with regard to man would be an account of the peculiar ways in which man is given to himself. To illustrate the need, one might point out that one's own body is given at best in a strangely distorted visual perspective, in which what are perhaps the most vital organs, including his major sense organs, and the whole back, are not given at all directly, but at best through mirror images in various degrees of indirectness. The consideration of these modes is even more important in the case of the subconscious.

(4) Yet all these undertakings would deal only with the static phenomenon of man. But man is anything but a static being. His life is not only a temporal structure, but in a distinctive sense a historical one. He passes through definite stages in his development. This raises the question of the connections between these temporal phases and stages. How far are they understandable? What would such understanding mean in comparison with mere causal explanation? To give such understanding by an exploration of the concrete connections would be the concern of an interpretive phenomenology. Its goal is the kind of understanding which goes by the seemingly untranslatable German term "verstehen." In a sense all essential insights are cases of such understanding. Under the name of "hermeneutic phenomenology" Heidegger has made a special effort to penetrate into the deeper and less obvious meanings of human existence. Man in his short-range and long-range enterprises certainly poses peculiar challenges for such an undertaking. In any event, the understanding of what can be found out about the essential motivations of human behavior is a legitimate concern of phenomenology, especially when these motives are given in direct experience.

In short a phenomenological anthropology so conceived is one in which man is to be studied as he appears to himself, with his human consciousness, his experienced body, and his experienced world in their historical development. Such an approach does not exclude the possibility of, and in fact the need for, complementary approaches in order to complete the task of a comprehensive philosophical anthropology. This philosophical anthropology would have to include the more objective information supplied by the biological sciences and other studies that could contribute to a panorama like that of Teilhard de Chardin.

What then is the peculiar significance of phenomenology in anthropology? Why should there be such a special phenomenological anthropology? Why not also, for instance, a phenomenological physics or botany? Now it is true that there are phenomenological aspects even of these fields. But phenomenology has a rather different and more central significance for the sciences of man. For *man* is a being who essentially appears to himself. And this appearance makes an essential part of his very being, perhaps his most essential part. In this sense man, the object of anthropology, is essentially a phenomenological being. He and his behavior cannot be understood without knowing how he appears to himself. There is therefore every reason to take his phenomenal aspect of man seriously. This does not mean that phenomenological anthropology should be set apart from philosophical anthropology. But it may be worth considering whether phenomenological anthropology should not eventually be handled as a special division within the comprehensive framework of philosophical anthropology, the division which would explore man's experiences of, and perspectives on, himself.

III. PHENOMENOLOGICAL ANTHROPOLOGY THUS FAR

To the best of my knowledge there is not yet any systematic text under the title "phenomenological anthropology." Are there at least any solid preparations for one, perhaps under a different name?

As far as the philosophers are concerned, I know at least of one German book, *Die Philosophische Anthropologie,* by Hans-Eduard Hengstenberg (1957), originally a student of Max Scheler, which begins with a section "Concerning the Phenomenology of Man," followed by three more on the metaphysics of man dealing with his *Geist,* with human life, and with the human whole respectively. But even the part on phenomenology has little to do with the program I have outlined, concentrating as it does on the facts of human attitude such as man's capacity for objectivity (*Sachlichkeit*). So whatever may be considered as phenomenological anthropology in my sense could only be found under different labels.

Husserl, the fountainhead of the phenomenological movement, once mentioned the idea of a "phenomenology of man" (*Phänomenologie des Menschen*).[3] One of several phenomenologies, it was to be undertaken after the phenomenological reduction had surrounded the natural world with the appropriate brackets, and was to deal with "his personality, his personal qualities, and his (human) flow of consciousness." But he remained suspicious of all *Anthropologie* as another form of anthropologism, against which he had fought in his *Logische Untersuchungen* as a variety of psychologism, warning against it specifically in his lecture on "Phenomenology and Anthropology." [4] Yet indirectly he gave special impetus to the study of the human life-world by his late stress on the *Lebenswelt* as a particularly promising avenue to his transcendental phenomenology.

Heidegger protested vigorously against the confusion of philosophical anthropology with his existential analytics. But since he equated human *Dasein* with man himself, it was not surprising that his analyses of such conceptions as that of being-in-the world proved particularly stimulating for the later development of a philosophical anthropology based on man's appearance to himself.

Among the French, Gabriel Marcel ought to be mentioned for his new emphasis on the importance of the phenomenal body. This theme is developed further in Merleau-Ponty's *Phenomenology of Perception*, though it should be pointed out that the phenomenal body is by no means absent from the writings of such German phenomenologists as Husserl and Scheler. But all this is at best raw material for a real phenomenological anthropology.

For a more explicit formulation of this idea one has to turn to those psychiatrists who saw in phenomenology the most promising approach to a real understanding of man in his entirety, normal as well as abnormal. Ludwig Binswanger is the most prominent advocate

---

[3] *Ideen* I, § 76 (*Husserliana* III, p. 175).
[4] "Phänomenologie und Anthropologie," *Philosophy and Phenomenological Research* II (1941), pp. 1-14; translated by Richard Schmitt in Chisholm, R. M., ed., *Phenomenology and the Background of Realism* (Chicago, 1960).

of such an anthropology. Actually, it was he who gave the title "Concerning Phenomenological Anthropology" to the first volume of his major essays, when he republished them with an important introduction in 1947. As his reason for the choice of this title he gave that the method of these essays was phenomenological, "since they had resulted from his occupation with Husserl's phenomenology," and that their subject matter was the essential relations and structures in human beings. An even more impressive result of Binswanger's concern was his magnum opus of 1942 on the "Basic Forms and the Knowledge of Human *Dasein*" (*Grundformen und Erkenntnis menschlichen Daseins*). But even this work can hardly be considered a comprehensive system of phenomenological anthropology, nor did Binswanger make such a claim. For its major concern is the phenomenology of love in the sense of the loving relationships of men, culminating in "we-hood" (*Wirheit*). No other aspect of man is considered.

The situation is basically the same with regard to the otherwise very significant contributions to a phenomenological anthropology which can be found in the works of Viktor von Gebsattel, Eugène Minkowski, Erwin Straus, and F. J. J. Buytendijk, who are closest to Binswanger in objective and approach. All of them offer phenomenological treatments of certain aspects of philosophical anthropology. None of them claims to present a fully developed system.

What in recent years has been offered in the United States as existential psychology and psychiatry, and even as anthropological phenomenology (Rollo May, Adrian van Kaam), contains a number of promising themes. But it is thus far anything but a systematic realization of the program of a phenomenological anthropology.

It seems therefore safe to state that to this hour the idea of a genuinely phenomenological anthropology remains a program, though by no means any longer an empty one. It is more than likely to lead to more systematic and fruitful realizations in the near future. Perhaps the greatest promise for its fulfillment is the recent work of Paul Ricoeur in hermeneutic phenomenology.

IV. PFÄNDER AND THE PHENOMENOLOGY OF MAN

To connect the name of Pfänder with phenomenological anthropology may at first sight seem like an anachronism. For the term was not yet born when, around 1933, he had completed his main work in the field.[5] To attach this name to his phenomenological psychology requires therefore a generous extension of the label, making his a phenomenological anthropology *avant la lettre*, as the French would say. Nevertheless, as far as the substance is concerned, no other phenomenological enterprise comes so close to fulfilling the specifications of my program as Pfänder's phenomenological psychology, and particularly his last completed work of 1933, *Die Seele des Menschen*.

Just how close Pfänder's ultimate objective in psychology and even in philosophy was to the development of a philosophical anthropology can be seen most directly from the translation of an announcement of his last work, whose German original was never published.[6] This text may at first give the impression that Pfänder's main concern was still psychology, though it was a new psychology and especially a psychology focused on man, in this sense a humanist psychology, but not yet an anthropology, which would deal with more than man's psyche. However, a closer inspection will reveal that much more is involved.

To be sure, Pfänder's earlier work as a phenomenological psychologist was mainly an attempt to enlarge the horizon of traditional psychology for its *own* sake, which Pfänder wanted to turn away from its preoccupation with psychophysics and physiology. He also aimed at relieving the poverty of its psychological content by a fresh phenomenological approach to the basic phenomena and by introducing new ones which had escaped the eyes even of such perceptive psychologists as his teacher Theodor Lipps, of empathy fame. In this manner, Pfänder explored particularly the phenomena of the will, the subject of his *Phenomenology of Willing* of 1900, and added to this book in his even more influential essay on "Motives and Motivation" of 1911. A similar enrichment was his phenomenology of the sentiments (*Gesinnungen*) of 1913, showing new dimensions in

---

[5] Pfänder himself refers to the "old name 'Anthropologie'" as a possible label for a study of man as a unified whole, a label which, however, had recently acquired a "somewhat different meaning." (*Die Seele des Menschen*, p. 4). But all he promises is a psychology of man's psyche and its life.

[6] See the Appendix at the end of this essay as published in Alexander Pfänder, *Phenomenology of Willing and Motivation and other Phaenomenologica*. (Evanston: Northwestern University Press, 1967, pp. 133-136). It is omitted in the present version.

such familiar phenomena as love and hatred, a study which attracted the admiration and adoption of Ortega y Gasset. Finally, in his "Fundamental Problems of Characterology" of 1924, he broke completely new ground by developing a new framework for describing the varieties of human personality.

All this descriptive work, though not yet focusing on man explicitly, showed Pfänder's intense interest in the full concreteness of human life and personality. But his supreme bid for not only encompassing but understanding man in his entirety was his last book on Man's Psyche. The announcement of this work also contains a condensed abstract of its main argument. In the present context only those features of this conception need mentioning which are pertinent to the development of a phenomenological anthropology. I shall therefore confine my report about this 400-page work to the following sketch.

Basic is the distinction between the psyche's life and the psyche itself. As far as its life is concerned, Pfänder begins with a colorful survey of its varieties in its cognitive, affective, and practical manifestations. Special attention is given to its relations with the body and with the world in which it occurs. A detailed attempt to understand this life follows. Pfänder traces it back to a network of "drives" or fundamental tendencies, e.g., toward having or avoiding, toward achieving, toward acting, toward power, etc. These in turn are derived from man's original drive toward creative unfolding of his general and individual fundamental essence, with the essential cooperation of the active ego. This essence can be discerned by means of a peculiar theoretical idealization based on empirical observation. The essential structure of the human psyche thus revealed is that of a living being, directed toward a world, with an organized psychic structure, with a body, a being which is reflective, personal, i.e., controlled by an ego, ethical, social and religious. Psyches differ in volume, configuration, texture, etc. Eventually Pfänder tries to show that the psyche is a meaningful and understandable unit, understandable as tending toward the unfolding of its essential characteristics in the context of its world.

In what sense and to what extent can such an anthropology be claimed as phenomenological anthropology?

The first doubt may easily be: Does it really deal with man as a whole? It does deal with his psyche. But what about his body? Now this doubt would be well taken if we were concerned with the task of a comprehensive *philosophical* anthropology, which must of course take account of man's full bodily structure. And it is true that Pfänder deliberately ignores anatomy and physiology in the study of man's real body. But all the more does he deal with the *phenomenal* body, as it is experienced in the life of the psyche. In fact, Pfänder gives the body a much more important place in the psyche's economy than is done in most other psychologies and even phenomenologies. Thus he sees in the body neither the mere physical basis for the existence of the psyche, nor the mere vantage point from which we perceive objects outside, as often seems to be the case in Husserl. For Pfänder the body is also the mediator between the psyche and the world, and its fitting representative in and to it. What Pfänder has to say on this point and on the bodily, as distinguished from the psychic, belongs to the most original and colorful parts of his work. This is phenomenology of the body at its best and qualifies his psychology as a piece of phenomenological anthropology, if not yet as a philosophical anthropology.

In passing let me also point out the fact that Pfänder's psychology does not exclude the unconscious, little though it mentions it. But Pfänder never defined the psyche as the conscious, much in the spirit of his teacher Theodor Lipps, whose plea for the unconscious was such important academic support to the cause of Sigmund Freud.

Thus Pfänder's descriptive psychology certainly satisfies the requirements of a phenomenological anthropology as far as man's experience of himself, his experiencing acts, and the experienced objects (body and world) are concerned. It fulfills it to a possibly even richer degree in his attempt to supply insights into essential structures, especially as he undertakes to determine the fundamental essence (*Grundwesen*) over and beyond the empirical data of the human psyche. Furthermore, with his attempt to understand the psychic life and the psyche itself as issuing from its fundamental essence, this psychology comes close not only to a genetic, as opposed to a static, phenomenology, but also to a hermeneutic phenomenology which tries to interpret the more basic and less obvious features of human being in the world. Yet Pfänder always tries to submit his interpretations to phenomenological verification by intuitive demonstration based on examples from experience and free imaginative variation.

Pfänder also pays repeated and explicit attention to the way in which the world and the body are presented in our life as occupying a more or less voluminous place in it. These studies may well pass as attempts to show in what manner man is given to himself. To this extent Pfänder's psychology is also a phenomenology of the modes of appearance of man.

Only in one respect do I see a real gap in this psychology considered as a phenomenology of man: Pfänder does not discuss the question of how the phenomenon of man becomes constituted in his consciousness. How, for instance, does man's image of his own body or his self establish itself, how does it typically develop, become enriched or impoverished or otherwise modified? A complete phenomenology of man may well have something to say on these points. This would be the sort of constitution which Husserl had in mind when he spoke about the constitution of man's empirical ego in and by his transcendental ego. It could certainly be added to such a psychology, though it may not be needed by it for its own sake.

But then, how important and how fair would it be to make such demands on an enterprise which was not at all meant as a piece of phenomenological anthropology for its own sake as here outlined? Pfänder's interpretive psychology deserves to be studied on its own terms as an ambitious and fully-developed attempt to understand human life and the human psyche as an entity with an essential and understandable structure. If besides this primary goal it also fills the specifications of a more recent demand, so much the better.

So my final plea is that the anthropology embodied in Pfänder's psychology be considered as an alternative to the conceptions of more successful philosophers, psychologists, and psychoanalysts. It is certainly much richer in phenomenological content, especially as far as the multiplicity of fundamental drives is concerned, compared with the one or two drives with which other systems operate. Economy is not its prime feature. But it does not abandon the search for a unifying understanding of variety. It avoids hypothetical constructions that can be verified only indirectly. Everywhere it tries to supply direct verification by phenomenological exhibiting. It eschews, perhaps excessively, the discussion of specific rival theories. Some of its underlying conceptions, such as those of fundamental essences, may be in need of further development and scrutiny. It is certainly too theoretical and complex for clinical and therapeutic applications.

All that Pfänder offers in this regard is the concluding sentence of his brief preface:

May this book help many people to better understand themselves and other human psyches, and may it besides find people to correct and to perfect it!

15. CHANGE OF PERSPECTIVES:
CONSTITUTION OF A HUSSERL IMAGE*

"To be forever imperfect is essential to the unbreakable correlation of 'thing' and thing-appearance" (Husserl *Ideas* I, § 44; Husserliana III, 100 f.). This insight of Husserl is in a heightened sense true of the correlation between 'person' and 'person-appearance.' How much more does it apply to a personality such as Husserl's. Not all of these appearances are equally characteristic. If the following reminiscences of my encounters with Husserl can claim more than personal meaning, this cannot be based on the extent and intensity of these contacts. My reflections will present merely a series of close and distant perspectives in time and space which are meant as testimonies to the inexhaustible multidimensionality of Husserl's personality, as these perspectives involve varying "intentions," fulfillments, disappointments, and revisions. As such they may show a certain typicality.

PRE-PERSPECTIVE FROM HEIDELBERG

My first picture of Husserl goes back to the year 1922, when this Heidelberg Gymnasium student was forming his first impressions of the philosophical celebrities who dominated the local scene. It was illuminated by the Olympian clarity and eloquence of Heinrich Rickert. The restless genius of the ex-psychiatrist Karl Jaspers seemed almost an intruder. But even then the name of Husserl appeared over the horizon and served as a warning against academic provincialism. The fact that he had replaced the tradition of the Southwest German School in Freiburg gave cause for thought. His exhortation to philosophy as a rigorous science still shone as a beacon. His

* A German version of this article appeared in *Edmund Husserl: 1859-1959*, Phaenomenologica 4 (1959) pp. 56-63.

Logical Investigations were mentioned even in Heidelberg as the most important work of philosophy in the new century.

Two years later, now as a university student, I became more clearly aware of the significance of the change in Freiburg. Increasing dissatisfaction with the surface clarity and the schematic symmetry of Rickert's system and, even more, the persistent but unconvincing polemics which he directed from his chair toward his rival in the south (who, as I did not know at the time, had actually been appointed at Rickert's suggestion), increased my curiosity and finally made me study Husserl's writings intensively by myself. Then in the summer of 1924 I decided to spend a free semester of my law studies in Freiburg, a decision which at that time in Heidelberg sounded like philosophical treason.

CLOSE-UP PERSPECTIVE FROM FREIBURG

In the winter semester of 1924-25 Husserl lectured on history of philosophy, a lecture course which did not attract the phenomenological novice particularly. But he also gave a phenomenological seminar for advanced students on Berkeley's *Treatise on Human Knowledge*. In spite of my insufficient preparation for an advanced seminar, I decided to make at least an attempt to be admitted as an auditor. Thus I had my first chance to see Husserl during his office hour in person. Erect, the striking head somewhat tilted backwards in a manner which made him look less physically undersized, he mustered me with a penetrating glance. What a relief it was when he recognized my preparation as adequate and my reasons for early admission as sufficient.

The two-hour weekly seminar took place in one of the smaller lecture rooms of the old university building. Berkeley's *Treatise* meant not much more than the take-off point for Husserl's philosophizing, triggered off by minutes of the discussions of the preceding sessions by a seminar member at the beginning of each meeting. The balance of the session consisted almost exclusively of Husserl's monolog. But this monolog was fascinating in its intensity, even though, especially in the beginning, Husserl often repeated himself. He never used the lectern. Mostly he stood in front of the first bench fixating his audience. But at times he also walked back and forth in meditation. His peculiarly insistent high-pitched voice with the

Austrian intonation still rings in my ears. He talked without notes. Only rarely did he stop. His style was often involved. Sometimes he displayed a somewhat grotesque humor, even at the expense of a seminar member. I still remember how at one time, in order to explain the essential relationship between body and ego, using free varying fantasy he converted one of the older members into a huge paper ball. Only rarely did he direct his questions at the audience. Once when a member raised a point, he interrupted: "Please talk slowly. You must know it is very difficult for me to transpose myself into the thought of others."

This is not the place to describe the content of the seminar. But I want to mention the deep impression which some of Husserl's incidental pronouncements left on me and which I recorded in my notebook. Thus, Husserl talked about the need to learn phenomenological inner viewing (*Innenschau*), not differently from the way one has to learn observing in the natural sciences. As he put it, phenomenology means the use of one's own eyes, abandoning tradition, especially the tradition of language, and all one has been merely told. Thus Berkeley, the first philosopher Husserl had studied, as he told us, was one of the exemplary phenomenologists. "The phenomenologist must study history, he must not push it aside, he must hold conversations with its creators." However, "the mere reading of books as books must cease, one has to read books as the works of living persons in order to understand them as live works." Then came an exhortation to the study of the much-neglected British empiricists, generally considered as outmoded, starting with Locke and using the original text rather than translations such as Kirchmann's. This exhortation was for me a first incentive for studying English and English philosophy intensively.

But the most vivid impression I received of Husserl's personality was on the occasion of a seminar reception in the Husserl apartment on the second floor of the apartment house on Lorettostrasse 40. Here Husserl circulated informally from group to group, asking and answering questions, and then commenting and philosophizing in free style. Thus he compared Heinrich Rickert's writings to huge colonnades whose clarity he could enjoy aesthetically when he read them for the first time, but which on repeated reading no longer seemed meaningful. Of Max Scheler he remarked that, in spite of his genius, he was merely a "fool's gold" phenomenologist (*"Talmi-

phänomenologe"): "One needs bright ideas, but one must not publish them." He called Alexander Pfänder "our most solid craftsman." When asked about Kierkegaard and Theodor Häcker, one of the German Catholic writers of the time, he responded sympathetically. Of the "History of German Literature" by Hermann Hettner he spoke with spontaneous enthusiasm. Since I was technically a law student at the time, he referred me to Adolf Reinach, an ex-law student who had written on the phenomenology of law, adding however that something more was needed than Reinach's ontology, namely a phenomenology of the consciousness of law, of which he developed, by way of improvisation, a picture which fascinated me. But what stands out most vividly in my memory is Husserl's plea for thoroughness at any price. "One must not consider oneself too good to work at the foundation." He himself did not want to be anything but a worker at foundation walls. This was the spirit of the specialist of rigorous science. There was a certain bravado in the way in which he expressed his commitment, but it was genuine.

RETROPERSPECTIVE FROM MUNICH

Extraneous reasons of my major study at the time, i.e., law, were mostly responsible for my moving on to Munich after only one semester in Freiburg. But other considerations entered, such as the realization that Freiburg phenomenology demanded a total commitment to the master Husserl for which, as a beginner, I was not yet ready. For I had serious doubts about Husserl's later views, and also about the picture which Oscar Becker, Husserl's younger teaching associate at the time, gave of the much discussed new phenomenology of Martin Heidegger, then still in Marburg. In Munich I was also attracted by Pfänder, to whom Husserl had given such high praise at the seminar reception. At that time Pfänder was still the acting editor of Husserl's phenomenological yearbook. The Munich group considered themselves as a "liberal" version of phenomenology. Their point of departure was the philosophy of Theodor Lipps, from whose "psychologism" they had emancipated themselves. Husserl's *Logical Investigations* had become their main aid in this struggle. But they were watching Husserl's later development with growing misgivings. The main stumbling block was Husserl's phenomenological idealism, for which the Munich group failed to find compelling evidence. Also, they were disappointed by the multi-plying programmatic promises in Husserl's publications following his *Ideen* of 1913, promises whose concrete phenomenological fulfill-ment failed to materialize. All this appeared to the novice arriving from Freiburg not unjustified, although the Munich position struck him in many regards as too naively realistic. But he enjoyed the new undogmatic freedom of phenomenologizing in the Munich style, which made it possible for him to find solid ground for a doctoral thesis in phenomenological ontology. It was therefore a happy sur-prise to him that this thesis was accepted for publication in the last volume of Husserl's yearbook.

But I was even more surprised when Husserl responded to the reprint I had sent him with unchanged friendliness and encourage-ment. This was repeated even after later publications. True, Husserl never concealed his disappointment with all those who had neglected what he had written after the *Logical Investigations*, held off by what in some of his notes to me he called "the barriers which con-ceal the new dimensions that I have opened up in the past decades to so many who have remained stuck in ontologism and realism." And he did not leave any doubt about the fact that he considered the writings of the Munich phenomenologists not genuine phenome-nology and not even philosophy, but merely achievements in the special sciences.

I saw Husserl last on October 8, 1936. The year before, at the end of one of his postcards he had encouraged me to see him for the purpose of *symphilosophein* (philosophizing together). But it was not until a year later that I could take up this suggestion. However, the one hour of conversation I then had was most frustrating and actually embarrassing. It became clear to me at once that now he saw in me only the representative of the Munich group, which he felt no longer cared about him and did not even read his recent publications. When referring to Eugen Fink's article in the *Kant Studien* of 1933, with which Husserl had identified, I expressed the hope that he soon would publish specimens of the productive phenomenological constitution which Fink had announced, he told me impatiently to wait for a forthcoming two-volume joint work on time. Husserl spoke almost uninterruptedly with alarming agitation and painful bitterness, which made it plain that there was no hope of reassuring him. It was clear that from his side the break with the Munich group had become irreparable. And yet Husserl's unbroken courage and energy at 77, in spite of all the hardships and threats of the Hitler period, aroused new admiration. Also, in the retrospective light of some of the correspondence which I have seen since then, I can understand much better the grounds for the tragic estrangement from the Munich group and for Husserl's bitterness. Ultimately it all went back to his disappointment over the failure of collaboration on a cause which Husserl had never abandoned, not even during the almost solipsistic isolation of his last years.

FAR-OFF RETROSPECTIVE FROM AMERICA

More than twenty years have passed since then, which meant for me the transplantation into the Anglo-American world. A year in England introduced me to the philosophizing of G. E. Moore, C. D. Broad, W. D. Ross, and A. C. Ewing, a way which in many regards seemed to me to have achieved insights parallel to those of phenomenology. Then came the acclimatization to the even opener atmosphere of North American philosophy, whose level of achievement, especially as far as clarity and precision of argumentation were concerned, impressed me at once. Many of the conditions which in Germany explained Husserl's success, such as the predominance of psychologism, had been overcome independently under the influence of William Whewell and Bertrand Russell. On the other hand, Husserl's turn to Cartesianism and transcendental idealism went counter to the American anti-Cartesianism and to its naturalistic realism. But even more significant were the differences of philosophical climate: I was attracted immediately by the unpretentious soberness, the intenseness of philosophical discussion without personal animosity, the skeptical caution and, last but not least, the live sense of humor in Anglo-American philosophizing. It was only natural that in such a climate the logical positivism of the Vienna and the Berlin circles made a stronger impression than phenomenology, and that the therapeutic approach of Ludwig Wittgenstein won out. It was unavoidable that the first look back at continental philosophizing induced a shrinkage effect and gave fresh nourishment to my constant suspicion that once again I had been a victim of a provincialism which had made me overestimate the celebrities of my native haunts. What had seemed to be seriousness and dedication to a cause now often appeared as pomposity, thoroughness as pedantry, terminological innovations as neglect of common sense and the wisdom of ordinary language.

In such an atmosphere it was not easy to demonstrate the relevance of phenomenology, and especially of Husserl's potential contribution, to the philosophical problems of the Anglo-American world. In spite of the open hospitality of American philosophy, and of the serious efforts of native and immigrant phenomenologists, the task has not yet been accomplished. Thus in the Anglo-American world Husserl is still chiefly the big name for an enigma which does not fit into the pattern of contemporary philosophy, except as a preparation for existentialism.

And yet for this transplanted European the shrinkage effect has not persisted. Entering the much clearer and soberer world of Anglo-American philosophizing revealed to me in the end a relative dearth of phenomena and a hardening of problems. The new analytic philosophizing is too often merely analysis of language, not of phenomena. This realization is now spreading. It opens up new possibilities to reactivate phenomenological insights. The inestimable enrichment of our knowledge of Husserl made possible by the Louvain edition of the *Husserliana* means a new help. Also, Husserl's research manuscripts, now made accessible, not only reveal the intensity of his thought, but also his readiness to revise and to start anew, which is illustrated best by the new phenomenology of the life-world.

TOTAL PERSPECTIVE

Which one of all the perspectives that I have tried to present deserves precedence? None and all. All are obviously conditioned by circumstances and developments, including my own. And yet the identical core, in Husserl's terms the noematic core, is unmistakable. It explains to a certain degree the necessity of the change of perspectives. It is part of the essential nature of this identical core that it permits and even requires the rise of ever new perspectives. It would be the end of Husserl's significance if his picture ever became rigid, if it did not unfurl ever new aspects and new meanings in renewed constitutions.

INDEX OF NAMES

NOTE: In the case of such names as Edmund Husserl this index lists only passages with substantially new information.

INDEX OF SUBJECTS

NOTE: This index includes chiefly items not easily traceable by consulting the Table of Contents.